ORDER AND ORGANISM

SUNY Series in Philosophy
Robert C. Neville, Editor

Order and Organism

Steps to a Whiteheadian Philosophy
of Mathematics and the Natural Sciences

Murray Code

State University of New York Press
Albany

Published by
State University of New York Press, Albany

©1985 State University of New York

For information, address State University of New York
Press, State University Plaza, Albany, NY 12246

Library of Congress Cataloging in Publication Data

Code, Murray.
    Order and organism.

    (SUNY series in philosophy)
    Based on the author's thesis (doctoral—University of London, 1980)
    Bibliography: p. 248
    Includes index.
    1. Mathematics—Philosophy.   2. Science—Philosophy.   3. Whitehead, Alfred North, 1861-
1947.   I. Title.   II. Series.
QA8.4C63   192   84-8591
ISBN 0-87395-951-5
                                                    ISBN 0-87395-952-3 (pbk.)

Contents

Preface

This book grows out of the conviction that both philosophy and science make important contributions to the common thinker's picture of the way things in the world really are. This of course includes the relation between mathematics and reality. But understanding is blocked by the inability of both contemporary science and philosophy of science to come to grips with pressing questions about the nature of physical being. Thus it is far from clear just what degree of importance is to be attached to the plethora of frequently anti-intuitive pronouncements that emerge from both disciplines. This situation is more than a little unsatisfactory in view of that fact that scientific conceptions sooner or later become embedded both in ordinary and in philosophical language. Our talk about the things of the world is shot through with terms and notions that have their roots deep in scientific theories. Thus despite the putative metaphysical neutrality of science, its deliverances have a profound influence upon common beliefs not only about how the world is "really" constituted but also, although more indirectly, about the place of the human organism in the total scheme of things.

Among most contemporary philosophers there reigns a general antipathy towards anything that is reminiscent of First Philosophy. But to ask what anything is "really" about is to open wide the door to metaphysical speculation. One reason for this is that it is not possible to establish a clear boundary between the rational and the empirical. Nevertheless, it is commonly assumed that explanation and elucidation of the relation between the rational and the empirical may be carried out on a purely logical level of discourse. This move simply refuses to acknowledge the pertinence of questions which in the past have led to allegedly grandiose metaphysical schemes.

It is thus one aim of this book to show that such thinking is unavoidable if the question of the nature of mathematics is to be tackled at all. A second and intimately related aim is to show that Alfred North Whitehead's thinking on these matters is very much to the point, for he is able to respond to this question in a way which does justice to the broad spectrum of issues involved. The outcome is not intended to be a detailed and firmly fleshed out Whiteheadian philosophy of mathematics and the natural sciences. Rather, what I hope to show is that, in following Whitehead, one at least begins to move in the direction of a plausible and adequate conceptual structure. Also the breadth and profundity of Whitehead's thought is invaluable in providing insights into the real difficulties involved. And this is no small thing, for an initial hurdle in the philosophy of mathematics, as in any other specialized philosophy, is to distinguish the real problems from artificial ones.

One of the most problematic general notions involved in the question of the applicability of mathematics is the concept of order. It is becoming increasingly clear that mathematics is unlikely to provide a universal language for the complete expression of all important aspects of order in the physical world. It seems that the emergence of order in biological systems, for example, is an essentially inexplicable fact of physical being. But we are only beginning to consider this possibility seriously, and to grasp the related fact that the success of the Galilean-Newtonian programme to mathematize physical science does not lead directly to a plausible metaphysical description of the world. The purely mathematical approach in fact raises into prominence the question of what we mean by 'order,' and what might reasonably be expected of any attempt to explain it.

One of Whitehead's basic ontological premises is that order is generic: the world is layered in respect to types of order. It is thus a natural epistemological consequence of the Whiteheadian view that there are distinct and essentially incommensurable modes of knowing which require different modes of logical expression. Whitehead is therefore able to present us with an important alternative to the all-pervasive scientistic conception of explanation wherein the scientific mode of knowledge-gathering is held to be the paradigm of human cognitive activitity, and the method of mathematical deduction the principal means of establishing its soundness. This view receives its most seductive expression in the claim that science is ultimately capable of providing a comprehensive and adequate explanation of the workings not only of matter but also of mind.

The underlying theme of this book is that the Whiteheadian approach not only provides a reasonable response to pertinent metaphysical problems connected with the relation between matter and mathematics, but it also is a timely contribution to the problem of how to redress the imbalance in philosophy of science which has been created by the excessively immodest scientism of the not-so-distant past. This is not to suggest that we no longer need to take science very seriously. On the contrary, one of the more important aspects of Whitehead's theory of organism is that it shows us, through the use of the analogy of organism, how to go about doing just this. For this type of conceptual tool, notable for its absence from much of contemporary philosophy, is indispensable if we are to make any sense of some of the bizarre reports that issue from the frontiers of scientific research.

The book is based on a thesis which I presented as a doctoral dissertation to the University of London in 1980. It is published with the help of a grant from the Canadian Federation for the Humanities, using funds provided by the Social Sciences and Humanities Research Council of Canada. Most of the third chapter has appeared in print (with the exception of some revisions to the penultimate section) in *Nature and System*, vol. #4, 1982, under the titles "Zeno's Paradoxes I: The Standard Mathematical Response" and "Zeno's Paradoxes II: A Whiteheadean Response."

Parts of the final draft were written while I was on sabbatical leave in England in 1981–82. Hence I wish to thank the Nuffield Foundation for a Travelling Fellowship which helped to make this leave possible. In addition, I want to express my gratitude to the Mathematical Institute of the University of Oxford for their generous provision of working space, and to the Fellows of Corpus Christi College, especially Dr. J. D. Murray, for their kind hospitality. I am highly in debt to a number of readers of the manuscript, whose anonymity in some cases prevents me from recording the extent of my indebtedness. Among the known readers I especially wish to thank Professor C. W. Kilmister, whose comments and criticisms have been an important stimulus in the attempt to introduce greater clarity and coherence into the work. My greatest debt is to my colleague and wife, Lorraine Code, whose editorial suggestions and philosophical criticisms have been invaluable in the struggle to shape and express thoughts on matters that invariably seemed to lead to topics lying beyond my competence. Of course, none of the above-named should be held accountable for the final product, all of whose errors and shortcomings are my full responsibility.

Murray Code
Guelph, 1984

Abbreviations

In citing Whitehead's writings I have used the following abbreviations throughout. Full publication data may be found in the Bibliography.

AI	*Adventures of Ideas*
AE	*The Aims of Education and Other Essays*
CN	*The Concept of Nature*
ESP	*Essays in Science and Philosophy*
FR	*The Function of Reason*
IM	*Introduction to Mathematics*
IS	*The Interpretation of Science*
M	"Mathematics" (in *Encyclopaedia Britannica,* eleventh edition)
MT	*Modes of Thought*
PNK	*An Enquiry Concerning the Principles of Natural Knowledge*
PM	*Principia Mathematica*
PR	*Process and Reality*
P Rel	*The Principle of Relativity*
SMW	*Science and the Modern World*
UA	*Universal Algebra*

Chapter One. Introduction

> You may polish up commonsense, you
> may contradict it in detail, you may
> surprise it. But ultimately your whole
> task is to satisfy it.
>
> A. N. Whitehead

1. What Mathematics is All About

For all the attention that the problems of the scope, the nature, and
the growth of scientific knowledge receive in the philosopy of science,
comparatively little notice is taken of the related problem of
determining the place of mathematics in scientific knowledge. The
remarks of an eminent physicist, Eugene Wigner, are thus well worth
noting, for they touch upon what deserves to be an underlying theme of
any study of this kind. After examining some of the more salient
features of the applications of mathematics to physics, Wigner
concludes that

> the miracle of the appropriateness of the language of mathematics for
> the formulation of the laws of physics is a wonderful gift which we
> neither understand nor deserve.[1]

It is not just Wigner's confession of complete puzzlement that is
worthy of note. His conclusion aptly hints at an unseemly lack of
modesty prevalent in current estimates of the nature of this problem.

One aim of this book is to show that any attempt to account for what
Wigner rightly sees to be a remarkable but mysterious fact must lead the
philosopher of mathematics into many areas of investigation hitherto
conceived as the proper concerns of other specialized domains of
philosophical enquiry. One simple reason for this is that the question
"What is mathematics all about?" is part of the still larger question of
what science is all about. For it is through its usefulness in the growth of
scientific knowledge that mathematics acquires its significance as
something more meaningful that a mere game of symbols and rules for
their manipulation. If mathematics were *not* thus useful, it is doubtful if
many philosophers would think a philosophy of mathematics worth
having at all. So the lack of attention given to the mathematical side of
the problem of scientific knowledge may be the result of an extremely

uncritical attitude towards mathematics itself: that as the chief guarantor of the meaningfulness of the term 'exact' in the expression "exact sciences," mathematics can be regarded as unproblematic in this respect.

Hence it may be useful to expand a little on Wigner's suggestion that our failure to produce a satisfactory explanation is nothing less than we deserve. In the first place, the complexity of the problem is seldom acknowledged for what it is. Its very nature defies a simple non-controversial answer. For the problem of understanding the application of mathematics to reality elicits the question of what the relationship is between conceptual structures and the real "external" world. Thus even before one takes up the question of relationshop *per se,* the whole vast Pandora's jar of Western philosopy has been unsealed. And what appears foremost in the buzzing swarm of puzzles is the vexed notion of reality itself, and the problem of how we shall know it if and when we stumble upon it.

Secondly, where the problem of relationship is directly tackled, whether in an explicitly realist or idealist setting, the treatment is seldom exempt from the charge of question-begging. This is especially evident, as I shall try to show, in modern mathematical responses to ancient puzzles first raised by Zeno of Elea. These illustrate vividly how a deep faith in logic and mathematics has helped to keep the storehouse of possible responses to our large question in a state near bankruptcy. One might expect that this situation would have generated much concern within the philosophy of science, for the traditional belief that we need only look to mathematics and logic for final answers has been increasingly undermined by advances in science itself. Nevertheless, there remain a significant number of active supporters of the traditional view. Yet the history of science amply confirms that, despite the fact that our knowledge of the physical world has grown increasingly more sophisticated, science, mathematics, and reality have gained rather than lost in mystery. Indeed, there is no obvious reason why progress in mathematics and in physical science *should* lead directly to a deeper understanding of the connection between mathematical abstractions and concrete physical events.

One thing at least emerges clearly from all this: it cannot be held as self-evident, a some of our ancestory have claimed, that the royal road to certain knowledge of the world lies through mathematics. Mathematics, the erstwhile bedrock beneath the shifting sands of uncertain belief, suffered a dramatic upheaval in the nineteenth century with the introduction of non-Euclidean geometries. The erosion has proceeded apace in our times with the discovery of the celebrated "limitative" theorems of Goedel *et al.* These make the hope for secure foundations of mathematics and logic seem a dubious product of wishful thinking. But even if foundations could be established, it is by no means clear that these would provide a sufficient ontological ground upon which to build a story of what mathematics is about.

Taking another tack, if one adopts the more circumspect view that mathematics is not the repository of ultimate ontological entities, but is instead a special kind of language, with the peculiar capablity of mirroring fundamental aspects of the order in the physical world, no immediate way out of our puzzlement presents itself. For the mirroring relationship between mathematical entities and their ontological referents, if any, is no less problematic than the parallel relationship between ordinary linguistic entities and their ontological referents, if any. The work of Wittgenstein, among others, has established that the notion of mirroring is far from clear. In any case, to hold that our problem reduces to a problem of reference is to prejudge issues that are as much ontological as they are epistemological. For the idea of reference, if it is to do any ontological work at all, inevitably evokes demands for ontological explicitness and commitment. But this is a controversial matter, and one to which I will return at various junctures in the development of this study. For the moment it is enough to say that the problem of reference in the context of the philosophy of mathematics may not only be refractory, it may involve asking entirely the wrong sort of question in the first place.

It is often argued that the undeniable efficacy of mathematics in physical science may be adduced as evidence for its special metaphysical significance. But the usefulness of mathematical modes of expression does not in itself provide much enlightenment about the meaning of such expressions. It is still reasonable to wonder if any significant metaphysical conclusion can be drawn from the predictive and practical successes of mathematical reasoning. Can purely verbal reasoning not also boast of dramatic successes? Apart from what language conveys and unveils of the intricate world of mind and feeling though poetry, literature, and drama, which is surely no small thing, the efficacy of non-mathematical symbolisms in human cultural, social, political, and scientific life is arguably just as remarkable as it is in the case of mathematical symbolisms. This is not to deny, for what the observation of ultimately worth, that the universality of the mathematical mode of communication would seem to put it in a category quite distinct from that of other modes of communication. But the admission of significant differences in kind is not equivalent to an admission of significant difference in cognitive *value* so far as power to reveal the real is concerned.

Philosophers of mathematics, with few exceptions, have been largely silent in the face of these fundamental metaphysical issues. Questions about the meaning of certainty, necessity, exactness, and so on, are frequently begged by the assumption that these important terms will eventually be fully explicated in terms of a perfected system of logic. Reality, in other words, is frequently assumed to be essentially and simply logico-mathematical.

From a metaphysical point of view, then, the philosophy of mathematics is, for the most part, a desolate region. It is populated, at one extreme, by astonishingly liberal doctrines of platonistic realism which lavishly grant high ontological status to such things as "actually infinite" classes of abstract mathematical objects on the strength of their apparent indispensability in mathematical theory. At the other extreme we find the severely conservative neo-Kantian doctrines of constructivism and intuitionism which rigidly deny that there is any meaning in a mathematical statement that cannot be proven by constructive methods. Behind the former position, it is possibile to detect the the anti-metaphysical positivism of Newton, Boyle, and many others, who seem to haunt the philosophy of mathematics just as doggedly as they do the philosophy of science.[2] While intuitionists generally display a much deeper awareness of the complexities of the philosophical issues involved, the full scope of these is obscured by neo-Kantian assumptions about the privileged position of mathematics in knowledge.[3]

If one turns instead to the empirical sciences in anticipation of enlightenment in respect to the physical side of the issue, what immediately strikes the enquirer is how much one needs to take on trust. For there is a deep gulf between commonsense beliefs about ordinary human experience and most scientific descriptions and explanations about the way things "really" are in the world. Progress in scientific research often reinforces the widespread conviction that common sense and scientific knowledge must grow ever further apart.

This gulf is evidenced by the seriousness with which immaterialist arguments are received in interpretations of formal advances of physics, especially microphysics. Here it is as if we were being persuaded, if not forced for want of a feasible alternative, to accept the sort of conclusion arrived at by Bishop Berkeley from a different direction. In the words of Yeats, Berkeley

> ...proved all things a dream,
> That this pragmatical, preposterous pig of a world, its farrow that so solid seem,
> Must vanish on the instant if the mind but change its theme. . . .[4]

Similar conclusions regularly issue from interpreters of researches in microphysics. We are, for example, invited to believe that the solid causal world of the commonsense realist is nothing but an ephemeral play of (possibly mind-spun) gossamers of things about which it is not possible to speak, at least in a coherent manner. Moreover, the whole puzzle is often glossed over with speculations that, in effect, hypostatize the mathematical formalisms which are so instrumental in linking the observables of physical experimentation into logical system. It thus seems but a short step from the immaterialism of Berkeley to what might be called the "mathematical materialism" of modern science.[5] For this has all the flavour of an up-to-date version of immaterialism, despite its air of sympathy toward the view that there is an external physical reality.

Faced with this confused and confusing situation, the commonsense realist might understandably be moved, if asked to choose between the two, to give up scientific and mathematical explanations altogether, rather than give up the palpable world of everyday experience with its plurality of contingent mind-independent objects and events. For despite the respect which science so obviously deserves, there is no difficulty in continuing to believe in a substantial Johnsonian foot meeting real resistance from a real stone. Moreover, the stone will no doubt be there whether kicked or not, and will remain long after the kicker and his pain have vanished from the world. The years which have intervened between us and Dr. Johnson have not turned up an acceptable answer to his implied criticism: if logical argumentation leads to an immaterialist and, as with Berkely, to an extreme idealist point of view, wherein reality is ascribed ultimately to the workings of the mind, then so much the worse for the deliverances of logic.

<u>Time</u> has shown the supreme difficulty, if not the impossiblity, of *TIME* providing an adequate answer to Dr. Johnson in purely logical (and this also means mathematical) terms. The world awaits explanation as a "solid" fact which, in some sense, simply must be taken as given: as beyond final explanation. Persistent emphasis upon logical argumentation as the core of good philosophy has diverted attention from this important truth. The only reasonable form which an adequate reply to the Johnsonian criticism *can* take, I shall argue, is that of the "story." <u>That is, in philosophy as in literature, what we want, in the end, is a sort of tale capable of co-ordinating the facts of feet and stones and pains in a</u> *story* <u>plausible system.</u> And, as with ordinary story-telling, the final assessment of the adequacy and the plausibility of the story will include judgements about how well the story "rings true," in addition to judgements about how well the facts are ascertained and described.

I am claiming that we must recognize that we have reached a point in our thinking about science where claims about the cognitive significance of logic and mathematics must be treated with great caution, indeed with considerable skepticism, and the deliverances of common sense listened to with more care, than has been the case in philosophy for some time. This is so despite the fact that common sense appears to have been left hopelessly behind by scientific progress, which owes many of its most dramatic successes to the use of higher mathematics. For it is also a fact that the facts of science are never unproblematic. Without gainsaying the importance of the mathermatical method, common sense notes that, when it comes to interpreting formal theories of science, whose formality increases as its subject-matter recedes ever further from the range of ordinary human sensory perception, the scientist is not on much firmer ground than the so-called plain man. Both must sooner or later appeal, if only covertly, to a world view sufficiently broad to be able to span an entire range of factors that extend from everyday human experience to the evidence underlying the theories of elementary particle physics.

Thus while the common thinker must rely upon the expert to explain what scientific theories are really all about, and to designate the truly significant facts, he or she is never wise to proceed without great circumspection. For it is an unfortunate truth, as Susan Stebbing has so well documented and argued, that the popular expositors of science do not always serve us well.[6] Stebbing supports this observation with an extensive critique of the writings of Sir Arthur Eddington and Sir James Jeans of the field in mathematical physics, but the main thrust of her criticism is far more broadly applicable.

There are good reasons, then, why the common thinker must constantly worry about *how seriously* the pronouncements of scientists should be taken. The situation poses something of a dilemma. On the one hand, while it would be highly irrational to suggest that the common thinker need not take science seriously at all, it is clear that it must not be taken too seriously. Science is being taken more seriously than it deserves when its method is held to be paradigmatic of legitimate philosophical method. And it seems an almost irresistible temptation of our age to believe that what does not come within the compass of the scientific method simply does not exist. Thus a dominant characteristic of many interpretations of scientific explanation is an uncritical, not to say presumptuous, attitude toward explanation *per se*. This attitude represents the negative contribution which the founding fathers of the Galilean-Newtonian revolution in science have made to the philosophy of science. In Burtt's succinct phrase, the temptation is still very much alive to

> make a metaphysics out of [one's] method, that is, to suppose the universe ultimately of such a sort that [one's] method must be appropriate and successful.[7]

We have here, it would seem, one of the main reasons why the choice of philosophical positions from which one can begin an examination of our large question is severely limited. By contrast, Whitehead's writings stand out as a rare peak in an otherwise extremely depressed metaphysical landscape. If only because he faces squarely the confusion and inadequacies imported into interpretations of modern scientific developments by the post-Newtonian metaphysics of method, he deserves much more attention than he is at present receiving. But I shall *whitehead* argue that he has a great deal more to offer. He <u>provides not only a</u> <u>thoroughgoing critique of the shortcomings of the metaphysical</u> <u>assumptions behind many key scientific and philosophical concep</u>ts, <u>assumptions which vitiate much</u> current philosophy of science, but also <u>puts forward a thoroughgoing</u> metaphysical response which is capable <u>of meeting that most insistent and reasonable demand of common</u> <u>sense, that scientific knowledge be intelligible knowledge</u>. That is to say, under the Whiteheadian approach the educated layman is not obliged to subjugate entirely his hope of understanding the nature of the physical to the dominion of the experts. Not since Kant has such an ambitious and far-reaching reform been attempted in philosophy. A rough comparative sketch of Whitehead's and Kant's attitudes in respect to the place of mathematics in knowledge may thus be useful at this point.

2. *Mathematics and Knowledge*

Kant and Whitehead share the desire to reconcile science with ordinary experience. Furthermore, they both begin with a first-hand ✓ acquaintance with and respect for contemporary mathematics and science, and they give ample evidence of the conviction that, as means to secure reliable knowledge of the world, science and mathematics must be taken very seriously indeed. Whitehead explicitly insists that mathematics must be counted as knowledge in its own right, and not merely as a means to this end. Thus he agrees with Kant, against Leibniz and Hume, that the truths of mathematics are not merely analytic. But the truths of mathematical knowledge cannot ever be confidently described as completely objective. It is at just this point, where the question of *how* seriously mathematics is to be taken, that one can begin to pinpoint some of the issues that irreconcilably divide Kant and Whitehead.

For Kant, science is the source of certain knowledge. He thus invests the Newtonian physics of his day with, as it has turned out, an unwarranted authority. Whitehead, on the other hand, seems never to have been tempted by this sort of idea. That Kant was in fact seriously mistaken in his attempt to ground his search for objective knowledge in mathematics and science is now fairly widely accepted. The important point that Newtonian physics is false under certain conditions and that all scientific theories share this characteristic has been pursued vigourously by Kuhn, Popper, Feyerabend, *et al.* While the debate about the nature and the growth of scientific knowledge seems far from over, enough has now been said to tarnish, probably forever, Kant's ideal of secure objective scientific knowledge.

A similar fate awaits the ideal of objective and incorrigible mathematical knowledge. It appears to have been entirely wrong of Kant to decide to spare mathematics from his critical gaze. The subsequent discovery of non-Euclidean geometries, comparatively recent developments of alternative set theories, and even of alternative logics, all have rendered extremely doubtful a fundamental Kantian assumption, namely, that mathematics is the home of synthetic a priori truths.

Whitehead's approach is, in this respect, much more realistic than Kant's. For Whitehead, mathematical knowledge is inherently corrigible, in so far as it is knowledge of reality at all. Indeed, Whitehead from the beginning of his philosophical investigations consistently maintains a skeptical attitude toward the notion of completely objective knowledge. In one sense, however, he adheres more closely than Kant himself to the latter's major epistemological insight, that perspectiveless knowledge is impossible. This point depends of course upon what one makes of the notion of perspective, so it may be worth exploring it a little further.

A denial of perspectiveless knowledge is one that a commonsense realist can readily allow. To common sense it is a palpable everyday truth that the world is both transparent and opaque. So far as knowledge of any of its many aspects is concerned, human understanding seems able to penetrate just so far and no further into the nature of, and interconnections between, its objects. Viewing is always dependent upon the particular perspective chosen. Sooner or later every essay at grasping the truth falters and fumbles—the world recedes into opaqueness and resists further penetration, at least from *this* particular direction, whatever that may be. For the commonsense realist, then, the notion of knowledge constrained by perspective is easily assimilated under the analogy of earth-bound perception, which is always knowledge of that thing *there* as seen/felt/tasted/heard from this standpoint *here*. There is no viewing which does not presuppose that one has some bit of ground upon which to stand, and there is no good reason to believe that viewing of any kind is privileged enough to be able to select an ideal standpoint from which everything can be grasped absolutely clearly, not to say at once.

This analogy aptly conveys the extent of the divergence between the Kantian and the Whiteheadian approaches to problems of knowledge. There is, says Whitehead, simply no reason to believe in the existence of a certain comprehensive and complete conceptual framework, finally and securely founded upon a basis of synthetic a priori intuitions, a framework which will support the *ne plus ultra* of platforms from which the whole world can be viewed. The notion of completely objective knowledge is a myth; this does not mean, however, that the notion of objectivity is completely empty. For there is also no reason, in Whitehead's view, "apart from dogmatic assumption, why any factor in the universe should not be manifest in some flash of human consciousness."[8] Or, to put this another way, the world *is* essentially (albeit only partially) transparent with an unclear line of division between what can be discerned and what lies beyond the possibility of discernment in any given perspective. The upshot is that we must take seriously what we have come to call our insights, however difficult it may be to explain their nature and genesis.

If both common sense and Whitehead are essentially right on this crucial point, it is clear that a primary problem for the philosophy of mathematics is to determine what role mathematics performs in *helping* to make the world partially transparent. Kantian ways of thinking, however, have blurred the distinction between 'helping' and 'prescribing'. Indeed, Kant may even be accused of contributing substantially to the present divorce between science, mathematics and common sense, a divorce which could at present hardly be made more complete. It would be no small achievement, then, if Whitehead's approach were able to help common sense find a way out of the current impasse.

One of the chief obstacles between common sense, on the one hand, and science and philosophy, on the other, is the assumption that science grows ever more objective and exact as it grows ever more mathematical. But common sense may legitimately object that if knowing is dependent upon perspective, and if there is no privileged body of knowledge which can guarantee the objectivity of any one perspective, then surely mathematical knowing is also subject to the uncertainties of perspective. For it is a major and, as Whitehead rightly insists, an unwarranted presupposition that the mathematical mode of knowing will not, in any one of its particular uses, sooner or later run up against the boundaries of the opaque. Put another way, there can be no guarantee that mathematical reasoning, however pure, is necessarily reasoning about the real necessities of the world. It may be partially expressive of absolute universal necessity (as Whitehead thinks it is), but there is no reason to suppose a priori that it is necessarily expressive-without-remainder in any of its applications.

[handwritten margin note: math. is not necessarily applied to the real.]

Thus the whole question of the nature of mathematical knowing is thrown wide open once the cogency of the Kantian assumption of the existence of synthetic a priori mathematical truths is denied. And it must be allowed that when this prop is removed, it becomes imperative for any philosophy of mathematics and the natural sciences to recognize that there is a difficult problem of choice involved in the making of conceptual frameworks, or viewing platforms. To abandon the ideal of

completely objective foundations is to make the question of what *are* the
most suitable underpinnings of conceptual frameworks an especially
urgent one.

Any choice of fundamental concepts which leads to a radical
separation of epistemological matters and ontological matters seems
bound to end in failure. In the absence of absolute foundations for
knowledge it is not easy to see how it would even make sense to try to
pursue the question of the role of mathematics in scientific knowledge
in any way which maintains a separation of problems about the *manner*
of knowing from problems about *what* is known. This is a view,
however, which is not widely held. So I shall now attempt to support it
with some observations that touch, although only lightly, upon the
tricky problem of whether, and in what way, concepts can be held to be
fundamental.

3. *On the Relation Between Epistemology and Ontology*

The object of our knowledge is the world: this includes not only all
that belongs to the external world, it includes also cognitive processes
themselves, and their apparently ever-changing perspective-governed
systems of knowledge. On the face of it, then, both the world and our
knowledge of it would seem to be so deeply interwined that it is unlikely
to exhibit its fundamental secrets to us in any clear way. This is only
partly because of the world as we know it is thoroughly imbued with
mutability.[9] Cognitive activity itself seems intrinsically bound up with
the mutable.

This is one of Whitehead's central beliefs. It runs directly counter to a
deeply embedded assumption of Western philosophy. The notion that
uncertainty is inherent even in our best cognitive efforts, an uncertainty
which infects all our knowledge of the world with an ineradicable
mutability, offends against the hopes and explicit beliefs of many of the
greatest thinkers in the Western philosophical tradition. Plato
articulates the clearest response to this wish to overcome or circumvent
the elements of mutability in our knowledge of the world when he holds
that the very mutability of the physical world is a barrier to its
intelligibility. In direct contrast, Whitehead holds that mutability is the
sine qua non of all our assumptions about the possibility of knowledge.

The latter phrase evokes once more the name of Kant. It seems clear
that one would be on the wrong track from the outset if one's initial
conception of knowledge entailed a denial of the Kantian truth that we
are in an important sense capable only of seeing what we look for, and

that our seeing is guided, it not entirely controlled, by the conceptual framework we happen to be living in. But for all the truth of this insight, a puzzle still surrounds the fact that we are capable of obtaining new knowledge of the world and its workings. The open and fluent character of knowledge systems, either in respect to actual novelty in conceptual content or to novel reorganizations of existing conceptions, is itself a candidate for truth which common sense is justifiably reluctant to deny. One good reason for doubting the existence of certain and immutable knowledge is the supreme difficulty of showing that the possibilities of novel cognitive achievements are actually bounded by a definite number of explicitly formulable categories or a priori forms of thought. And the main force of Kant's point of view is highly dependent upon there being a set of unabiguously definable fundamental concepts or categories.

The category of substance, for example, is of particular interest in this context. It is not easy to elucidate it without invoking preconceptions about the metaphysical status of matter. In Kant's account, at any rate, substance is dubiously founded upon notions which stem from Newtonian physics and a subject-predicate view of matter. On this view, substance is somehow to be conceived as the support or carrier of properties. Yet once this manner of thinking about substance is shown to be mistaken and misleading, as Whitehead among many others has argued, not only does the concept of substance become problematic, so do a good many that are related to it. The question thus arises which, if any, concepts might actually be fundamental.

The notion of fundamental concept is extremely obscure. Hence one important reason why Whitehead's view can be described as more realistic than Kant's is that his estimation of the actual status of concepts in organized thought is far more circumspect and less constrained by dubious presuppositions about fundamental concepts. This does not mean that Whitehead's approach involves an outright denial of the possibility of fundamental concepts; rather it rests upon a much less rigid notion than Kant's idea of indispensability. And the Kantian programme comes to grief when it runs up against the apparently insurmountable difficulty of having to satisfy its self-imposed requirement that certain key concepts be *demonstrably* indispensable. Yet Kant's failure to find proof of the indispensability of the fundamental categories does not point to the conclusion that all concepts are equally dispensable. Some concepts are less dispensable that others, not by virtue of their superior clarity and precision but rather, it would seem, for just the opposite reasons. The character of *not* being amenable to an analysis that fully accounts for them as short-hand expressions for a particular body of theories and definitions may be central to their very usefulness.

The concept of matter is a case in point. At any one stage in its history, 'matter' carries with it an only more or less well articulated corpus of meanings. Its meaning as a concept seems never capable of exhaustion by an itemization of its theoretical contents. The concept itself acts more like a pointer indicating vague and imprecise general truths about reality. Or perhaps the proper analogy is closer to that of wavering sign-post, which points us in different directions according to how we are disposed to assign weights to general conceptions about the nature of the physical. In the case of the concept of matter, we are directed to look at the physical world in quite different ways depending upon whether we are inclined to adopt notions expressive of activity or of passivity as qualifying matter. This decision makes all the difference to subsequent descriptions of the fundamental underpinnings of various instances of matter, and, perhaps even more importantly, to the very formulation of the whole problematic of matter. The history of this concept provides ample evidence that Westen philosophy has, by stressing the aspect of passivity in the underpinnings of the physical, pointed itself in entirely the wrong direction in this respect. Whether or not this in fact *is* a basic deficiency in our thinking about matter is a question of primary importance for the philosophy of mathematics and the natural sciences.

A full treatment of this problem would lead us far beyond the scope of this book.[10] But I shall maintain and attempt in various ways throughout this study to show that Whitehead's many thoughts on the subject are not only valuable and timely, they are also fully in accord with common sense, as well as with the findings of modern science. Moreover, inasmuch as modern physics has rendered unintelligible the traditional notion of substance as comprised of independent existents which passively support properties, Whitehead can claim empirically based confirmation for one of his major premises. For underlying his whole thought is the assumption that matter has as many characteristics of activity as it has of passivity.

So it may be useful to focus this necessarily brief excursion into the problem of fundamental concepts by considering some general reasons why a Whiteheadian conception of matter might be justified.[11] I am suggesting that he finds much support in the meaning of some extremely basic, although perhaps not absolutely indispensable, ordinary concepts. We shall see that the notion of "differences" plays a central role, both in an epistemological and in an ontological sense.

One of the more significant ontological aspects of the general concept of matter that arises from the results of elementary particle physics is a notion which is fully in accord with a basic conception of common sense: whatever deserves to be called matter must be capable of being described in terms that convey a fundamental "capacity to make and to *matter = possibly of difference.*

register differences." For only when interpreted in this way can the term rest easily with some of the more ephemeral entities of modern physics. This definition is of course vague and inprecise, but unavoidably so, granted that the concept of matter is one of those that cannot be precisely pinned down. And this latter point emerges more clearly from some general reflections that find the notion of differences close to the heart of common sense.

In the first place, it seems impossible to conceive of a world arrested and devoid of process, that is, a world stripped of all its past, present and future differences. In such a world, one would be faced with the impossible task of conceiving of things that were incapable of making any difference to anything else. Indeed, a world that stood thus completely still would have no need for description in terms of spatial or temporal differences. It would have no need for description or explanation at all: what existed, if anything, would just be.

In the second place, it is evident that both science and philosophy presuppose a world of real differences. Indeed, this is implied in every meaning of 'cognition'. The intuition of time presupposes the intuition of differences: a world without temporally unfolding differences would for all purposes be a world which stood absolutely still, and so would be no world, or at least no knowable world. But once we are led to acknowledge the existence of real differences in the world, we are inexorably led to ask: what sort of differences and differences between what and what?[12] The point is that the notions of cognition and intuition invoke deep ontological questions along with epistemological ones.

The notion of differences is also intimately bound up with the apparently indispensable concept of experience. Indeed, it seems that a large part of the mystery surrounding the concept of matter can be traced to the rigid separation maintained in the post-Galilean scientific tradition between matter, on the one hand, and experience, on the other. It is one of the more unsatisfactory aspects of the Kantian view that the meaning of cognition and experience are firmly tied to meanings associated with human life. It appears to be a tacitly held assumption of epistemologists in general that experience *can* only be conceived as a peculiarly human phenomenon. But while it may be true that our descriptions of the world are closely tied to human experience, this does not entail that the meaning of experience is tied exclusively to this realm.[13]

Here we meet another reason, then, to say that Whitehead's approach deserves the name 'realistic.' His conception of experience is more abstract than, say, Kant's. Whitehead does not presuppose that experience is a concept applicable only to a single domain of organic existence. Indeed, it is extremely difficult to see how anyone who is

prepared to take the concept of organism seriously could consistently
and coherently take any other view, short of abandoning all claims to
take science seriously. For the very term 'organism' essentially
presupposes a capacity of something, more or less determinate and
individual, to discern, to suffer and to effect real differences in other
external things.

It might be objected at this point that the attempt to express one of
the central features of the concept of matter by saying that matter is
"that which is capable of making and suffering differences" is to suggest
a definition which is much too vague and all-inclusive to be of much use.
Are not concepts, one might ask, "things" that also have such capacities,
at least under certain circumstances? But to respond either in the
affirmative or the negative would be inappropriate without a prior
investigation of the meaning of the concept of interaction in a full-
blown metaphysical context. This is exactly what Whitehead provides in
his detailed treatise *Process and Reality,* which can be seen as a
monumental essay in the elucidation of the generic concept of
experience.[14] Here we must merely note that this is very much an open
question. In the light of the above remarks, it seems far from obvious
that there is *no* fundamental connection (as received opinion would
have it) between the concepts of matter, interaction, experience,
causality, and even of value. In short, there may be, as Whitehead thinks
there is, a fundamental link joining the concepts of matter and
mattering, where the latter has the ordinary meaning of "making a
significant difference."[15]

I began this discussion by suggesting that mutability is implicated in
the very notion of knowledge. The notion of mutability presupposes the
notion of differences. And the fundamental nature of the latter concept
again emerges when we consider another aspect of the problem of
knowing. In this case, the point is illustrated vividly by raising that most
general of metaphysical questions: what can we say about the
universality of metaphysical principles? Or, to put this another way, is
there any reason to think that we could acquire certain knowledge of
ultimate metaphysical principles? Such principles, if there were any,
would presumably express the necessary conditions to which all
manifestations of order in the process of the world must conform.
Whitehead's answer must surely be the right one. To discover ultimate
metaphysical principles we should have, in his words, to "catch the
actual world taking a holiday from their sway."[16] But an assertion that
here such principles apply but *there* they do not is precluded by their
very nature. In a word, where differences are indiscernible, the
possibility of knowledge completely vanishes.

The consequence of this general observation about differences is of great significance for philosophy. It means that any attempt to frame ultimate metaphysical principles is inescapably dependent upon empirical observation, inference, and conjecture, that is, upon observations and principles of a relatively high degree of particularity. This means that the construction of a categoreal scheme, such as Whitehead attempts in *Process and Reality,* must inevitably be speculative and tentative. Metaphysics would seem to be intrinsically permeated with uncertainty in respect to the appropriateness and adequacy of its basic concepts and principles. We touch here an underlying theme of this study. The crucial question for the philosopher who wishes to explain the connection between mathematics and reality is not whether we can do without metaphysics but whether or not we can do without categoreal schemes such as Whitehead's.

The foregoing discussion indicates that common sense alone can find reason enough to give the edge to Whitehead, and not to Plato or to Kant, at least in respect to understanding the essential nature of our conceptual schemes. These appear to be inescapably imbued with mutability, and not merely because of limited human capacities for knowledge. More specifically, Whitehead's primary epistemological assumption, that there can be no "transcendental deduction" which will somehow guarantee the validity of ultimate metaphysical principles,[17] seems entirely the correct one. Not only is the process of attempting to establish metaphysical principles and fundamental concepts subject to the constraints and uncertainties of a chosen perspective, that is, to contingent factors which involve the time and place of world-viewing, it seems a complete mistake to regard 'mutability' as somehow antithetical to 'knowledge.' While the notion that change should somehow be the *condition* of intelligibility appears at first glance perverse, if not actually heretical, we see that the ascription of heresy is in fact more apposite. Enough has now been said, I think, to show that Whitehead is in conflict here with prejudice and not with reason.

To sum up the discussion so far, I have touched upon some general reasons for supposing that the ineradicable perspectival element in cognition leads to the general epistemological conclusion that certainty is not the ultimate or even a reasonable ideal of human knowledge-seeking. Moreover, the above discussion indicates that we cannot proceed very far if we hold to a predominantly Kantian type of epistemological investigation, as if exploration of knowledge pertaining to matter and experience does not evoke equally difficult and crucial ontological questions. In a word, we are pointed in the direction of making ontological commitments in the traditional manner. To speak of things which are capable of making a difference is to elicit the demand to make clear what are the things that are the propagators as well as the receptors of differences.

4. On Conceptual Complementarity

What is both exemplary and likely to be of lasting importance in the ambitious and extensive writings of both Kant and Whitehead is the consistent effort to find a proper balance between the rational and the empirical, one which is able to reconcile the legitimate claims of ordinary experience, common sense, and science. Both philosophers attempt to find a middle path between rationalism (as exemplified by Leibniz) and empiricism (as exemplified by Hume).[18] By contrast, post-Humean philosophy of science has failed even to acknowledge the breadth and depth of the problems involved. This is so despite exhaustive studies of logical systems and despite endless debates over the empirico-theoretical structures of science. A major reason for this failure is that the modes of philosophizing usually referred to as rationalist and empiricist have been wrongly construed as representing incompatible alternatives. Thus the best efforts of a great deal of Western philosophy have resulted in the widening of the gulf between reason and experience, the gulf which Kant tried so hard to close.

The failure to come to terms with the rational and the empirical appears largely due, on the one hand, to a dogmatic and narrow conception of rationalism, wherein the rational is essentially identified with what is amenable to logico-mathematical expression.[19] On the other hand, a less than adequate conception of the empirical has followed from the empirically unwarranted decision to make the meaning of 'experience' depend solely upon factors arising in sense perception. In current philosophy of science, both preconceptions have somehow come to be closely connected. That is to say, a narrow view of empiricism is shored up by an uncritical adoption of the mathematico-deductive view of the rational, and *vice versa*.[20] It seems characteristic of the positivistic mind that it sees no difficulty in assuming an intimate connection between what has in fact come to be sharply separated. I am suggesting that unless a reconciliation is attempted we have reached a permanent stalement in our efforts to understand the relation between the rational and the empirical.

The correct view is the one which Kant to some extent advocates but fails to consolidate: the rational and the empirical modes of reasoning require each other for their completion. For it seems impossible to conceive of anything being designated as rational knowledge of the world on grounds that make no appeal whatsoever to the empirical. (The exception is of course an appeal to a transcendent authority, but this requires revelation as distinct from justification.) A rational cognitive enterprise sets out to explain and describe *this* world, and regardless of what possible worlds must be invoked on the way, it is to *this* reality that the explanations and descriptions must ultimately refer. To put this point in another way, a rational account of this world can be called rational only insofar as the world itself is rational, that is, comprised of intelligible instances of order, system, pattern, and so forth. This observation can be dismissed as a truism only so long as the sheer contingency displayed by the onrush of world-events is either ignored or denied. For this reason, and on account of the strong inclination of Western though to adopt the latter course, it is worth noting well one of Whitehead's basic tenets. He puts the crucial point thus:

> You can push contingency back and back, but you never seem to get rid
> of it. . . . You can't give a reason for history.[21]

Briefly, <u>the pursuit of rational explanation is always confronted sooner or later with the problem of what to make of the contingent aspects of order, of that which just *is*, as pattern, system or whatever.</u>

But the nature of the problem of the ontological *ground* of rationality does not receive much attention in current philosophy. Epistemological concerns predominate; in particular, concerns about the justification of knowledge occupy the center of attention. But the quest for completely justified knowledge elicits a more fundamental worry: in order for such a quest to justify its own *raison d'etre*, it would first have to establish reasonably secure grounds for *expecting* that it is possible (without in the end having to appeal to empirical evidence, with all its attendant uncertainties) to find a fully justified account of rational enquiry.[22]

On the other hand, there is no way to give meaning to the notion of empirical facts which does not in some manner appeal to factors belonging to the domain of the rational. Such facts are not regarded as contributions to our knowledge of the world unless and until they are linked into a conceptual scheme by means of logical inferences, or according to some metaphysical categoreal framework, or, perhaps better yet, by a combination of both, as Whitehead claims needs to be done. Isolated facts (and it is highly doubtful if there really are such things) are, in themselves, of little significance. Significance derives in good part from relational standing. Isolated facts, if there are any, are most likely facts in transition, awaiting absorption into novel conceptual schemes.

The import of these observations for any enterprise that seeks to explain the relation between mathematics and the empirical is that it will not be proceeding either safely or sagely if it directs its attentions to only one half of an essentially inseparably reciprocity. For the terms 'rational' and 'empirical' do not denote independent or contrary notions but rather refer to different but mutually dependent aspects of one reality. In other words, these concepts are cardinal instances of what may be called complementary concepts; they are complementary in the sense that neither concept is capable of being fully understood in the total absence of reference to the other.

An acute awareness of the importance of conceptual complementarity is therefore one of the most salutary features of Whitehead's thought. A general sensitivity to the complementarity of the rational and empirical manifests itself in the stress which he places upon the complementarity inherent in many important conceptual dyads: necessity and contingency, atomicity and continuity, actuality and potentiality. All of these, I shall subsequently maintain, must figure centrally in an adequate account of the nature of mathematical and scientific thought.

As I have already mentioned, Whitehead is in sympathy with Kant's criticism of rationalism (i.e., Leibniz's) and of empiricism (i.e., Hume's). In the former case, a serious mistake is involved in the attempt to subsume sensations under concepts of the understanding. In the latter case, an equally serious mistake is perpetrated by trying to construe concepts on the model of sensations. But while agreeing on the diagnosis, Kant and Whitehead are divided as to the proper cure of these fundamental errors. The essential differences between their respective attempts to reconcile sensibility and understanding can, I think, be generally characterized in terms of 'complementarity.'

Kant speaks of two faculties of mind, the sensible and the intellectual, which deal with sensations and concepts respectively. His conception of the two faculties and of the their need for synthesis is not here in question. In the words of Scruton's clear restatement of Kant's position, it seems true that "A mind without concepts would have no capacity to think; equally, a mind armed with concepts, but with no sensory date to which they could be applied, would have nothing to think about."[23] But the epistemological problem predominates in Kant's treatment: in order to achieve his goal of establishing a foundation for objectively valid judgments of things, he argues for a "conjunction" of mental faculties. His synthesis is in the end elicited by and subordinate to his insistence upon a transcendental solution to the problems of knowledge.[24] It seems not much more than a problematic juxtaposition of essentially unreconciled concepts.

The grounds for a proper synthesis, Whitehead would maintain, need to be present at the outset of the philosophical enterprise, embedded in its very fabric, as it were. The fundamental complementarity of the Kantian faculties of the sensible and the intelligible seems to require an even more fundamental complementarity involving the general categories of the physical and the mental. While a full discussion of the point is outside the scope of this study, it is arguably just this feature of Whitehead's thought which enables him to proceed further than Kant with the attempt to reconcile the common sense world of science and everyday experience with the more esoteric and remote abstractions of mathematics and science.

We are now in a better position to describe the general character of a Whiteheadian philosophy of mathematics and the natural sciences.

Whitehead is both rationalist & empiricist.

Whitehead's way of thinking can be described as both rationalist and empiricist. But here 'empiricist' means 'radically empiricist,' where the roots of the concept of experience are not prematurely and arbitrarily trimmed by the presupposition that experience is completely reducible to sensory perception. On the other hand, it is rationalist enough to admit that mind is capable of partial penetration into the nature of the order of the world, with the assistance of logico-mathematical modes of thought.[25]

Without the hope of Kantian foundations upon which to found a rationalist-empiricist enterprise of the Whiteheadian kind, the problem of conceptual choice emerges as paramount and urgent. For it is evident that there is extreme difficulty in awarding just estimates of trustworthiness to the multitude of abstractions which compete for the thinker's allegiance. If the answer to our question "What is mathematics all about?" is not to be presupposed by according to the abstract system of mathematics some sort of ontological and epistemological privilege, it seems unavoidable that crucial decisions must be made at the outset about the relative significance of the many abstractions which arise from scientific and philosophical thought. The question is not only which concepts are to be trusted most, but also which of the many complex factors arising from the domains of the empirical and the rational deserve pre-eminence in a comprehensive scheme of thought.

There can be no final answer to such a question. Nevertheless, if one eschews the idea of re-building the world on the basis of the high abstractions of mathematics and logic (whose degree of abstractness can be roughly described in terms of their remoteness from ordinary experience), some sort of answer must be attempted. That is to say, there seems no escaping the necessity to choose governing concepts from the plethora of low abstractions (i.e., concepts whose vagueness and generality is compensated for by the breadth of their scope). Since such initial choices are crucial in that they control the whole programme of description and explanation, this topic deserves some special attention. I shall therefore take it up again in a later chapter. In what immediately follows, I will confine my observations to Whitehead's own approach.

Whitehead proposes that one of the large descriptive generalizations in which it is reasonable to place our trust is "process." It would be well to point out immediately that Whitehead's conception of the world as process does not imply that all aspects of reality can be subsumed under the category of the dynamic. Indeed, an indispensable element in Whitehead's attempt to account for the fact of order in the world is the hypothesis that there is a realm of enduring forms or potentialities ("eternal objects"), and these cannot be said to be in process. Nonetheless, such objects also have a claim to be included in the real, for they provide the abstract possibilities for the existence of types of order of any sort whatever. Thus process is not exhaustive of reality; rather process is that aspect of reality which falls under the category of the concrete. And, as Whitehead forcefully and (I will argue) rightly urges, the concrete ineluctably evokes its complement, the abstract. In the Whiteheadian approach, the factor of complementarity thus receives general recognition in the dictum that the actual facts of the concrete world cannot be fully understood without postulating a complementary realm of abstract possibilities or potentialities for order.

It is in the category of the purely abstract, or, in other words, in the realm of pure possibility, that Whitehead believes the elucidation of mathematical order must be based. But the complementary duality of the concrete (i.e., the dynamic process of world-events) and of the abstract (i.e., the static realm of possibilities), which reflects the general complementarity of the rational and the empirical, imports an ineradicable element of uncertainty into mathematics. This point becomes relevant whenever mathematics is viewed as knowledge of the intrinsic factors of necessity in the world. In brief, the so-called timeless truths of mathematics are in the end inexplicable without reference to the concrete contingencies of the world-in-process-as-we-know-it.

A similar consideration affects all discussion of the generic notion of order. Since the dynamic invokes its complement, the static, embodied in enduring static forms of order, the concept of order becomes fully intelligible only when it is regarded as one half of a complementary duality. This is completely in accord with common sense. For it is a fact that the notion of order is intimately connected to the notion of disorder. The evidence is overwhelming that the world is not the scene of perfect harmony, governed by eternal and perfect laws. To hold that the world exemplifies order by no means entails the extreme and simplistic rationalistic view which might be expressed concisely thus: *"Everything* in its proper place at its appointed time." Whatever conception of reality one finally arrives at, it must be capable of accommodating the facts of disorder, as well as the facts of order. Or, in short, talk about evil must be considered just as meaningful as talk about good. To deny this is to fall prey to the lure of false dichotomies, wherein one or the other half of a complementary duality is emphasized at the expense of the other half, thus relinquishing any hope of arriving at an adequate and plausible account. In this respect, then, Whitehead's whole approach begins on a very sound footing.

Since this discussion began on an epistemological note, with a suggestion that our knowledge of the world can, at any one time or place, achieve only a more or less satisfactory balance between the transparent and the opaque matter of fact, it is fitting that it should close in a like manner. It is Whitehead's contention that Western philosophy has not only been one-sided in its neglect of ontological questions and in its over-emphasis upon the epistemological problem of the justification of knowledge, it has also been one-sided in its failure to come to terms with the inherent complementarity of the knower and the known. This failure is reflected in mistaken and misleading basic preconceptions about perception.

In traditional approaches to problems of perception one finds competing, but equally narrow, conceptions of the relation between the perceiver and the perceived. The narrowness of these conceptions can be traced to a neglect of the inherent complementarity of the transparent and the opaque in our viewing of the world. Ian Hacking's succinct description of the change in the usage of the term 'perception' at the end of the eighteenth century may be pertinent here. He remarks that

> Cartesian perception is the active rendering of the object transparent to the mind. Positivist seeing is the passive blunting of light rays on opaque, impermeable 'physical objects' which are themselves passive and indifferent to the observer.[26]

I am suggesting that both types of viewing are necessary. The working of some sort of Cartesian viewing is evident in the very fact that the world grows more and more intelligible to us. Rational schemes of thought do evolve, and by their means we are led to new and surprising empirical discoveries. Modern physics, for example, has shown the power of rational conceptual systematic thought to penetrate into some very remote corners of the physical world. Such successes do not come about solely by means of deductive or of inductive procedures: they rely upon the insights of gifted individuals, that is, upon acts of creative imagination. Such insights seem to require for an adequate description reference to private acts of rational Cartesian viewing, although they are of course never purely private. They always occur in some historical and cultural setting which possesses strong elements of public viewing.

On the other hand, it is undeniable that positivistic viewing is an important element in the evolution of public or intersubjective knowledge, especially of scientific knowledge. The renowned testability of scientific theory depends upon this type of viewing; here the importance of the repeatability of sensory observations is hardly in need of emphasis. Yet the growth of scientific knowledge cannot be accounted for by concentrating upon one type of viewing to the exclusion of the other. The successes of science are due to what appears to be a delicate balancing act involving the complementary modes of Cartesian private and positivistic public viewing.

I will return briefly to this line of thought in the next chapter when I discuss some of the implications of the method of scientific discovery. The main point which I wish to make here is that either type of viewing, when carried over into philosophy, and emphasized at the expense of the other type, inexorably leads to a distorted conception of the relationship between the rational and the empirical. Indeed, to overemphasize either one of the two modes of perception seems to result in a world-view which Whitehead aptly describes as a "bifurcation of nature." Thereby one arrives at the philosophical impasse wherein the world become a mysterious, inexplicable interplay of "disembodied minds," on the one hand, and "isolated structures," on the other. The act of bifurcation thus inevitably generates a need for an *ad hoc* hypothesis in order to bring these divided realms together again. But apart from the philosophical objections which can be brought against this sort of move, it can be argued that it offends both against common sense and against current science.

It offends against the former in its denial of the complementarity of the transparent and the opaque. It offends against the latter in that it ignores or fails to take seriously enough what modern science has to tell us about the structure of the physical world. For developments in both physics and biology indicate that the world is in some profound sense evolutionary. And under a thoroughgoing evolutionary view, which Whitehead consistently urges, it does not make much sense to speak of an external world as if there exists a passive terminus 'out there' which patiently awaits isolated and independent acts of perception. This last consideration seriously undermines the once commonly held assumption that it ought to be possible to draw a distinct line of separation between the knower and the known. The perceiver, or better, "percipient event," to use Whitehead's more suggestive terminology, is part of the "ether of events" which go to make up the world. In Whitehead's characteristically vivid language,

> Mind is inside its images, not its images inside the mind: I am 'immersed' in a topic in mathematics, not the reverse. We are actors in scenes, not the scenes inside us.[27]

This consideration needs to be taken seriously once it is allowed that it is unwise to ignore or deny the interdependence of Cartesian and of positivistic modes of viewing.

Returning to the topic of mathematics and the problem of its role in world-viewing, it is highly unlikely that a simple straight-forward answer to the question of what mathematics is about will ever be found. At the outset, in quoting the remarks of Wigner, I suggested that a fairly large measure of humility might not be out of place. Once again, Whitehead strikes the right note. In contrast to Kant, who at times expresses remarkable confidence in the sufficiency of his metaphysical reforms, Whitehead reminds us of the immense difficulty of the problems we face:

> We have to remember that while nature is complex with timeless

subtlety, human thought issues from the simple-mindedness of beings whose active life is less than half a century.[28]

What follows, then, must be regarded as a tentative enquiry into whether or not Whitehead offers us a reasonably plausible and comprehensive account of the role of mathematics in our quest to know what there is and how it all hangs together. I shall try to show that he gives considerable satisfaction to the commonsense realist in so far as he provides a way to meet an essential requirement for an adequate story of the world: that is, whatever the difficulties in explaining them, he does not sacrifice the everyday facts of vivid observational, aesthetic, and ethical experiences to logical expediency.[29] At the same time he preserves the basic insight of idealism, the Kantian insight that it is impossible to stand off from the world and view it as a thing-in-itself, thereby obtaining objective knowledge of it independently of the fact that it is being viewed. In sum, Whitehead's account is founded upon the general awareness that not much progress can be expected if the complementary demands of epistemology and of ontology are not always kept in sight. But whether or to what extent Whitehead is successful in reconciling the rational and the empirical is a large and extremely complex question.

Chapter Two. Whitehead on Mathematics and Philosophy

> Only the mathematicians contrived to
> reach certainty and evidence, because
> they started with the easiest and the
> simplest.
> Descartes, *De Methodo* (transl. by H.
> Weyl)

1. *The Many-Sided Character of Mathematics*

There is never any doubt that Whitehead regards mathematics as one of the most impressive achievements of human thought. He says, for instance, "The science of Pure Mathematics, in its modern developments, may claim to be the most original creation of the human spirit."[1] This is a bold statement, so it is well to warn the reader that we shall not find in Whitehead a simple account of creativity in mathematics. In particular, he cannot be said to come down on either one side or the other in the historical debate over whether the genesis of mathematical system is to be explained in terms of 'invention' or in terms of 'discovery'. Typically and, one might add, realistically Whitehead's position is that every mathematical creation probably contains a good measure of each.

One good reason for describing Whitehead's attitude as realistic is that this sort of debate tacitly assumes that the question requires an either-or type of answer. But this may simply reveal how easy it is to insert red herrings, in the form of doubtful dichotomies, into the discussion of our large question. It also shows how tempting it is to deny or ignore significant aspects of the whole mathematical enterprise. For it is undeniable that elements of both creativity and discovery can be found in abundance in the history of mathematics. Reports from notable practitioners and users of mathemataics continually attest to the care and effort required in the expression of mathematical ideas, and to the significant difference which the choice of a symbolism can make to progress in the subject. On the other hand, there are also many impressive accounts of happy occurrences of the unexpected, of gratifying flashes of insight.

24

In the previous chapter, I have put forward some general reasons why we should regard putative dichotomies, such as the above, with considerable suspicion. In the context of the philosophy of mathematics, they do not outline crucial alternatives so much as they illustrate the difficulty in articulating just what is problematic about our large question. One worry which needs to be kept near the forefront of our concerns is the correctness, or otherwise, of the widespread assumption that the meaning of terms such as 'truth,' 'exactness,' 'necessity,' and 'certainty' are peculiarly unproblematic in the context of mathematics.

An expression of skepticism here is not tantamount to a denial that mathematics is in *some* sense intimately involved in the exact and necessary characteristics of physical reality. A denial of this sort would make a total mystery of the fact that mathematics plays an indispensable role in the discoveries of the so-called exact sciences. But there is a profound difficulty in explaining just what is meant by 'exact' and 'necessary' when these adjectives refer to the actual physical world. To hold that mathematics has something significant to reveal about the meaning of 'order' in the world is to raise profound metaphysical problems about the meaning of 'order' *per se*. Behind every use of this term lie philosophical assumptions whose coherence and intelligibility are very much part of our whole problem.

If one grants the truth of these observations, one is well on the way to admitting that much current philosophy of mathematics falls well short of being able to respond satisfactorily to the question of what mathematics is about. Whitehead's thinking about mathematics is an outstanding exception to this state of affairs. Long before he became a philosopher with an interest almost solely devoted to the construction of metaphysical system, even before he became a philosopher of science, Whitehead proved himself to be an insightful philosopher of mathematics. He adumbrates in his early writings a position which is compatible with and which points the way to many of his mature metaphysical reflections.

In what follows, I shall try to outline Whitehead's position by drawing attention to some of the more significant of his observations on mathematics and related topics.

It seems appropriate to begin by exploring the idea that mathematics is knowledge of a sort. I have already indicated that Whitehead is disposed to regard mathematics in this light. This does not entail, under his view, that mathematics possesses the degree of certainty which so many admirers of the subject have accorded to it. This idea, in its boldest form, is that mathematics leads to an infallible body of knowledge consisting of absolutely true conclusions deduced by means of universally valid laws of inference from certain and necessary premises.

As such, it supposedly lends to scientific theory whatever exactness the latter can claim. Taken to its extreme, this view issues in the scientistic faith that only that which can be explained and described in mathematical terms is knowledge, or at least the only knowledge worth having.

But Whitehead is not completely out of sympathy with the notion that only through mathematics can we obtain exact knowledge of the world. Indeed, he states explicitly that mathematics is "necessarily the foundation of exact thought as applied to natural phenomena."[2] His view accords with the now commonly acknowledged fact that mathematics does seem to be indispensable as a means to establish necessary and exact conclusions about events in the physical world. But the necessity and the exactness of mathematical applications seems never, and Whitehead argues *can* never be, pure and unqualified. The distinction between the extreme view of mathematical necessity and Whitehead's view of mathematical necessity is thus a central theme of this study, and one which I shall subsequently explore from a number of different angles. Let us first consider the notion that mathematics is a kind of exact knowledge.

This idea is, and has been throughout history, a highly controversial one. A central problem is the degree of certainty entailed in logico-deductive structure. Should the very nature of this structure allow one to assert dogmatically that if one knows mathematically then one knows with certainty? Or is a skeptical position more reasonable: that even in logic and mathematics we cannot ever know with certainty, or at least cannot know that we know?

This epistemological challenge has generated three types of response: they are, in Imre Lakatos' terminology, 1) the Euclidean programme, 2) the Empiricist programme, and 3) the Inductivist programme.[3] All programmes are in agreement on the indispensability of the logico-deductive method in the systematization of knowledge. But they differ radically as to the significance which is ultimately to be ascribed to the logical structure and its primitive foundations.

The Euclidean programme, according to Lakatos, is characterized by the search for a finite set of trivially true premises from which the truth of all propositions in the system can be deduced.[4] Thus the foundations of the subject are to be found at the top or axiomatic level of the deductive system. The strong appeal which the Euclidean programme has for its followers lies in the belief that, once the search for self-evident or trivially true first principles is successfully completed, truth will inundate the whole system by reason of what might be called, says Lakatos, the super-triviality of the deductive structure. This last assumption, that certain logical structures are wholly and transparently right, is one of the major weaknesses in the programme. The establishment of the truth of the logical first principles or inference procedures can never be made as secure as the spirit of the programme demands.

In the Empiricist programme, on the other hand, the foundations of truth and meaning are situated at the bottom of the deductive structure. Here, it is hoped, a primitive level of perfectly well-known empirical truths can be established. In Lakatos' view, the chief difference between a Euclidean and an Empiricist theory is that the direction of the flow of truth is from top to bottom in the former, while there is a counter-flow of possible falsity from bottom to the top in the latter. The falsity of an empirical statement at the end of a deductive chain puts the whole structure into question, whereas a demonstration of the truth of an empirical statement is no guarantee of the truth of its premises or the validity of its inferences. This means that an empiricist theory "is either conjectural (except possibly for true statements at the very bottom) or consists of conclusively false propositions."[5]

The above observations point to an important distinction which bears on the problem of the essential character of a deductive system. A deductive system, according to Lakatos, is characterized by the principle of the retransmission of falsity; that is, a counter-example to a conclusion must be regarded as a counter-example to at least one of the premises.[6] The principle of the transmission of truth, on the other hand, asserts that if there is no counter-example to any of the conclusions, then the deductive structure is a reliable link between premises and conclusions. Lakatos' distinction between these two principles shows that the principle of the transmission of truth, which expresses a common view of deductivity, is the weaker of the two. For it requires, in the absence of a formally established principle of induction, an act of faith before the reliability can be taken in any way as complete.

This indicates that the third programme, Inductivism, is a form of Euclideanism, at least insofar as its own search for foundations is based upon the presupppostion that it is possible to make these secure. Thus a pure inductivism would reflect an unswerving belief in the existence of a fundamental set of primitive empirical and logical entities, as well as the existence of formal means to justify the inductive process by which these are established. When regarded in this light, pure inductivism is a particularly clear instance of the Euclidean enterprise.

The spirit of Euclideanism has been extremely influential not only in the philosophy of mathematics but also throughout the whole of philosophy. As Whitehead puts it, philosophy has been misled by it into the temptation to seek "premises which are severally clear, distinct, and certain; and to erect upon those premises a deductive system of thought."[7] Russell's search for foundations of knowledge distinguishes him clearly from Whitehead in this respect. Under the above classification, Whitehead must be counted among the Empiricists, at least in spirit, and for reasons which I have already touched upon in the previous chapter.[8] More specifically, his views on the nature of deductivity exemplify a belief in the strong principle of the retransmission of falsity (that one counter-example to a conclusion puts the whole deductive system into question). And here Whitehead is surely on solid ground, for while we have good reason to believe that such systems *help* us to discover empirical truths, we have no reason to believe that we thereby obtain an absolutely firm grasp of them. And even if, *per impossible,* we could establish the primitive concepts as indubitable truths once and for all, we would still require a leap of inductive faith in order to assert that our particular deductive system was just the right one to organize our thinking around them. Being especially responsive to considerations such as these, Whitehead can be described as a particularly thorough empiricist. That is to say, he gives priority to evidence over system and is especially critical of the tendency of many philosophers and scientists to do violence to the meaning of the former in the name of the latter.

Whitehead's philosophy of mathematics is essentially irreconcilable with any other philosophy which exemplifies the Euclidean spirit. In this category are the well-known programmes of intuitionism and formalism. The intuitionist, such as Brouwer, seeks to found a secure reconstructed mathematics upon a self-evident basal intuition, the intuition of "two-oneness". The formalist, such as Hilbert, looks for error-free proof procedures. Formalism shares with intuitionism the basic philosophical presupposition that security and certainty are the proper goals of a reconstructed mathematics. Both programmes stress the importance of justifiable constructive methods. They differ in their respective identifications of the key to mathematical exactness. To answer the question of its location, as Brouwer succinctly puts it, "the intuitionist says: in the human intellect, the formalist says: on paper."[9] But the certainty of "self-evident" intuitions is always questionable, and, as I have noted previously, it is far from obvious that this approach could ever issue in truly secure foundations.

While the formalist and the intuitionist are concerned with mathematical certainty, they are not directly concerned with the exact validity of mathematical laws as laws of nature. The stress placed upon constructivist standards of proof, which follows from the belief that it is both necessary and possible to eliminate all sources of error in mathematics, illustrates an extremely narrow view of the problems involved, which arises perhaps from a Kantian misjudgement of the meaning of mathematics. Evidence for this exists in the minimal contribution that the programmes of intuitionism and formalism have made to the philosophical problem of explaining why mathematics works.[10]

But while Whitehead is an empiricist in the sense of rejecting an important tenet of the Euclidean programme, that the logico-deductive method of mathematics is somehow capable of guaranteeing certain and exact knowledge, it is important to note that this does not detract from his contribution to the logicist programme. For it might appear, at first glance, that here we will find Whitehead to be something of a Euclidean. As it happens, Whitehead's logicism is closely bound up with his empiricism.

For the moment, however, we note that Whitehead is far from exemplifying an ordinary empiricist view of mathematics. His approach is at least sophisticated enough for us to dispose at once of the worry that is often expressed as an obvious objection to an empiricist philosophy of mathematics: that it is impossible to devise direct empirical means to test the truth of mathematical theories. Such an objection rests upon the false assumption that tests of this sort are appropriate to mathematics. But <u>it is clear that a mathematical theory is not a scientific theory in having the character of direct empirical testability</u>. On the other hand, enough has now been said to throw some doubt on the notion that mathematics is merely a means to an end in the establishment of scientific knowledge. It may also be a kind of knowledge in its own right which receives indirect empirical confirmation whenever mathematically-based scientific theories receive empirical confirmation. This raises a question which is crucial to the whole issue. If mathematics does not merely serve to guarantee the respectibility of scientific knowledge but rather receives support for the claim that it is itself a certain kind of knowledge from the fact that it works in the creation of scientific knowledge, what is the genesis of the latter kind of knowledge?

2. *The Method of Retroduction*

My discussion so far leads to the following formulation of our large problem: how is it possible that logico-mathematical systems developed under the dominant constraint of self-consistency, and tied at certain points to non-intuitive (in many modern instances) physical hypotheses, can be so successful in the organization of our knowledge of the physical world? I am maintaining that we shall not get much further in assessing the strengths or weaknesses of Whitehead's views on the applicability of mathematics unless we become clearer about the scientific method of establishing and organizing knowledge in the first place.

A common view of scientific method, which is summed up in the claim of Newton's that he did not invent hypotheses, seems largely mistaken. For the most far-reaching advances in scientific theory appear to be the result neither of purely deductive nor of purely inductive procedures, but rather of an amalgam of both. This synthesis involves a large measure of creativity. Contrary to the Newtonian dictum, scientific premises are often the result of a speculative and creative framing of hypotheses. N. R. Hanson designates the type of reasoning actually used, at least by the forerunners in scientific advances, as retroduction (following C. S. Peirce who used the term 'abduction'). It is most in evidence when major concept-leaps occur in scientific theory.[11]

retroductio

Hanson describes the method of retroduction as a search for hypotheses which is prompted by the discovery of inexplicable phenomena. It is a type of imaginative reasoning which proceeds from the contemplation of surprising data (i.e., data which does not conform to existing patterns of explanation) to the formation of a new theory. The process both illustrates and arises from the scientist's deep desire to establish a coherent (preferably mathematical) system based upon a minimal set of premises.[12]

It is a salient characteristic of this mode of explanation that the things which demand explanation always become the means of testing the explanation. Moreover, the unifying hypothesis is not required to have the same order of comprehensibility as the phenomena which it helps to organize. This aspect is especially evident in modern physics where the trend is toward increasingly formal (i.e., mathematical) theories whose interpretation in terms of classical concepts becomes ever more problematical. Modern physical theories are, in fact, explanations only in a special sense of the word.[13] They do not organize knowledge in terms of deductive systems based upon premises which are simpler or better understood than the phemomena which are to be explained.[14] The ideal of comprehensibility has taken second place to the ideal of comprehensiveness. In other words, the search for unified systems, and ideally for one monolithic system, has rendered the notion of intelligibility subordinate to something like 'grasp of formal pattern.' Whether this is an inevitable consequence of scientific advance or whether it is even a reasonable view of scientific explanation is thus a pertinent question in a study such as this and one which I shall return to in Chapter 4. At this point I wish only to stress the importance of the method of retroduction in the establishment of some of our more significant scientific theories about the world.

It is possible to see the method of retroduction at work in the nonempirical mathematical sciences. Indeed, Whitehead's article "Mathematics" (published soon after the completion of *Principia Mathematica*) indicates an acute awareness of the significance of the retroductive method. Addressing the problem of the nature of the relationship between pure and applied mathematics, he notes that while every piece of mathematics, whether it is called pure or applied, may be viewed simply as mathematics (that is, as a formal construction proceeding to interesting conclusions from fixed premises by means of strict logical deductions),[15] there is nevertheless between pure mathematics and applied mathematics a fundamental difference in method.

> In 'applied mathematics' the 'deductions' are given in the shape of the experimental evidence of natural science, and the hypotheses from which the 'deductions' can be deduced are sought. Accordingly, every treatise on applied mathematics, properly so-called, is directed to the criticism of the 'laws' from which the reasoning starts, or to a suggestion of results which experiment may hope to find. Thus if it calculates the results of some experiment, it is not the experimentalist's well-attested results which are on trial, but the basis of the calculation.[16]

While this passage refers only to the retroductive procedures of applied mathematics, it is noteworthy to find that the concept of retroduction applies to Whitehead's and Russell's major reorganization of thought in logic itself. The method of retroduction underlies their attempt to express mathematics in terms of primitive logical concepts. In the preface to *Principia Mathematica,* with reference to the non-philosophical and dogmatic character of their investigation into the principles of mathematics, they write:

> The chief reason in favour of any theory on the principles of mathematics must always be inductive, i.e. it must lie in the fact that the theory in question enables us to deduce ordinary mathematics. In mathematics, the greatest degree of self-evidence is usually not to be found quite at the beginning, but at some later point; hence the early deductions, until they reach this point, give reasons rather for believing the premises because true consequences follow from them, than for believing the consequences because they follow from the premises.[17]

This may be taken as an apt description of the retroductive method as it applies to the programme of logicism. In logic, as in natural science, the primary concepts and premises do not have a claim to self evidence. Entities with such a claim appear further down in the deductive chains of reasoning, if they appear at all.

It is possible to find throughout Whitehead's work remarks on the purpose and methods of philosophy which are distinctly retroductive in import. For instance:

> Philosophy is the search for premises. It is not deduction. Such deductions as occur are for the purpose of testing the starting points by the evidence of the conclusions.[18]

I am suggesting that Whitehead's interpretation of the logicist programme must be seen in this light. In his early work, the retroductive point of view appears in his frequent appeals to Occam's Razor. For example, the authors of *Principia Mathematica* take pains to point out that they are not attempting to make a definitive and exhaustive analysis of existing mathematics in order to establish once and for all a unique and minimal set of basic premises. Rather, they say they are seeking to establish an adequate framework of logical concepts for the reconstruction of

> as much as may seem necessary of the data previously analysed, and as many other consequences of our premises as are of sufficient general interest to deserve statement.[19]

They do not assert that the analysis has been carried as far as possible. They affirm only that "the ideas and axioms with which we start are sufficient, not that they are necessary."[20] Again, one finds in the article "Mathematics" an independent expression of Whitehead's belief in the value of Occam's Razor. He notes that the procedure of defining number in terms of the general properties of classes and relations has two complementary features. The procedure "exacts a greater attention, combined with a smaller credulity; for every idea, assumed as ultimate, demands a separate act of faith."[21]

It is on this basis that one can distinguish Whitehead's and Russell's interpretations of the logicist programme. For Whitehead, the important aspect of the programme lies in the successful application of Occam's Razor to reduce the number of acts of faith required if a large number of mathematical premises is to be affirmed. For Russell, the programme is, at least before the discovery of the logical paradoxes undermines confidence in it, aimed at establishing logical foundations for mathematics, on the basis of which mathematical structures might finally be reconstructed free from perplexing uncertainties.[22] Thus, while Whitehead endorses Russell's general characterization of mathematics as the "science concerned with the logical deduction of consequences from the general premises of all reasoning,"[23] he cannot be described as a logicist in the same sense as Russell. In the last analysis, the two thinkers are of such different philosophical temperaments that, after their collaboration on mathematical logic, they were bound to take quite different philosophical directions.[24] Nevertheless, they share a deep respect for mathematics and logic as a powerful tool. It is a shared retroductive urge to clarify and unify the foundations of mathematics which underlies their successful collaboration on *Principia Mathematica*.

A proper description of Whitehead as a logicist, therefore, is incomplete without the following qualification: he is a pragmatic logicist in the sense that he aims at the simplification through unification which has been an undeniably important achievement of the logicist programme. But for him the chief significance of the programme is that it enhances our understanding of the complex interrelatedness of mathematical structures. It is perhaps worth stressing that, in Whitehead's view, this sort of understanding does not lead directly to an explanation of these structures in so far as they relate to or express something about the structure of reality. Nor is there, on the face of it, good reason to suppose that they should.

This partly accounts for Whitehead's somewhat pragmatic approach to various problems which are usually regarded as purely logical. For instance, he voices early approval of the theory of types as a device for preserving for mathematics the valuable theory of classes and relations. But he is careful to emphasize that the theory of types only resolves the difficulties which arise out of the *use* of the concepts of class and relation. It "does not decide the philosophic question as to the sense (if any) in which a class in extension is one entity."[25] He is very much aware, in other words, that the theory of types has metaphysical implications. In fact, Whitehead generally regards the difficulties surrounding the concept of a class to extend much further than the domain of logic.[26] Even at this early stage, he sees quite clearly that this problem encompasses an ancient philosophic dilemma, which he refers to as the dilemma of "the one and the many."[27]

The retroductive reorganization at the foundations of mathematics, to which Russell and Whitehead made such a significant contribution, continues to have profound consequences. Not least of these is the support lent by subsequent foundational studies to the view that the foundations of mathematics are ineluctably conjectural. The hope of ultimately establishing a final and secure basis for truths about reality in terms of classically certain mathematical or logical structures may finally be receding into the limbo of misbegotten human enterprises. Thus one consequence of logicism is reminiscent of the drastic alteration in our conception of the physical world which follows from the adoption of the quantum hypothesis. In mathematics, as well as in science, large cracks have opened in hitherto "sound"conceptual structures. Not even logic has been spared. The lesson for philosophy seems to be that in order to deal at all adequately with the cracks in this last bastion of certain knowledge, it may be impossible to avoid the risks inherent in the invention of hypotheses which are designed to account for what we want to save and explain.

3. *Pure Mathematics and Applied Mathematics*

As noted above, Whitehead maintains a clear distinction between pure mathematics and applied mathematics. The chief activity of the pure mathematician, he remarks in one place, is rule-following.[28] In this

sense his view is thoroughly modern. Pure mathematics has indeed
become the science of formal systems, of abstract symbols combined and
manipulated according to explicit and definite sets of rules. By contrast,
the work of the applied mathematician exemplifies, says Whitehead,
"covert inductive intention overlaid with the superficial forms of
deduction."[29] Or, in other words, the applied mathematician tends to
follow the methods of retroduction for which there are no definite rules.

Since pure mathematics need only display internal consistency in
order to justify itself, the question arises of the place of conventional
definitions in mathematical creation. On what grounds can one deny
their predominance, other than by dogmatic fiat? Whitehead would
quite properly refuse to allow that the question deserves an either-or
answer. There is, he suggests, very likely some truth in the claim, as put
forward in analytic philosophy, that the ground of mathematics and
logic is a body of analytic propositions connected by the powerful device
of symbolic reasoning. But once one admits the *usefulness* of pure
mathematical theories, it is simply not reasonable to regard them as
mere collections of tautologies. That is, not unless one is prepared to
regard the world as, in some profound sense, "tautological." And this
would be an unlikely metaphysical proposition, at least for a process
philosopher of Whitehead's bent.

There is probably a closely interwoven mixture of existential and
conventional content in mathematical definitions, and there is no
reason why one aspect should be clearly distinguishable from the other.
An important factor is the manner of the origin of definitions. In
Whitehead's estimation

> A mathematical definition with an existential import is the result of
> an act of *pure abstraction.* Such definitions are the starting points of
> applied mathematical sciences; . . . they require for verification more
> than the mere test of self-consistency.

As for conventional definitions, they cannot be regarded as entirely
arbitrary, despite their name, if the theory is to have survival value:

> In order that a mathematical science of any *importance* may be
> founded upon conventional definitions, the entities created by them
> must have properties which bear some affinity to the properties of
> existing things.[30]

Here, in these two early passages, taking note of the emphasized words,
we have an adumbration of Whitehead's philosophy of the mathematical sciences.

The position in outline is this: the question of the significance with
respect to reality of a mathematical theory is bound up with an
estimation of its importance; i.e., its actual or potential explanatory or
descriptive usefulness. And this may be evident in nothing more
substantial than the interests of a more or less influential group of

mathematicians. If the theory turns out to have, in the long run, no useful application it is not unreasonable to hold that it is merely conventional.[31]

For Whitehead the account of the existential status of definitions and the meaning of mathematical concepts is closely linked to the notion of abstraction. Pure mathematicians create abstract theories on the basis of a finite set of abstract concepts. How these abstractions actually come into the mathematical world is not a question which can be settled simply or easily. It requires, in fact, the prior development of a substantial metaphysical background, and so an answer can only be attempted at the end, and not at the beginning of an enquiry such as this. Granted that Whitehead's notion of "an act of pure abstraction" is loaded with philosophical difficulties, some such concept is necessary in order to bridge the gap between the purely formal and the practically useful. I have earlier suggested that one might think of this problem in terms of the complementarity of Cartesian and positivistic viewing. If one puts all one's emphasis upon the latter type of viewing, one fails to treat with due respect the fact that logic and mathematics actually work. This fact surely tells us *something* about the world, if only that its structures are of a certain kind, more or less. But the central puzzle still remains: how much more or less?[32]

For my present purpose it is enough to note that Whitehead's notion of "act of abstraction" is compatible with the fact that many premises and definitions of mathematical structures are established retroductively. The primitive notions are selected from an infinite variety of possibilities because they happen to be the ones which are of interest in a given historical or cultural scientific setting. The act of mathematical creation may thus involve acts of abstraction which, perhaps only fortuitously, introduce existential content into conventional definitions. Whitehead is not guilty here of blurring his own distinction between existential and conventional content, because for him an act of pure abstraction cannot result in a final and complete acquisition of essentials. In this respect, his early views are consistent with the more explicit philosophical constructions of his later work.

The unclear line of division between the existential and the conventional content of definitions exists because

> mathematical definitions are always to be construed as limitations as well as definitions; namely, the properties of the thing defined are to be considered for the purposes of the argument as being merely those involved in the definitions.[33]

This is an important epistemological point for a realist. To put it another way, the process of abstraction is a process which inexorably separates fundamental characteristics of objects or events into those belonging primarily to a foreground and those belonging to a background. That the latter are usually ignored does not entail their permanent irrelevance.

There is, therefore, reason to doubt that a unique and exhaustive description of the essential characteristics of a real object or event is ever achieved. What is relevant in one context may not be in another. Indeed, if the world is, as Whitehead believes (and here modern physics bears him out), essentially a dynamic plurality of interlocked events, rather than a static aggregate of independent entities, we seem to be led inexorably to the epistemological conclusion that even the most rigorously logical system of knowledge is inherently limited. But this observation anticipates a general conclusion which it is the ultimate aim of this study to show.

At this stage, we can adduce partial support for this view by noting that the application of even the most elementary theory of mathematics elicits deep metaphysical problems. Consider the process of ordinary counting. This applies the mathematical theory of cardinal numbers to the description of classes of physical entities. So it is a matter for experience, and not for logic, to decide whether the process of counting gives the true cardinal number of the class. For, as Whitehead puts it,

> It is perfectly possible to imagine a universe in which any act of counting by a being in it annihilated some members of the class being counted during the time and only during the time of [the act's] continuance.[34]

In other words, the inexactness of individuals in actuality requires a (usually suppressed) assumption about the application of arithmetic. In asserting a correspondence between the formal rules of arithmetical addition and the process of physical addition, we are simultaneously asserting an extra-logical principle. That is, we are relying upon "some inductively inferred law of permanence during that process."[35] Thus the meaning of 'exactness,' or even of the 'truth,' of the most elementary and simplest arithmetical proposition, such as '1 + 1 = 2,' is different in pure and in applied mathematics. The distinction cannot be discussed adequately in the total absence of an explicitly stated physical context. Regarded as a proposition in pure mathematics, the above statement is demonstrably true as a theorem in the theory of cardinal arithmetic. However, when regarded as an empirical statement, the final appeal as to its truth rests with experience.

This point may appear at first glance to be somewhat picayune, especially when viewed from the perspective of the macrophysical world of apples and sheep. The contrary is in fact the case. At microphysical levels of reality, for example, where myriads of "particles" undergo, so we are told, a ceaseless "dance" of activity and transmutation, the result of adding one to 10^{27}, say, may simply not obey the rules of arithmetic. Depending upon the types of entities involved, the result may be instead a tremendous release of energy. Furthermore, the operation of counting at the quantal level is surely a problematic concept, for to count is first to observe and, as quantum theory tells us, we cannot observe the objects of a quantum phenomenon as if they belonged to a closed system in complete isolation from the observer. In short, it is questionable if the standard example of '1 apple plus 1 apple = 2 apples' is at all paradigmatic of the most important applications of mathematics. At the very least, one must take into account the possibility, which if often overlooked, that a given mathematical theory is severely restricted in respect to its proper range of applicability. This is a crucial consideration and one which cannot be passed over in any attempt to estimate the place of mathematics in the rational elucidation of the empirical facts of the physical world. Indeed, it seems highly presumptous to decide this question before determining and stating explicitly what kind of world we actually live in.

4. Some Problems in the Philosophy of Mathematics

If Whitehead is correct in regarding process as a fundamental characteristic of reality, the fact that the apparently timeless abstractions of mathematics are somehow intimately involved in the transitory processes of the world (in so far as they are a part of applied mathematics) requires a particularly subtle explanation. For the profound problem of the meaning of 'order' immediately steps to the forefront of our puzzle. A world in process is a world in ceaseless transition. Hence to talk about the reality of this world is to speak of a plurality of events, none of which can be regarded as permanently enduring, free from all of time's implications of mutability. In other words, reality can never be caught unawares, as in an instantaneous photograph with all its elements of order on view: it is the *flux* of events which is on view, for this constitutes everything that there is to be viewed. Yet within this flux it is possible to discern pattern and structure. The question now arises whether the intimate connection which mathematics has to this structure is not ultimately explicable, at least in principle, solely in terms of its efficacy in the organization of our empirical knowledge of this structure.

For it is not to be denied that the persuasiveness and impressive precision of mathematical argument arises in good part from the efficiency of its symbolic mode of communication. Indeed, of all the symbolic structures that organize and express human thought mathematics is arguably the one that can claim to be the most efficient in terms of economy of mental effort. Whitehead's oft-quoted remarks on the symbolic aspect of mathematics are well worth repeating:

> By relieving the brain of all unnecessary work, a good notation sets it
> free to concentrate on more advanced problems, and in effect increases
> the mental power of the race.[36]

Moreover, this capacity to increase the power of thought through
formal symbolic manipulations constitutes, Whitehead believes, the
main difference between science today and the science of antiquity:

> then as now, a regularity of events was patent. But no minute tracing
> of their interconnection was possible, and there was no knowledge
> how even to set about to construct such a science.[37]

This point elicits another, closely related one: it is not simply the
efficiency of mathematical symbolic manipulation that is actually
impressive. We are ultimately impressed by the power of symbolic
structures to establish connections between apparently unrelated
concepts and ideas, or groupings of concepts. Thus a study devoted
exclusively to an investigation of its symbolic structure will not provide
complete elucidation of the fact that mathematical arguments are
meaningful in real physical contexts.[38] For this reason Whitehead holds
the view that the simplification of a good symbolism has two significant
aspects: it is not only of practical value, it is of great interest because "it
represents an analysis of the ideas of the subject and an almost pictorial
representation of their relations to each other."[39]

This suggestion, that the search for the meaning of mathematics
must take account of the non-verbal, diagrammatic nature of its
symbolic patterns, may be evident to any lover of geometry. For
instance, it is hard to believe that one's appreciation of the surprising
and beautiful theorems of projective geometry would not be seriously
impoverished if one were kept in ignorance of their pictorial (synthetic)
representations. But the importance of pattern is evident in algebra as
well. As Whitehead points out, the chief difference between verbal
expression and algebra is that algebra is "essentially a written language,
and it endeavours to exemplify in its written structures the patterns
which it is its purpose to convey."[40]

It is worth noting in passing that Whitehead's early work reflects a
deep conviction that mathematics has great significance for our
understanding of symbolic reasoning. In *Universal Algebra,* described
by Whitehead as a study of some recently invented algebras, or "systems
of Symbolic Reasoning allied to ordinary Algebra," he notes that he has
a dual purpose in studying such systems.[41] For they can be regarded
either as pure mathematics or as applied mathematics. As pure
mathematics, they are "systems of symbolism" and worth studying for
"the light thereby thrown on the general theory of symbolic reasoning."
On the other hand, as applied mathematics, they are useful "engines for
the investigation of the possibilities of thought and reasoning connected
with the abstract general idea of space."[42]

It is often remarked that the potential usefulness of mathematical systems is not a major source of inspiration behind their creation. This seems especially true of the work of algebraists. We thus come to another point which needs to be taken into consideration. It is a fact that aesthetic considerations figure greatly in the mathematician's acts of "pure" creation-invention. Indeed, we have here a secondary, but no less difficult, aspect of our large problem. There is a deep and far from clear connection between aesthetic feeling and abstract mathematical pattern. To hold that mathematics is merely a short-hand form of symbolic communication is to dismiss as irrelevant a large part of what makes mathematics *interesting* to the mathematician.

It appears, then, highly risky to prejudge this issue by concentrating upon the argumentative aspect of mathematical reasoning.[43] Both the search for pattern and the satisfaction experienced when it is found are as much in need of explanation as the fact that mathematical pattern is sometimes of great practical usefulness. In sum, the efficacy of mathematical reasoning is not explicable solely in terms of the utter generality of its symbolic structures and of the resulting deductive efficiency.

It is the latter fact, however, which presents us with the primary puzzle so far as the philosophy of mathematics is concerned. Mathematical systems are the most effective means, among all other means of symbolic representation, of organizing thought. It is virtually a commonplace that this is what makes it so valuable to science. Whitehead even goes so far as to say that "all science as it grows towards perfection becomes mathematical in its ideas."[44] But this remark is as much a reflection upon the nature of scientific thought as it is upon the nature of mathematics. The aim towards perfect generality is, *pace* the scientistic way of thinking, quite a different matter from the aim towards complete understanding. Whitehead's point is that perfect generality requires the highest abstraction for its expression, and, in his opinion, only mathematics is fully capable of this.[45] Of highest significance, therefore, is the thorny issue of the meaning of 'understanding.' Since our understanding of 'understanding' is far from clear, a host of questions would be simply begged if understanding as a whole were conflated with mathematical understanding. And there is a strong tendency to do just that in much current philosophy of science.

This observation brings us back to the heart of our problem. Here the practicality of mathematical reasoning contends for our attention with the element of reasoning-for-its-own-sake. These aspects of reasoning are very likely not completely separable. However much mathematicians appear to be playing a self-contained game, the possibility always exists that even the most esoteric of games may, sooner or later, turn out to be useful. The intermingling of the concrete and the practical with the abstract and the theoretical is, as Whitehead notes, one of the most remarkable features of scientific thought. That it is difficult to explain this conjunction become more and more obvious as we contemplate physics becoming less and less physical, which is to say, more and more reliant upon mathematical formalisms. While these undoubtedly help us to unify empirical observations, it is not so obvious that they lead in any direct way to explanations of physical phenomena. We are thus confronted once again with the question of method. If explanation is not going to come from one or another direct encounter with mathematics, no more will it come from a direct encounter with uninterpreted formal mathematical physical theories. We must adopt a roundabout way to balance the respective claims of the practical and the theoretical. As I indicated earlier, the method which underpins Whitehead's whole approach is that which appears to have been most effective in the scientific enterprise itself: the method of retroduction. It has profound implications for metaphysical investigations as well as for scientific investigation.

5. On Mathematics and Metaphysics

If one holds that the presence of features of regularity within the flux of events is neither completely fortuitous nor completely fictional (which is not to deny that every event has its contingent aspects), one is led to postulate retroductively a non-contingent source of forms of order. At the basis of process there must be, in Whitehead's view, abstract possibilities ("pure potentials" or "eternal objects") which are in some sense outside the flux. This type of thoroughgoing metaphysical response is, at present, very much out of fashion. So before pursuing this topic any further, it may be well to summarize some of the general considerations which point to the conclusion that this sort of metaphysical talk is not only appropriate in the context of modern philosophy, it may actually be unavoidable.

I have already discussed some of the reasons why the metaphysical question, how to account for those apparently permanent aspects of order and necessity that are manifest in our transitory world, is not only extremely difficult, but also wide-ranging. For it elicits all sorts of questions touching upon the problem of the relation between the rational and the empirical. I have argued in the previous chapter that it does not make sense to think that the pursuit of this kind of philosophical enquiry can proceed very far if epistemological questions about the manner of knowing are not closely linked to ontological questions about what is known. The widespread belief that a more or less clean division can be maintained between these two realms of philosophical enquiry seems to be intimately bound up with a misconception of the place of mathematics in the quest for rational explanation and description of what there is. By this means, philosophy, or at least that part of it which takes science seriously, has put itself seriously off balance when it comes to explaining the connection between the rational and the empirical. This is one good reason why much of what it has to say about the nature of the relationship between mathematics and reality is suspect and in need of radical revision.

This point turns in part on whether or not the method of retroduction is in fact as deeply implicated in a philosophical investigation of this kind as it is in science. Whitehead is in no doubt that this method has broad implications for philosophy as a whole. In his remarks upon the nature of scientific enquiry he explicitly points out that science is never capable of proceeding very far by the methods of pure deduction or of pure induction alone. Instead, the method used in practice is always a synthesis of the two modes. Whitehead's metaphor which likens thought to the flight of an airplane vividly illustrates this fact. He observes that if science had consistently followed the method of pure induction, it would have remained precisely where it started:

> What Bacon omitted was the play of a free imagination, controlled by the requirements of coherence and logic. The true method of discovery is like the flight of an aeroplane. It starts from the ground of particular observation; it makes a flight in the thin air of imaginative generalization; and it again lands for renewed observation rendered acute by rational interpretation.[47]

As for the method of pure deduction, Whitehead believes it has had a pernicious influence on philosophy, however great its significance is for scientific method:

> The method of philosophy has. . . been vitiated by the example of mathematics. The primary method of mathematics is deduction; the primary method of philosophy is descriptive generalization. . . . [Deduction takes its] true place as an essential auxiliary mode of verification whereby to test the scope of generalities.[48]

Thus Whitehead sets himself fully against the inclinations of many present-day philosophers with his retroductive statement of the final aims of rational enquiry:

> The verification of a rationalistic scheme is to be sought in its general success, and not in the peculiar certainty, or initial clarity, of its first principles.[49]

Moreover, his aims are the aims of the commonsense realist who is concerned to make sense of the apparently significant discoveries of rational science. Both this kind of realist and the rational scientist share what Whitehead refers to as the "hope of rationalism," that "we fail to find in experience any elements intrinsically incapable of exhibition as examples of general theory."[50]

For Whitehead, then, there is no escaping the (to many, uncomfort-able) conclusion that talk connected with the aims and methods of rational enquiry (e.g., about justified knowledge, or about 'verification' or 'confirmation' or 'interpretation' of scientific theories), is subordinate to talk about metaphysically ultimate entities. And if it is correct that the retroductive method of enquiry is all we have to go on, it does seem an inescapable conclusion that if we want satisfactory explanations of the world and its workings, we must first have a metaphysical system. This means we must either construct or make tentative ontological commitments to categoreal schemes in the manner of Whitehead.

This point, however, is an extremely controversial one, for it turns on the tricky issue of what a satisfactory explanation might be. Hence I will return to it in chapter four. For the present, if we grant that it is necessary to postulate some kinds of metaphysically ultimate entities, it is clear that real difficulties arise over which particular concepts might be adequate as a basis for a plausible programme of "descriptive generalization."

It must be acknowledged that to follow Whitehead's lead in this matter is to throw oneself immediately into the deep end of metaphysical waters. It is perhaps for this reason that few care to follow. Be this as it may, it is often objected that Whitehead's introduction of eternal objects and of actual entities, as fundamental metaphysical categories pertaining to respectively the abstract and the concrete aspects of reality, evokes out-moded Platonistic conceptions which have no place in modern explanations of the events of the world.

Skepticism about such things as eternal objects and actual entities is not easy to respond to, if for no other reason than that the question of what constitutes an adequate explanation is extremely complex. It may help to consider briefly the analogous situation in particle physics. Here there is no quibbling about any lack of direct access to elementary particles. Not even electrons, whose existence is perhaps least in doubt, must submit to the indignity of being pointed out as individuals, even supposing this were a physical possiblility. Likewise, the existence, or otherwise, of eternal objects and actual entities is not one which could be resolved in a metaphysically neutral fashion by pointing, say, to certain empirical facts concerning 'order.' There would be no point in complaining, for example, that it is extremely difficult to produce a clear and unproblematic instance of an eternal object in real events. Such entities can no more be produced for critical inspection than an actual entity or an electron could be plucked, as it were, out of the onrush of events and examined under a microscope.[51]

In short, metaphysically ultimate entities, like fundamental physical entities, are thoroughly permeated with possibly extraneous trappings of theory and conjecture. The main difference is that elementary particles possess, at least for the trained physicist, who knows *how* if not *where* to look, a higher degree of accessibility than metaphysically ultimate entities. Nevertheless, it is nothing like *direct* accessibility. Elusiveness and ephemerality are primary characteristics of such things. In a word, as with quarks and their "strange" properties, so (almost) with actual entities and eternal objects.

Indeed, all metaphysically ultimate objects owe their existence to the demands of rational-empirical theory construction, that is, to the retroductive method. In the end, the only justification for introducing them is that without them it is not possible to make sufficient sense out of all the factors which are judged to be significant and indispensable. And science bears witness that it is a delicate and extremely difficult task to separate highly conjectural and corrigible theoretical considerations from more observationally accessible, and thus more certain, empirical data. Whether or not particular elements of an explanation can be dispensed with, on the grounds that they introduce unnecessary complications, or that they fail to contribute to the adequacy of the final account, or even that they fail to satisfy intuitive conditions of plausibility, is a question which can only be decided once a fair sample of all the relevant factors have been inspected. And what is acceptable as a fair sample is not always obvious or easily decidable.

Thus the appropriateness, or otherwise, of Whitehead's retroductive postulation of two fundamental complementary realms of reality, the realm of the concrete and the realm of the abstract, is intimately linked to the vital question of what are the most relevant and salient facts which explanation in philosophy and science must take into account. So not only does Whitehead raise the important question of just *what* is to be explained, he raises the even more fundamental question of what an adequate explanation would look like in the first place.

To return now to the problem of explaining mathematics, it appears at first glance that Whitehead's general stance puts him squarely in the camp of the Platonists. So it is first necessary to point out that Whitehead's position has only a partial resemblance to Platonism. The theory of eternal objects is in fact only a quasi-Platonic theory of forms. This theory is subordinate to Whitehead's primary metaphysical concerns which are generally aimed at avoiding the temptations of vicious dualisms. In particular, he is careful not to adopt a conception of the abstract in which this is set over against the concrete. Thus Whitehead's is a Platonism in which the abstract entities are not to be conceived as essentially divorced from life and motion.[52]

The essential nature of mathematics, in Whitehead's view, is that it is capable of expressing some of the relations exemplified by and existing between these forms of order. It is their connection with process which, in Whitehead's opinion, saves mathematics from collapsing into mere tautology.[53] Therefore, in order that the forms may not be divorced entirely from reality, Whitehead insists upon their immanence as well as upon their transcendence. We thus return to a fundamental characteristic of his thought, which I have called "complementary dualism."

I have maintained in the previous chapter that a constant awareness of the complementarity in key conceptual dualisms is necessary for an adequate treatment of many philosophical problems. Such an awareness is essential, in any case, for a proper understanding of Whitehead's approach. In the context of the philosophy of mathematics, the complementary duality of the abstract and the concrete, which is intrinsic to Whitehead's fundamental metaphysical categories of eternal objects and actual entities, precludes any identification of his type of Platonism with more standard versions of mathematical Platonism. But there are other reasons of a less technical nature for withholding this appellation from a Whiteheadian philosophy of mathematics.

A major issue in the philosophy of mathematics is the meaning of 'mathematical truth.' Traditional Platonists, along with intuitionists, want to to be able to say unequivocally of any individual mathematical statement that it is either true or false.[54] Yet it seems a rash prejudgment, if not a gross over-simplification, to demand that mathematical statements have such a direct connection to truth. It seems much more realistic to assume, at least to begin with, that the meaning of mathematical statements may simply not be capturable by a bivalent notion of truth.

The reason for this is that to claim that a particular statement is determinately either true or false is, in effect, to hold that each statement must refer in some fundamental and unproblematic manner to reality. It is only by means of this sort of assumption that the intuitionist or the traditional platonist can hope to be talking sense when speaking of "mathematical reality".[55] The central issue of truth, however, involves not the nature of mathematical reality but rather the nature of reality *per se*. And the fact that the nature of reality is extremely problematic makes the concept of truth equally problematic.

Whitehead is well aware of this consideration. For him, questions about the meaning of mathematics are inseparable from questions about the meaning of a whole complex interrelated structure of concepts. In other words, his approach is thoroughly holistic in the sense of adhering closely to the view that mathematical statements must be regarded as part of a body of statements, no one of which can be regarded as having a truth content which is entirely independent of other, extremely elusive and debatable, truth claims.[56]

Hence the fundamental question in a Whiteheadian approach to the philosophy of mathematics is not whether or not mathematical concepts or structures are true independently of our knowledge of them or of our possession of the means to prove them. Nor is it the question which so exercises intuitionists and constructivists: whether mathematical statements within particular structures are only deserving of being designated as true and meaningful according to whether or not there exist legitimate constructive means to decide the matter. Rather the real difficulty is to decide what view of reality is most compatible with the fact that mathematical structures are capable of opening a window through which we can discern particular types of order which are actually involved in the obscure processes of the physical world. It is this consideration which drives a holistic thinker, such as Whitehead, to refuse to separate questions of meaning in specialized languages, such as mathematics, from more metaphysically significant (and committed) languages, such as the language of the physical sciences.

It seems hardly necessary to add that the Whiteheadian view explicitly denies another common Platonistic assumption, namely, that reality itself is comprised of abstract mathematical structures. In fact, Whitehead's sophisticated Platonism is of such a different order from that which is usually understood by the term that it scarcely warrants the same name. For traditional mathematical Platonism seriously misapprehends the nature of the whole problem. Apart from the tendency to hypostatize abstract entities, it frequently errs with an uncritical adoption of the assumption that crucial debates about meaning in the philosophy of mathematics and the natural sciences can be resolved within the confines of this specialized area of enquiry. In this respect, it closely resembles the more philosophically sophisticated but ultimately unsatisfactory doctrines of intuitionism and constructivism.

Whitehead's sophisticated Platonism is not, therefore, subject to the general charge which can be levelled at most philosophies of this sort. They simply do not take the whole problematic of 'order' seriously enough. And this problematic raises difficulties for the whole of philosophy of mathematics which extend far beyond those that are generally recognized as properly belonging to this specialized discipline. One of the more outstanding of these problems concerns the question, raised at the end of the previous section, of the extent to which a mathematical theory can be said to be representative of actual order.

Any claim that mathematics expresses something of the character of the order which permeates process does not necessarily entail the proposition that any mathematical theory, however well-adapted it is to the description of physical reality, is of necessity (or can, in principle, be reconstructed so as to become) a complete or exhaustive or exact expression of actual order. On Whitehead's view, mathematical theories are to be regarded as constructions in the realm of potentiality. This is a reasonable hypothesis, given that there is no reason to believe that a particular mathematical construction will necessarily have *complete* relevance to actuality, assuming it has any at all. The limitative theorems of Goedel *et al* would seem to provide sufficient reason for a cautious approach in this respect. But there are stronger reasons of a metaphysical nature which, as I shall try to show, emerge as we try to come to grips with what modern science has to say about reality. The upshot of these is to support the general Whiteheadian view that a mathematical theory is very much like any other theory in respect to what it has to say about reality. This means, among other things, that it very likely has only more or less clearly definable domains of applicability.

From the epistemological point of view, there is no compelling reason to believe that that part of mathematics which deserves to be called knowledge can be entirely subsumed under either a correspondence theory of truth or a coherence theory of truth. For such a theory need not be true merely on account of its consistency. On the other hand, its applicability to the physical world (supposing it has any) does not necessarily guarantee the existence of all the structures of order which are implicated. Here again, Whitehead's view that the abstractions of mathematics may only partially correspond to their concrete counterparts, if any, and only partially express pure necessity seems generally on the right track. And if Whitehead is correct in his overall assessment of the situation, it is likely that a similar conclusion must apply to the logical structure underlying mathematics. Indeed, under the Whiteheadian view, logical patterns, as patterns expressive of abstract potentiality, are *ipso facto* subject to the same limitations as mathematical patterns.

Whitehead not only brings out clearly reasons to believe that most approaches to the philosophy of mathematics are far too simplistic, he sets us on a path of inquiry which does much to reveal the immensity of the whole problem. He makes us face the fact that whatever will deserve to be called an adequate and comprehensive philosophy of mathematics must be one which attempts to explain not only *how* but also to *what extent* the abstractions of mathematics are involved in the concrete world.

Since his response to the problem of explanation sharply divides Whitehead from the mainstream of the philosophy of mathematics, I shall explore it in greater detail in the following chapter. There I will attempt to demonstrate, through a discussion of certain puzzles which stem from Zeno, that Whitehead's metaphysical approach comes much closer to providing an adequate reply to Zeno than does the more standard mathematical approach. Following this discussion, I will argue further in support of my contention that certain mistaken assumptions about the nature of scientific explanation effectively stand in the way of progress in this whole problem area.

Chapter Three. Zeno's Paradoxes: Mathematical and Metaphysical Responses

> There is no religious denomination
> in which the misuse of metaphysical
> expressions has been responsible for
> so much sin as it has in mathematics.
> L. Wittgenstein, *Culture and Value*

1. Zeno Versus the Mathematicians

A common assumption in modern responses to Zeno is that purely mathematical arguments have an important role to play in the resolution of his paradoxes. My purpose here is to attempt to show that the mathematical response to Zeno is not the appropriate one. I shall argue that the importance of mathematical arguments to Zeno's paradoxes has been largely over-rated: they simply fail to do any justice to the complex factors of both a physical and metaphysical nature which his problems inevitably evoke. This is because the mathematical solutions depend upon arguable presuppositions about the physical interpretations of mathematical formalisms, which in turn cannot be separated from their metaphysical backgrounds. The philosophical core of Zeno's arguments is too remote from the mathematical treatments to be adequately dealt with by such means. Abstruse and elaborate mathematical discussions thus add little to the resolution of the profound difficulties which the arguments of Zeno perennially reincarnate. Moreover, the inadequacy of mathematical arguments in modern attempts to counter Zeno's arguments contributes to the doubt that one of the traditional assumptions about the applicability to physical continuity of the mathematical continum is valid. This is the hypothesis that the mathematical continuum accurately and exhaustively mirrors the physical continuum.

As Whitehead observes, it is the mark of a good philosophical problem that it should constantly inspire the invention of arguments claiming to meet all its difficulties. Such are the problems of Zeno, he says: "No one has ever touched Zeno without refuting him, and every century thinks it worth while to refute him."[1] In the past century, mathematical arguments have dominated discussions of Zeno's problems, no doubt on account of significant advances in both mathematics and mathematical physics. For it is maintained that the successful establishment of logical foundations for analysis, due to Cauchy, Weierstrass, Dedekind, Cantor and many others, has contributed greatly to the solution of certain forms of Zeno's puzzles. Bertrand Russell, for example, confidently asserts that it is just the lack of a tenable theory of infinite numbers, subsequently supplied by George Cantor, which vitiates the contributions of previous generations of thinkers.[2]

On the other hand, there is much to be said for the view that Zeno's arguments do not demand refutation so much as they require accommodation. Whitehead himself maintains this minority point of view; for him they indicate the metaphysical truth of atomism. But in order to understand why Zeno's problems should lead to, if not logically entail, this metaphysical conclusion it is first necessary to become clear about the shortcomings of the majority view. I shall begin by dealing with the question whether Zeno can, even in principle, be satisfactorily answered within a non-metaphysical, indeed purely mathematical, setting. Then I shall explain why I think Whitehead's approach is more promising.

Discussions of Zenonian arguments against common sense beliefs in the existence of plurality or of motion in the physical world, or against then current forms of Pythagoreanism which underlay attempts to describe and explain it,[3] naturally reflect assumptions about the nature of the physical world. The perennially pertinent message conveyed by Zeno is that the nature of physical continuity is not well understood; yet mathematical treatments presuppose a clear understanding of continuity. For on the matter of continuous extension, to be able to counter Zeno is to be able to reply, without falling into contradiction, to the question: Is it intelligible to conceive of the world, at least in its spatio-temporal aspects, as made up of geometrical (i.e., extensionless) points? If so, how shall one conceive of the building up of extended events from unextended points, or, conversely, how shall one conceive of the deconstruction or division of extended entities into extensionless points?[4] This general question underlying Zeno's arguments is one which I shall take as central to my discussion.

In mathematical texts the paradoxes of Zeno are often used paedagogically to demonstrate the value of acquiring a familiarity with the theory of infinite series. It is frequently claimed that this theory dispenses with at least some of the Zenonian puzzles once for all.[5] A brief examination of the Bisection Paradox will expose the dubiety of this claim. In one form of this paradox a finite line segment is conceived as a finite distance to be traversed. Zeno's argument is that this can only be achieved by successively traversing an infinite sequence of subintervals obtained from the whole interval by repeated bisection. This bisection, from the whole to a half to half the second half, and so on, generates an endless sequence of successively shrinking finite intervals. A contradiction emerges once it is admitted that it is impossible to sum an infinite sequence of finite lengths. Hence the traversal of a finite interval is impossible.

Before considering the standard mathematical solution, it is well to note the problematic nature of the formulation itself. As with a related problem, the Paradox of Achilles and the Tortoise, it contains confusing and irrelevant references to time and motion (i.e. to traversal of intervals). Indeed, one's very first step into the profundities of Zeno's problems cannot help but be muddled if one does not first distinguish between the paradoxes of motion and the paradoxes of plurality or extension. For kinematical descriptions assume pre-established properties of space and time. Thus the problems of extension have a claim to priority over the problems of motion, at least to the extent that the latter add to the complexity of more fundamental puzzles. Furthermore, the above standard formulation of the Bisection Paradox raises the important question of whether it is even intelligible to apply the term 'movement' to geometrical (i.e. extensionless) points.[6]

The conflation of the puzzles of motion and extension probably owes much to the Newtonian conception of a line segment as the path generated by a moving extensionless point. It may be that many of the muddles arising from confusing or incoherent formulations of Zeno's puzzles are traceable to the Newtonian world-view, which still permeates much of our everyday, and even scientific, language.[7] At any rate, formulations of Zeno's problems which refer, even if only covertly, to moving points tend to lose their intelligibility in concert with the Newtonian cosmology. For this world-view is based upon the assumption that it is meaningful to speak of instantaneous punctiform existences, but this notion becomes less and less credible with every advance in modern science.

Even from the most elementary point of view, that of extension alone, the mathematical solution leaves us in puzzlement. For the Bisection problem in its original spirit implicitly demands an explanation as to how the sum of an infinite number of finite distances can be reconciled with the notion of the physical summation of a finite number of finite distances, the latter alone being accessible to common sense. The mathematical solution does not meet this demand, for the solution appeals to the comparatively sophisticated mathematical theory of an infinite series of a real variable. The mathematical answer takes the form of a demonstration that the infinite sequence of bisected lengths forms a geometric sequence of lengths whose infinite "sum," according to the theory, is a definite number which is equal to the original length of the interval. Hence, the sum of the infinite sequence of bisected subintervals clearly does exist after all and Zeno is refuted.

But what is meant by the sum of an infinite series is not what is meant by the sum of a finite series. For the sum of an infinite series is defined in terms of the concept of the limit of a real-valued function, while the sum of a finite series refers to the quite different notion of ordinary arithmetical addition. It might be objected that the definition of infinite sum is a consistent generalization of the notion of a finite sum, and so it is in the sense that the former reduces to the latter in the finite case. Nevertheless, the definition of the infinite sum presupposes the definition of a limit of a real variable, and this in turn presupposes a consistent formalization of the real continuum, not to mention an assumption about the intelligibility of full mathematical continuity in descriptions of the physical world. Hence the generalization adds considerable novelty and complexity to the ordinary notion of addition which is, in physical contexts, ultimately understood in operational terms.

But the question then arises, if the two uses of the term 'sum' are not interchangeable, what *does* the mathematical solution really signify? As R. L. Goodstein points out, it would have been no surprise to Zeno that the sum of an infinite geometric series of bisected subintervals is equal to the length of the whole inteval. For the subintervals are the result of a subdivision of the entire interval in the first instance.[8] We have, with the mathematical theory, merely found the means to add them up again. Without the leap of blind faith which is required by the postulate that the real continuum actually mirrors the physical continuum, it is difficult to understand why one should conclude anything more definite than that the theory of the mathematical continuum can accommodate consistent usages of terms such as 'sum', 'length', and so on. And this seems hardly surprising in view of the fact that the theory of the continuum has developed, at least in part, from the explicit desire to establish a consistent mathematical theory of mensuration. If nineteenth-century mathematicians had failed to find a consistent mathematical theory of infinite series which was also compatible with our physical intuitions and expectations, it is doubtful that the theory would have gained anything like its present prominence. But the mere fact of its usefulness does not in itself throw any light upon the question as to *why* one should conflate the meanings of finite and infinite sums.

Such considerations make it evident that mathematical solutions do not, at any rate, provide universal remedies for Zenonian troubles. Indeed, in the case of the above formulation, the mathematical treatment does not even approach a satisfactory resolution. One lesson that emerges clearly is that *how* one formulates Zeno's problems is of utmost interest. In other words, it does not suffice simply to refute Zeno in terms of the explicit premises of the particular variation of a Zenonian puzzle which happens to be under discussion. Zeno's problems are not merely dialectical exercises wherein the chief aim is to avoid or dispel apparent contradictions. For should a Zenonian argument be accepted as completely successful it would entail the admission that the world is, at any rate, not like *this* (whichever view is implicated in the premises of the argument). Frequently, however, key metaphysical presuppositions are imported into the discussion as part of the phraseology whose intelligibility is dependent upon a presupposed world-view. Thus what is of chief interest to Zeno is only briefly or tacitly alluded to and attention is focused upon the argument itself. The result is an unsatisfactory treatment with a residue of unanswered questions belonging to some neglected but crucial perspective. This fault is especially characteristic of putative mathematical resolutions of Zenonian problems.

2. *The Exact-correspondence Hypothesis*

In general, then, mathematical treatments of Zeno's puzzles evoke the whole difficult philosophical problem of the applicability of mathematics. In terms of physical continuity, this problem takes the form of how to conceive of the correspondence between the formal properties of the mathematical continuum and their actual, or perhaps fictional, physical correlates. It is a common assumption held by many mathematicians, philosophers of science, and scientists that the mathematical continuum exhaustively and accurately reflects the properties of the physical continuum, assuming that there is one. This assumption, which I shall designate as the exact correspondence hypothesis, is thus of primary importance in mathematical responses to Zeno. However, to doubt its veracity is to plunge directly into the heart of the profound question of the relationship between the exact concepts of mathematics and the inexact concepts which pertain to the physical world. Small wonder, then, that the exact-correspondence hypothesis is so popular.

Nevertheless, recent developments in physics, and particularly in quantum theory, have given new impetus to speculations that matter and space-time possess an irreducible granular texture. Thus from the physical point of view the exact correspondence hypothesis has lost some of its former self-evidence. But there are more immediate and intuitive grounds, as well as historical grounds, for doubting it.

A recurring problem for intuition in the attempt to understand the physical continuum, under the exact-correspondence hypothesis, is the sheer oddness of the formal mathematical notion of continuity. The intelligibility of the latter is dependent upon the intelligibility of the concept of the actual infinite. Ever since Georg Cantor succeeded in making this concept not only compatible with the intuitive notion of a finite set (at the cost of making the notion of the finite secondary to that of the infinite) but also exceedingly fruitful in terms of novel mathematical concepts, mathematicians have tended to believe that the intelligibility of the actual infinite is somehow guaranteed by the consistency of the formal system of real numbers. While this consistency is recognized as one that cannot ever be established as absolute, a widespread confidence in its comparative security is responsible, no doubt, for the ease with which mathematical continuity is conflated with physical continuity.[9] But it is no easier now than it was for Aristotle to conceive of the actual infinite as playing an actual role in the concrete world. Indeed, this conceptual task is even more difficult for the modern enquirer because the concept of mathematical continuity confounds the intuition with an astonishing multiplicity of numbers extending over quite diverse species. Certain of these species cannot, in principle, even be enumerated, that is, ticked off one by one: which is to say that there are more of them than could possibly meet the eye, assuming that it makes sense to speak of counting aggregates of extensionless entities.[10] The so-called irrational numbers do seem to be, from a physical point of view, an embarrassing and unreasonable surfeit in that they have no practical value so far as the operation of measurement is concerned. Their non-denumerable totality, when conceived as geometrical points packed into a line interval, lends an air of mystery to the latter in so far as geometric line intervals are assumed to have real physical significance. It is just this mystery which is open to the modern Zeno to exploit.

There are also reasons of an historical nature for doubting the exact-correspondence hypothesis. The standard theory of number evolved in tandem with the calculus. The history of the latter is a history of a struggle to overcome the incoherencies both logical and metaphysical arising from vague and ill-defined concepts. The currently accepted rigorous formulation of the real number system as an abstract axiomatic structure is thus the result of an historically protracted quest for a sound and intelligible foundation upon which to base the quantitative study of spatio-temporal phenomena. It gradually reversed the ancient Greek conception of number as the expression of immediately accessible intuitions of continuous geometrical magnitudes. The modern concept of real number stresses the logical completeness of the systematic expression of real numbers over the intelligibility of their correlates in terms of geometric intuitions. The development of the concept has thus resulted in a highly non-intuitive conception of number. The modern non-geometrical or "arithmetical" number is a mere symbol whose meaning derives from its role in a system and is nothing in itself. In other words, it is a primitive undefined entity satisfying the formal conditions of a complete Archimedean ordered field. Supporters of the exact-correspondence hypothesis, however, propose that we should now make an about-face in this historical process and, by fiat, as it were, reinvest the formal elements of this abstract system, which has been purged of its intuitive content, with physical meaning.

Here we meet what is described as the semantical problem of finding coordinating definitions between key mathematical terms and their physical referents. It is now generally recognized that to find suitable definitions which coordinate the formal system with the physical system one does not need to find physical referents for *all* the formal entities of the mathematical system. Nevertheless, some sort of reification has been granted to individual extensionless geometrical points in mathematical treatments of Zeno's problems. Otherwise it would be nonsensical to speak of actually infinite sums as if they were physically meaningful. The semantical difficulties raised by Zeno's problems thus include but extend beyond the need to clarify the equivocation in the use of terms such as 'sum' and 'length'.[11] Indeed the whole mathematical approach is closely bound up with the semantical problem of the meaning which is to be ascribed to the formal elements of the mathematical system. Nevertheless, certain responses to Zeno are offered as if it were possible to make a clear division between the semantical and the mathematical aspects of certain Zenonian problems. Wesley Salmon, for example, believes that Adolf Gruenbaum successfully deals with the "purely *mathematical* problem of providing a consistent account of the extended continuum" as opposed to the "*semantical* problems that arise when we consider the application of mathematical systems to physical reality."[12] But an examination of Gruenbaum's discussion raises the doubt that such an approach could, even in principle, ever provide a satisfactory response to Zeno.

3. *The Metrical Paradox of Extension*

Gruenbaum's declared aim is to provide a comprehensive philosophical and scientific treatment of Zeno's paradoxes insofar as they can be interpreted as posing intellectual difficulties for modern mathematical physics. I propose to consider only Gruenbaum's "metrical paradox of extension:" this involves the contradiction which a modern Zeno can claim to find in the notion of the real line interval conceived as a plurality of dimensionless points. In his words, the question to be resolved is

> How can the definition of length *consistently* assign zero length to *unit* point-sets or individual points while assigning positive *finite* lengths to such unions (sums) of these point-sets as constitute a finite interval?[13]

Gruenbaum's treatments of Zeno's metrical paradoxes of spatial and temporal extension are meant to defeat the objections of critics of the mathematical theory of space and time (who at the same time challenge basic Cantorean conceptions of contemporary point-set theory). William James and F. W. Bridgman, for example, maintain that it is paradoxical to conceive of a geometrical line as literally an actually infinite assemblage of points of zero length. Such a radical view, Gruenbaum rightly points out, "calls into question such philosophies of science as rely on these conceptions for the interpretation of our mathematical knowledge of nature."[14] Gruenbaum's discussion is thus important not only in that he responds to Zeno in the context of recent developments in modern mathematics and physics and, in particular, in terms of the mathematical theory of the continuum. He also aims to make clear "what kind of mathematical and philosophical theory does succeed in avoiding Zeno's mathematical (metrical) paradoxes of plurality."[15] My contention is that Gruenbaum fails to achieve this clarity, by virtue of the emphasis which he places upon the mathematical aspects of the problem.

I want to consider first Gruenbaum's physical interpretation of the formal mathematical theory. Gruenbaum's conception of how the real continuum is actually involved in physical reality differs from the ordinary notion of a one-to-one correspondence between physical point and mathematical point. It is erroneous, he points out, to picture the physical correlates of abstract real numbers as occupying the line interval like beads on a string. Such a model of the real interval is vitiated by the property of denseness in the number system. For between any two beads on a string there is not always a third bead; that is to say, the bead model does not even reflect the fundamental property of denseness of the rational numbers, let alone represent the irrational numbers. Instead, Gruenbaum proposes that the correspondence between the physical and the mathematical continuum be expressed as an association of "the term '*linear continuum of points*' of our theory with an appropriate body in nature."[16] That is, Gruenbaum coordinates not individual points but individual finite line segments. By this means he disposes of the objection that the notion of a geometric line interval is counterintuitive or even paradoxical in the sense that it consists of an actual infinity of extensionless points. For the points of the abstract interval, which corresponds to the physical interval, are not to be pictured as individual concrete entities. As he puts it:

> By a point of this body we . . . mean nothing more or less than an
> element of it possessing the formal properties prescribed for points by
> the postulates of geometry.[17]

This key notion is at the base of Gruenbaum's mathematical refutation of Zeno. But it is meaningless to speak of the formal properties as prescribed by the postulates of the system without first assuming that the properties of abstract points are in fact relevant to the description of geometrical points in physical intervals. So there is, notwithstanding what appears at first glance to be a qualification which would surmount a dubious reification of mathematical points, an affirmation of the existence of non-denumerable actual infnites of concrete extensionless points. What else could one mean by "an element of it possessing the formal properties prescribed for points by the postulates of geometry" if one did not mean that there were such points in actual physical continua? The usefulness of Gruenbaum's coordinating definition lies solely in its ability to counter the objection that it is impossible to imagine an actual infinity of extensionless points because there is no intelligible macrophysical model (like that of beads on a string) which will do the job. Introduced apparently in order to make the notion of non-denumerably many physical points in a line interval appear less bizarre, Gruenbaum's coordinating definition in effect highlights the peculiar difficulties inherent in any attempt to correlate abstract and concrete concepts.

Thus Gruenbaum's coordination of physical and mathematical intervals is a form of the exact-correspondence hypothesis. For even if one coordinates finite intervals and not individual points, some sort of physical existence must be granted to individual mathematical (i.e. extensionless) points. Otherwise it would make no sense at all for Zeno to argue, and for Gruenbaum to counter Zeno, that it is unintelligible to speak of a line segment as composed of a non-denumerable infinity of points. Therefore, what Gruenbaum describes as an "arithmetical rebuttal" of Zeno is based upon the major metaphyscial assumption that physical line segments are composed of actually infinite, non-denumerable aggregates of extensionless points which obey the laws of the mathematical theory of the real continuum. We may, therefore, immediately dispense with the notion that Gruenbaum has effected a clear separation between the mathematical and the semantical aspects of Zeno's problem.

Gruenbaum also enlists the exact-correspondence hypothesis to counter the objection that it is inconceivable that a physical line interval could be divided and subdivided into an actual infinity of non-denumerable points. If the exact-correspondence hypothesis is allowed and if the consistency of the mathematical continuum is admitted, then, *ipso facto*, this division already exists. According to Cantorean theory the real continuum is not only potentially infinitely divisible but it is also in itself, or in any of its finite subintervals, actually infinitely divisible. A physical interval is potentially infinitely divisible into subintervals in the sense that it is possible to separate out an infinite collection of positive non-overlapping subintervals by repeated bisections. Moreover, an interval can be divided and subdivided indefinitely without altering the super-denumerable dividedness of each subinterval. It follows, then, that not only the Bisection Paradox but also Gruenbaum's generalization of it, the "metrical paradox of extension," can be coherently formulated. That is, no charge can be brought against the mathematical arguments which is based upon the claim that it is impossible to *effect* an actual division of the line interval into a super-denumerable aggregate of degenerate subintervals (i.e. points) of zero length. For Cantor assures us that these already exist in any finite interval. But the price for the passage to the mathematical stage of Gruenbaum's rebuttal of Zeno must be paid in metaphysical coin. That is, the evocation of the exact-correspondence hypothesis is a necessary (but arguable) metaphysical presupposition which must me made *before* Zeno's "metrical paradox of extension" can even be formulated. Indeed, some such metaphysical commitment is necessary before any mathematical rebuttal of Zeno can be attempted.

Gruenbaum's resolution of the paradox involves an analysis of the concept of length, as it is formally elaborated in the theory of measure of subsets of the real continuum. Zeno is ultimately refuted, he maintains, if the theory of measure is admitted as a consistent mathematical theory. For the argument which absolves the mathematical theory of the continuum of the charge of inconsistency shows that the super-denumerability of the continuum is in fact just what precludes the Zenonian anomaly that the positive length of a linear interval is the sum of an infinite number of zero lengths. Indeed, the theory of measure denies that this notion is meaningful in the case of the full continuum. Gruenbaum argues that the additivity rules for length and duration (or, more generally, for measure on subsets of the real continuum) presuppose countable collections of measurable sets. Thus, non-denumerable collections of degenerate subintervals (point sets) are not measurable and the Zenonian paradox of extension collapses.

Now Gruenbaum is aware that the above argument can be described as merely technical, and thus liable to the objection that it does nothing to remove the obscurity surrounding the Zenonian puzzle. His reply is that it is not the non-denumerability of the continuum alone which is instrumental in providing the means for an "arithmetical rebuttal" of Zeno. Super-denumerability is necessary if a paradox is to be avoided at all. For if spatial or temporal intervals are conceived as consisting only of infinite sets of *rational* points, the property of countable additivity will allow the Zenonian paradox. As he puts it

> If any infinite set of *rational* points were regarded as constituting an extended line segment, then the customary mathematical theory under consideration could assert the length of that merely denumerable point set to be greater than zero only at the cost of permitting itself to become self-contradictory![18]

However, a contradiction (that the countable sum of zero lengths is both zero and greater than zero) only follows from an appeal to the debatable premise that there *is* an exact and exhaustive correspondence between abstract and concrete line intervals, whatever their degree of cardinality. Whether we are speaking of irrational points or rational points does not matter from the point of view of Zeno's objection that it is not intelligible to speak of them at all. The question as to which theory of measure should be appealed to is, in this metaphysical context, secondary.[19] Thus the real difficulty is whether or not it is reasonable to hold the exact-correspondence hypothesis.

Now in discussing the notion that space may actually be "rational," Gruenbaum points to the fact that the framework of mathematics, as used in physical theories, employs the full continuum. He insists that "in the absence of a denumerable alternative to the standard mathematical theory which is demonstrably viable for the purposes of physics," a reconstruction of mathematical physics (such as might be advocated by a "radical operationist"), "must be rejected on logical grounds."[20] It is, however, not at all clear how such grounds could, even in principle, ever be made logical. For they must ultimately be based upon a prior decision as to the nature of the correspondence between formal systems of mathematics and physical reality.

There appears to be no strong empirical grounds upon which one can base such a decision. From the point of view of physics, atomicity appears to be a fundamental aspect of reality. Gruenbaum is, of course, aware of the objection that the quantum hypothesis runs counter to any identification of the real continuum with physical processes. But even if the conjecture of some quantum physicists is correct that there are minimal distances ("hodons") and minimal times ("chronons") in nature, standard physics refers to these minima, as Gruenbaum elsewhere points out, as "extensive magnitudes whose values are given by real numbers".[21] That is to say, there is no reason why these minimal distances and times cannot correspond to real linear intervals. He therefore correctly concludes that the quantum hypothesis entails the admission that some physical properties are quantized but does not thereby logically imply that continuous processes in the quantal world do not embody the full mathematical continuum.[22] However, if modern physics has little to say which has direct bearing upon Zeno's puzzles, it is not easy to understand why one should expect modern mathematics to have anything more substantial to add.

Although it is true that a large part of modern physics is logically grounded in the mathematical continuum, this fact in itself yields no logical warrant for the exact-correspondence hypothesis. For even highly successful physical theories are probably never more than approximate descriptions of nature. The extensions and modifications in, for example, the theory of mechanics which followed the development of Einstein's special theory of relativity are no doubt indicative of the fate awaiting most physical theories. If it is unreasonable to expect the laws of physics to provide exact and exhaustive descriptions of physical reality why should one expect mathematical theories to have this characteristic? Surely this is to place demands upon the mathematical substructure which are unwarranted in terms of the needs of the physical theoretical superstructure.[23]

In summary, Gruenbaum's mathematical discussion is grounded in the purely circumstantial evidence that standard mathematics is manifestly successful in standard physics and that there is no available or feasible alternative mathematical theory which does not employ super-denumerable sets. But this is no help in establishing what he takes to be the ideal answer to Zeno, namely a logical or mathematical refutation of his puzzles. There is, in fact, no connection at all between the mathematical and the physical premises which does not raise arguable extra-logical issues. He shows that there is a serious difficulty in the conception of a "rational" space-time maintained in conjunction with the assumption of the complete applicability of standard measure theory. But the force of this mathematical argument is dependent upon the full-blown metaphysical assumption of an exact correspondence between the mathematical and the physical continuum.

The denial of super-denumerability in nature may only in a weak sense be described as inconsistent with the present state of empirical science. It is merely out of step with current fashions in science and the philosophy of science, but not with more wide-ranging philosophical investigations into and critiques of conceptual structures. For there is no logical warrant for granting immunity to the conceptual structures of mathematics from broad semantical concerns; they too are subject to the general question as to the extent to which a conceptual structure can be said to mirror reality. There is simply no authority, apart from an appeal to their limited practical successes in providing approximate descriptions of the physical world, to warrant the supposition that mathematical structures are completely isomorphic to physical structures.

As for the mathematical method in Gruenbaum's refutation of Zeno, it suffers from a serious shortcoming which is peculiar to all purely mathematical solutions. For there is an element of circularity inherent in mathematical treatments of Zeno's problems which are based upon some form of the exact-correspondence hypothesis. The use of this hypothesis as a premise in a refutation of Zeno has the effect of begging his question. For if the Zenonian argument is understood to be directed against the intelligibility of the proposition that the physical world exhibits actually infinite (even non-denumerable) totalities of extensionless entities it is surely a dubious procedure to enlist this proposition as a major premise in its own rebuttal.[24]

Apart from drawing attention to the fact that the rules of countable additivity in standard measure theory are artificial, in the sense that they are formal logical extensions of the intuitive rules for finite additivity, Gruenbaum's mathematical argument indirectly throws into doubt their physical significance. Countable additivity is defined in a manner which is analogous to the definition of the sum of an infinite series as the limit of a sequence of finite sums. The introduction of the limit concept involves a subsequent equivocation in the use of key terms, such as 'sum'. Hence there is a similarity between the mathematical solution of the Bisection Paradox and Gruenbaum's mathematical resolution of the metrical paradox. Neither solution provides, in effect, much more than the reassuring but negative conclusion that the abstract theory of the continuum is not inconsistent with our physical intuitions. This is scarcely surprising, however, in view of the almost universal agreement as to its usefulness.

By committing himself to a version of the "extensionless point" model of physical spatio-temporal intervals, Gruenbaum not only fails to separate the mathematical from the semantical aspects of Zeno's problem. He also demonstrates, albeit indirectly, that our modern Zeno is unlikely ever to be answered satisfactorily in a purely mathematical context. The lesson to be learned from this discussion is that one must first distinguish between real or concrete Zenonian problems and abstract or artificial Zenonian problems (which are well represented in the literature by problems involving "infinity machines"). The latter are those which are amenable to purely mathematical treatments, perhaps because they are essentially about the consistency of mathematical systems; the former are too subtle to be caught in the meshes of a purely mathematical net.

One may go further than Whitehead, then, and say that with every century the problems of Zeno present increasing difficulties partly on account of extensive advances in our knowledge of the physical world and of our formal means of describing it. These advances have tended to obscure, rather than to clarify, the profound nature of Zeno's problems. For the sheer success of esoteric mathematical theories in describing and predicting physical observations has encouraged the over-simplified view, held by many scientists and philosophers of science, that the world is fundamentally mathematical. Such a view simply ignores many crucial philosophical considerations. Indeed, it seems that one of the chief benefits to be derived from modern treatments of Zeno's puzzles is their effective exposure of the artificiality of the boundaries which have evolved historically between the now separate disciplines of philosophy, physics, and mathematics. It is partly because it is impossible to make these boundaries incontestably distinct that Zeno's arguments are and will continue to be fascinating. But sophisticated mathematical arguments, if not treated with the skepticism which properly attends all philosophical argumentation, simply serve as elaborate means to evade Zeno's fundamental question. In the end, before any of the abstruse mathematical reasoning can be evaluated, one must deal with the philosophical problem of deciding, if one wishes to maintain that there *is* plurality in the world, what sort of things the units of this plurality can be.

4. *Zeno, Mathematics, and Reality*

If my assessment of the situation is correct, it adds to the suspicion, already well supported by developments in mathematics itself, that "quantity" is very likely not an important philosophical category. For despite its current dominance in the scientific description of the physical world, the mathematical concept of the continuum appears to have no major metaphysical significance. The above discussion indicates that mathematical resolutions of Zeno's puzzles are scarcely more than reassurances that standard mathematical theories (e.g. of infinite series or of measure) are not internally incoherent in their uses of the terms 'sum', 'length', and so on. But Zeno's arguments are only incidently about the *consistency* of the relevant conceptual system, which may be a complex amalgam of mathematical, physical and philosophical terms. A fundamental concern in assessing any response to Zeno is the question of its *intelligibility*. Mathematical arguments tend to gloss over what is most debatable and obscure on the geometrical side of Zeno's problems. That is to say, to answer Zeno with a mathematical argument is to raise ineluctably the related, and even more fundamental, question: What is the physical meaning of continuity and to what extent is it safe to assume that properties of the mathematical continuum are actually correlative with properties of the physical continuum? The strong assumption of an exact correspondence between the abstract and the concrete aspects of continuity thus evades the real issue.[25]

Now Gruenbaum upholds the validity of the exact correspondence hypothesis because the full mathematical continuum is at the basis of highly successful and widely confirmed physical theories. Moreover, he stresses the point that there is, at present, no feasible denumerable mathematical theory of measure which can replace the standard Cantorean theory. But this position appears to rest upon a debatable assumption about the role of mathematical theories in physical description: this assumption turns the tables on the ancient Greek approach. In discussing why Zeno's problems *were* problems for the Greeks, Gruenbaum observes that the Greeks brought certain preconceptions concerning the physical properties of measure to bear on the mathematical theory: contrariwise, Gruenbaum's approach is to make the properties of the mathematical system bear upon the theory of measurement.[26] Thus his belief that the usefulness of continuum-centered mathematics provides grounds for asserting the concrete existence of the full continuum rests upon a questionable methodology. On such grounds one could assert that it is permissible to reify the abstractions of any applied mathematical theory, however unrelated they may be to the initial interests which prompted the application of that theory, provided only that the theory was successful enough. In other words, it would make all characteristics of a mathematical system, many of whose properties arise out of purely logical considerations, in a certain sense "physically mandatory."

But apart from their doubtful relevance to questions of methodology, empirical considerations must still be given some weight. Modern physics has conferred renewed, and even increased, status on the concept of atomicity and, indirectly at least, has called into question the dominance in physical thinking of the concept of continuity. For an approach to accord with modern physics, then, it must take into account the empirically verified factor of atomicity. It appears that there is in the physical world a complementary duality between the discrete and the continuous. It is not only recent advances in science, particularly in quantum physics, that lend support to this view. Hermann Weyl points out that the duality of the discrete versus the continuous is "of fundamental importance for all morphological investigations. . . ."[27] There are, therefore, physical and philosophical, as well as historical, reasons for questioning the dominance of the concept of continuity in physical description. Doubts as to the propriety of this emphasis also extend *a fortiori* to the soundness of the exact-correspondence hypothesis. What is ultimately in question is the wisdom of inferring from the successes of continuum-based physics any conclusion of substantial metaphysical import about the role of the mathematical continuum in physical reality.

5. Number and the Continuum

The question as to *how* number is involved in continuous processes is one which has challenged thinkers at all stages in the history of natural science. One of the chief concerns of nineteenth-century mathematics was to clear up the logical anomalies which centered on the concept of real number and which plagued the development of the calculus. The result, the so-called "arithmetization of analysis," is generally regarded as one of the supreme achievements of mathematics. No doubt this has reinforced the view, which is one of the major presuppositions of modern science, that the Galilean programme which aims to quantify all physical concepts, not the least important of which are space and time, is fundamentally correct. Hence it seems at first glance perverse to deny that the mathematical continuum provides the final answer to the problem of the description of the physical continuum. Indeed, without the postulate of an exact correlation between mathematical and physical continuity it is difficult even to give a meaning to the concept of spatial or temporal continuity. At any rate, it is not difficult to understand the prevalence in scientific thought of the Pythagorean notion that there is a fundamental numerical structure at the base of the physical world: in the modern view, the primacy of the natural numbers has merely been superseded by the primacy of the real numbers.

From the standpoint of the concrete world, then, the continuum problem is that of trying to describe the mathematical continuum as some form of 'Being in itself'. According to Weyl, there have been three programmes which have evolved historically to meet this challenge; the first and most radical of these is the programme of atomism. Under this view, the physical continuum is believed to consist of countable discrete elements. But despite its "brilliant success" in modern physics, the atomistic conception, Weyl believes, has "never achieved sufficient contact with reality".[28] In support of this objection he observes that the atomistic conception raises the following paradoxical barrier to the understanding of the metric relations in space: "If a square is built up of miniature tiles, then there are as many tiles along the diagonal as there are along the side: thus the diagonal should be equal in length to the side."[29] On the other hand, he points out that it is impossible to posit the abstract continuum as a real thing "existing, closed and complete in itself". This is because, if space is conceived in terms of the continuum, we are obliged to regard it as "inwardly infinite" in the sense that any point of space can be approached only by a sequence of unending divisions. Thus we should have to deny "the resting and complete existence that intuition ascribes to space." For Weyl, then, the continuum problem "drives one toward epistemological idealism."[30]

But a complete submission to idealism is not the only way out of this difficulty. Weyl is aware that Leibniz, in order to find his own way out of the "labyrinth of the composition of the continuum," formulated a conception of space and time as orders of the phenomena. Because of its relevance to this discussion, it is worth reproducing Weyl's quotation from Leibniz in full:

> Within the ideal or the continuum the whole precedes the parts. . . . The parts are here only potential; among the real [i.e. substantial] things, however, the simple precedes the aggregates, and the parts are given actually and prior to the whole. These difficulties dispel the difficulties regarding the continuum–difficulties which arise only when the continuum is looked upon as something real, which possesses real parts before any such division as we may devise, and when matter is regarded as a substance.[31]

Leibniz thus puts his finger on some essential considerations, which one can neglect only at the risk of muddling the whole issue. His reference to matter reminds us that we are speaking not just about abstract mathematical concepts but instead are attempting to describe the relation between the abstract and the concrete. That is to say, we must not only understand the complexity within the potential (or the merely possible, as this is given in the conceptual, i.e. mathematical structure), but we must also relate the potential to the actual in some coherent conception of reality, and, in particular, of a more or less explicit conception of substance. Unless we are willing to grant absolute existence to space and time, it is not possible to speak of them without presupposing the existence of spatio-temporal entities. These entities must, following Leibniz, be the simple real things which are "given actually and prior to the whole" (i.e. spatio-temporal world).

Leibniz thus succinctly expresses the most promising approach to the continuum problem, although it is a path which Weyl does not follow. Nevertheless, it contains the solution to his puzzle about the metric relations of space. For it is enough to note that Weyl's objection is only cogent if it be first granted that space-time actually consists of countably many building blocks, or ur-tiles of space-time, and the meaning of extension is to be found in the counting of such tiles. But if it is possible to reconcile the Leibnizian view of space and time with the requirements of modern physics, as Whitehead persuasively argues can be done,[32] then Weyl's objection collapses. For when space-time is regarded as derivative from the more fundamental notion of event, the continuum problem takes on a wholly different complexion. The real difficulty is to determine the nature of the relationship between the spatio-temporal relations of ur-events, of which continuity is merely one aspect, and the extent to which these are reflected by the mathematical theories which are used to describe them.

That Gruenbaum shares Weyl's lack of sympathy for the atomistic view is not surprising, for he clearly believes in the soundness of the historical programme whose chief aim is to mathematize the world. Both he and Weyl, in fact, are representatives of that tradition, so characteristic of Western thought, whose ultimate goal is the expression of all physical knowledge in terms of secure and complete mathematical systems. Gruenbaum represents the school of thought which would save the continuum by means of the strong assumption of its total metaphysical and physical relevance. On the other hand, Weyl's approach, while similar in intent, is more cautious.

Weyl is in sympathy with the radical programme of intuitionism which denies not only the metaphysical but also the mathematical significance of the full continuum. Following Brouwer, he seeks a secure and true basis for mathematics in the intuition of two-oneness and in the proper use of the related principle of complete (mathematical) induction. Thus he denies the metaphysical relevance of the full continuum because he is wary of the paradoxical traps which await those who make bold "leaps into the beyond."[33] The excessive awkwardness of the intuitionistic reconstruction of standard analysis is the price which must be paid, in his opinion, for the security of a true mathematics. Hence Weyl's desire to found mathematics upon a secure basis of truth puts him well within the mathematizing tradition.

But the intuitionist's dismissal of the continuum is based upon a mistaken conception of the cognitive role of mathematics. In its attempt to found mathematics on a secure and self-evidently true foundation, the programme of intuitionism loses sight of the consideration that every interpreted mathematical system is inherently corrigble. As for the application problem, the programme of intuitionism, and the more general programme of constructivism, is imbued with the fault which underlies the entire aim of mathematization. The attempt to formulate true descriptions of the actual world by means of a radical reconstruction of mathematics is a misguided move in the Procrustean exercise of trying to fit the world into too narrow a frame.

With respect to Weyl's metric difficulty, its puzzling aspects completely disappear if one regards the mathematical theory of measure as a mode of expression of physical characteristics but not as necessarily containing entities present in the events which they describe.[34] That the Pythagorean theorem, for example, applies in actual physical description and that the length of the diagonal of a square is different from (indeed incommensurate with) the length of a side is no reason to believe that irrational lengths actually exist in nature. We may conclude only that we have some confirmation that space is locally Euclidean: that is, that the relationships between actual events exhibit regularities and patterns which, to an indeterminable extent, are predictable from a study of those present in the abstract theory. This view is more realistic than the purely Pythagorean view, which would reify irrational lengths, in that it accords with the fact that mathematical theories are always limited as to the scope of their application. Euclidean theory, for example, is probably only a reasonably accurate description of the macrophysical world of ordinary human sense perception. It is a highly conjectural proposition to assert that its applicability extends into the microcosmos or into the macrocosmos.

These considerations extend also to Gruenbaum's formulation of Zeno's "metrical paradox of extension." The paradox disappears because its force is entirely supported by the dubious exact-correspondence hypothesis. To deny the latter is not to denounce the application of continuum-based mathematics in physics nor is it to draw unwarranted conclusions from the quantum hypothesis. For Gruenbaum rightly points out that quantum theory does not logically entail the discreteness of space or time. The most we can say is that physical events, as distinct from space and time elements, appear to be discrete and have minimal spatial and temporal extensions. Yet here there is a danger of falling into confusion if one fails to maintain a clear distinction between *events*, which by all accounts of modern physics are neither instantaneous nor punctiform, and the mathematical structures which are used to describe and predict their behavior. As Gruenbaum himself observes, "Every point of continuous physical space is a *potential* sharply defined position of, say, an electron. . . ."[35] But the stress on the word 'potential' must be carried through to the rest of the statement. For the electron in question is an abstraction, i.e. a non-physical instantaneous and punctiform quasi-event. From this stand-point, many of Zeno's paradoxes, including the metrical paradox of extension, appear in a wholly artificial light—or, to put it another way, the paradoxes reduce to matters involving only mathematico-physical abstractions and thus evade Zeno's main philosophical point.

So it is a mistake to believe, as Gruenbaum apparently does, that the skeptic who claims that super-denumerability may be inessential to the understanding of physical continuity is also committed thereby to an attempt to erect a new physics on denumerable foundations. It does not follow that it is necessary *either* to accede to the super-denumerability of the physical continuum *or* to construct an alternative denumerable mathematical physics. This dichotomy overlooks the point that it is highly doubtful, whatever mathematical theory is adopted in any branch of science, that the theory could, even in principle, completely and exhaustively mirror the physical phenomena under consideration. Whatever the metaphysical import of the success of a theory is, it is surely not this. The involvement of the real continuum in standard physics can only be regarded as evidence for the general claim that mathematical patterns have *some* bearing on the description of the order intrinsic in actual events. The question of the nature of this relationship is bound up with profound philosophical problems about the nature of abstract knowledge and its relation to the concrete world.

Furthermore, from a practical point of view, the appeal to the fact that the full continuum is one of the basic tools of current physics is becoming less and less significant. There appears to be no substantial progress as yet in the search for alternative mathematical approaches. Yet it is clear that continuum-based mathematics is no longer entirely adequate for key physical theories, such as quantum mechanics, which require the means to study and express the behavior of discrete entities.[36] But perhaps we are so dazzled by the successes of continuum-based mathematics that it will be some time before appropriate combinatorial methods are developed. The predominance of continuum methods appears to owe everything to the assumption that continuous processes, as opposed to atomic processes, predominate in nature. Or perhaps physical science has, until quite recently, concentrated upon the continuous aspect of physical processes simply because it has possessed the means, in the calculus and other continuum-centered theories, to treat this aspect of nature successfully. At any rate, the problems of Zeno have always been at hand to remind us of the one-sidedness of physical investigations.

This observation brings us back to Whitehead, whose metaphysical theory of organism meets the requirement, implicit in the arguments of Zeno and in the demands of modern physics, that a reasonably adequate theory of reality must be one which can reconcile the concepts of atomicity and continuity.

6. *Whitehead and Zeno*

Whitehead is fundamentally in sympathy with the Pythagorean mind which conceives mathematical patterns as related to, or in some way indicative of, the order which is manifestly inherent in the physical world. In his view, the significance of mathematics lies much deeper than in the fact that it is a superb tool for the organization of scientific thought. Nevertheless, he is careful to maintain a clear distinction between the properties of actual events and the abstract concepts used in their description. He thus eschews the dubious tendency of modern Pythagoreans to reify mathematical entities. In the context of the present discussion, whatever may be the metaphysical significance of the real mathematical continuum it is unlikely that it exactly mirrors the fine structure of the physical world.

Whitehead's response to Zeno is to take the metaphysical bull directly by the horns, and so his account is essentially free, despite a minor lapse, from the circularity inherent in the mathematical approach. Rather than being intent upon refuting Zeno, he recognizes the metaphysical significance of his irrepressible arguments: they support the contention that "the ultimate metaphysical truth is atomism."[37] He does not thereby deny the existence of continuity in nature–rather he downgrades it from its current dominant, not to say tyrannical, conceptual elevation.

Whitehead's position is summed up in the following passage:

> There is a becoming of continuity, but no continuity of becoming. The actual occasions are the creatures which become, and they constitute a continuously extensive world. In other words, extensiveness becomes, but 'becoming' is not itself extensive.[38]

To understand his response to Zeno, then, one must begin where it is most salutary to begin, i.e. with his primary metaphysical presupposition. For it is a particular world-view which any Zenonian argument ultimately brings into question. In Whitehead's view, the world is a process of the becoming (and the perishing) of actual entities. These are not to be conceived as becoming in a pre-existent container of space-time. Spatio-temporal relations are derivative from the more fundamental relations of extension which govern becoming. They are therefore contingent upon the general characteristics of becoming which obtain in any given epoch of the world. There is no *a priori* reason, therefore, why any particular characteristics of continuity should exist in nature. Indeed, Whitehead goes so far as to say that not even the becoming of continuity need be regarded as an ultimate fact: "In the present cosmic epoch there is a creation of continuity. Perhaps such creation is an ultimate metaphysical truth holding of all cosmic epochs; but this does not seem to be a necessary conclusion."[39] This remark, however, is somewhat at odds with Whitehead's estimation of the real significance of Zeno's arguments. For he interprets Zeno as showing that there cannot be instantaneous and punctiform events in nature. Given the importance of polar concepts in Whitehead's thought, a commitment to the existence of some sort of continuity would seem to be entailed by the acceptance of the polar concept of atomicity. And Whitehead is quite clear about the second half of the polarity: Zeno's arguments oblige us, he says, to accept the general fact of atomicity.

The essence of Zeno's paradoxes is to be found, in Whitehead's opinion, in the conjunction of two premises: (i) That in a becoming something becomes, and (ii) that every act of becoming is divisible into earlier and later sections which are themselves acts of becoming. The successive bisection of a one-second act of becoming into an infinite regression of such acts, leads to the conclusion that nothing at all can become because there can never be a first act of becoming. As he puts it:

> Consider, for example, an act of becoming during one second. The act is divisible into two acts, one during the earlier half of the second, the other during the later half of the second. Thus that which becomes during the whole second presupposes that which becomes during the first half-second. Analogously, that which becomes during the first

half-second presupposes that which becomes during the first quarter-second, and so on indefinitely.[40]

But the argument really shows, contrary to the above conclusion, that becoming cannot be continuous: "If we admit that 'something becomes', it is easy, by employing Zeno's method, to prove that there can be no continuity of becoming."[41] For the argument calls into question the validity of the second premise; it is the assumption of the infinite divisibility of acts of becoming which is in doubt. This doubt is strengthened, for Whitehead, if one pursues Zeno's argument a step further, as follows:

> The difficulty is not evaded by assuming that something becomes at each non-extensive instant of time. For at the beginning of the second of time there is no next instant at which something can become.[42]

This observation, however, invites a closer examination of Whitehead's position, for it alludes, in the term 'next', to a correspondence between physical temporality and the rational denseness of mathematical instants. The matter of the existence and the nature of such a correspondence is just what is here in question.

It is thus helpful to look at Whitehead's discussion of a second form of the Bisection Paradox, which is a version of the Paradox of Achilles and the Tortoise, but from which all references to time and motion have been removed. Here, Zeno's paradoxical conclusion is that nothing can become. Whitehead's version of this form of the paradox deals with an act of becoming which is conceived as an infinite sequence of shrinking acts, with the first half-second as one act of becoming, the next quarter-second as another such act, and so on indefinitely. The paradox arises from the observation that such a sequence of acts can have no last act. Therefore, there can be no new act of becoming which follows this sequence of acts.

For Whitehead, these two forms of the Bisection Paradox are distinct. The argument of the first form fails because it appeals to the illegitimate second premise. That is, an act of becoming cannot be assumed to be indefinitely divisible, at least not without adding important qualifications. However, his argument against the second form of the paradox takes the mathematical approach:

> There is no need to assume that an infinite series of acts of becoming, with a first act, and each act with an immediate successor, is inexhaustible in the process of becoming. Simple arithmetic assures us that the series just indicated will be exhausted in the period of one second.[43]

While it is mathematically true that the sum of an infinite geometric series of durations of one-half second, one-quarter second, and so on, is one second, the total is not arrived at by means of simple arithmetic. The artificiality of the mathematical argument obscures Whitehead's main point, for mathematical considerations are actually irrelevant to his discussion.[44] At best, the mathematical solution merely offers the assurance that the formal mathematics which we use to describe and solve the abstract problem is not at varience with our intuitive expectation that a new set of becoming will follow upon such a sequence of acts.

As Whitehead elsewhere makes quite clear, the real problem raised by Zeno concerns the nature of being which, in his view, is essentially the outcome of "becoming." In fact, he refers to this second form of the paradox as a modification of the "Arrow in Its Flight" paradox, differing from the original version in that the notion of an arrow in flight brings in irrelevant details involving motion. Under Whitehead's conception of process, which I shall explore more fully later, the world is a hierarchy of organic structures of organic structures whose lower levels are occupied by irreducible spatially and temporally extended structures (actual entities). With this key notion, Whitehead renders all traditional references to motion in Zenonian problems irrelevant to their proper formulation. For "an actual entity never moves: it is where it is and what it is."[45] Under Whitehead's conception of the hierarchy of organisms, an arrow must be regarded as a material society, that is, as a relatively unorganized aggregate of more highly organized societies of actual entities. Its motion therefore cannot be conceived of or expressed directly in terms of the fundamental categories with which the world is to be described. In short, since 'motion' is a term which simply does not apply to actual entities, this Zenonian problem needs to be reformulated: as Whitehead succinctly puts it, "The true difficulty is to understand how the arrow survives the lapse of time."[46]

The second form of the Bisection Paradox would be more to the point, then, if it were put as follows: No act of becoming can ever be completed because the act can be divided into earlier and later acts of becoming. Thus an act of becoming in one second presupposes that an act is completed in the first half-second, a second act in the next quarter-second, and so on indefinitely. Such a sequence of shrinking acts of becoming can never be completed because there is no last act in the sequence. But this form of the Bisection Paradox, like the first form, appeals to the dubious second premise (that acts of becoming are indefinitely divisible) and disappears with its denial. That Whitehead is predominately concerned with the validity of the second premise and aware of Zeno's implicit demand that he counter with a coherent theory of becoming is evident from the following observation:

> Every act of becoming must have an immediate successor, if we admit that something becomes. For otherwise we cannot point out what creature becomes as we enter upon the second in question. But we cannot, in the absence of some additional premise, infer that every act

of becoming must have had an immediate predecessor.[47]
This indicates why Whitehead does not use the same argument in both formulations of the Bisection Paradox. There are some forms of the paradox which do not appear to contradict what he sees as essential to the concept of becoming. Thus he unnecessarily, and erroneously, dismisses the second form of the paradox as based upon "a mathematical fallacy."

But this point provides only a partial elucidation of Whitehead's position. For the question immediately arises, how exactly do the arguments of Zeno, especially those pertaining to the endless bisection of acts of becoming, support Whitehead's atomistic position? For Whitehead insists that his claim that there can be no continuity of becoming, even though there is becoming of continuity, follows from Zeno's arguments once one postulates that something becomes. The most general reply to this question is that what Zeno does for Whitehead is what he does (or at least should do) for all of his commentators; he forces him into metaphysical explicitness. In Whitehead's case, Zeno's puzzle elicits the following concise summary of 'becoming':

> The conclusion is that in every act of becoming there is the becoming of something with temporal extension; but that the act itself is not extensive, in the sense that it is divisible into earlier and later acts of beoming which correspond to the extensive divisibility of what has become.[48]

My next task is to try to elucidate Whitehead's position, and to show what are some of the implications for a just estimate of the real difficulties in Zeno's problems.

7. *Real and Artificial Zenonian Problems*

In what follows I shall be concerned mainly with that aspect of Whitehead's theory of becoming which bears upon his response to Zeno. As it turns out, however, an exploration of this topic also throws light upon the problem of the relation between mathematics and reality. The advantage of Whitehead's approach over rival treatments of this large subject depends, as I have argued previously, upon one of his major philosophical insights. Whitehead holds that there is an ineradicable element of reciprocity between certain key concepts, a reciprocity which I have called complementary dualism. It is a mistake, he rightly insists, to concentrate upon either half of a dualism to the exclusion of the other half. I shall argue that an important reason why Zeno's arguments have been, and still are, so profoundly and perennially puzzling is that they lead to the deep metaphysical problem of just how we should go about the reconciliation of the complementary factors of atomicity and continuity in the actual world. More specifically, I shall try to show that Whitehead's approach reveals some of the real difficulties involved. He also helps us to understand why a failure to effect a reconciliation between atomicity and continuity must inevitably result in a failure to distinguish real from artificial Zenonian puzzles.

Whitehead's metaphysics is a suitable candidate for an adequate treatment of Zeno's puzzles just because it is grounded upon what must be one of the most fundamental of all complementary dualities: actuality and potentiality. To see how Zeno's arguments actually bear on the relation between atomicity and continuity, we must take a (necessarily brief) look at Whitehead's theory of the relation between actuality and potentiality.

In Whitehead's view, the world is generally characterized as process, where process consists of changing relations between things that are in no way describable in terms of 'stuff' possessing properties or attributes. These things, he claims, are best understood in terms of the model of organism; that is to say, we may best speak of them as primitive organisms. This is a view which I shall examine in greater detail in the following chapters. Granted for the present that Whitehead is essentially correct in his choice of models, the consequence is that a fundamental real thing, which Whitehead calls an actual entity, is a structure of pure activity, as opposed to a structure of stuff, that is, something supported by an underlying "primary matter." In Whitehead's theory of becoming, the concrete world is built up from the continual formation of these individual but mutually interrelated units of structures of activity. Zenonian puzzles can be posed when it comes to the attempt to elucidate the process of formation and the interrelatedness of actual entities.

Let us consider the matter of their interrelatedness first. In Whitehead's conception, an actual entity stands, as it were, as the vital link between the past and the future: it is the means by which the order of what has come into being is transmitted to the future world. So its 'being' is both consequent upon what has already become and partly determinant of what is yet to come. Moreover, as structure of pure activity, it cannot be analyzed solely in terms of internal relations (what it is in itself) or solely in terms of external relations (what it is for other entities). Hence Whitehead professes a general principle of relativity: every fundamental entity is essentially related to all other such entities. In defence of this principle, he in effect argues that without it we would be faced with the problem of trying to conceive of a world in which the notion of order was essentially unintelligible.

An actual entity is a transmitter of order. As pure activity, it must be conceived as expressive of form, where form can only be analyzed in terms of the entity's mode of activity.[49] This means that when Whitehead explains order within process in terms of the endurance of form, it is not endurance in the sense of perdurance: rather order is established by the propagation of form from one atomic creature to another. And since the general principle of relativity asserts that actual entities do not become as isolated individuals, but rather as communities of individuals, we must look to the relations between and within the actual entities to determine what aspects of any account of the spatio-temporal elements of order might be subject to the objections of a Zeno.

It is here that the complementarity intrinsic to Whitehead's overall conception of becoming begins to be crucial. On the one hand, an actual entity may be regarded as a 'subject' in the sense that it is an individual act of experience; i.e., it is a 'concretion' of 'real' and 'pure' forms or potentialities into a determinate individual. It arises out of what has already become; the world at any stage in process is a reservoir of 'real potentiality' which conditions further process. On the other hand, an actual entity that has completed its activity of becoming is an 'object' of the public world in the sense that it is a factor of the experience of other actual entities. There is no 'subject' that is not also an 'object' and *vice versa.*

When regarded as a 'subject', an actual entity is the becoming of an individual whose very determinateness gives rise to the 'solidity' of the world. In particular, the interrelatedness of the community of actual entities gives rise to spatio-temporal order. In Whitehead's view, the becoming of an actual entity generates a spatio-temporal extensiveness which is peculiar to that individual. An actual entity, as Whitehead puts it, "enjoys" a definite quantum of space and time which comes into being in concert with the entity. Such extensive regions are divisible (i.e., continuous), but Whitehead maintains that the actual entity itself cannot be divisible. It is this fundamental point which we must examine more closely.

An actual entity is atomic in the sense that it is the final concretion of real and pure potentialities into determinate individuality. But the process of its becoming, Whitehead insists, cannot be instantaneous or punctiform; that is, there must be an element of continuity in the constitution of every atomic actual entity. This follows, he says, not only from Zeno's arguments, but also from the general principle of the relatedness of actual entities when these are regarded as "acts of experience."

The role which Zeno plays in Whitehead's account of becoming is actually more indirect than he claims. The argument goes like this. If we allow Zeno to assert the intelligibility of indefinite and endless divisibility of fundamental entities, any event would thus be divisible into an infinite sequence of shrinking events which either has no first member or no last member. Either way we must contemplate an event which is potentially non-extensive. In this way Zeno raises a metaphysical question of primary importance, which bears directly on the meaning of 'event'. If we further assume that the notion of event is intimately connected to the notion of becoming, as Whitehead does, we must focus our response to Zeno's challenge on Whitehead's point that an act of becoming cannot be completely devoid of extensiveness. And here he seems on solid ground, for it is undoubtedly extremely difficult to conceive of a world composed of extensionless events. If the physical contributions of fundamental events are essentially only analyzable in terms of pure activity, they can only be regarded as determinate to the extent that they become manifest through interactions. And the intelligibility of 'interaction' depends not only upon the prior intelligibility of spatio-temporal relatedness, it presupposes the existence of causal relatedness, of the capacity of 'something-here' with the means to effect, or be affected by, 'something-there'. In brief, the notion of non-extensive but interacting structures of pure activity seems incoherent. Hence, if one ascribes instantaneous and punctiform existence to fundamental entities of the kind we are considering, the physical structure of the world simply collapses. In particular, one would have replaced this dynamic world with an entirely static one, and one, moreover, that is unlike anything that science sketches for us.[50]

To summarize, it is Whitehead's view that an actual entity can only be understood in terms of the notion of activity, and hence in terms of the related concept of experience. Furthermore, the generic concept of experience is simply incompatible with the concept of instantaneous punctiform existents, notwithstanding the overweening popularity of the latter notion. Thus his point that there can be no becoming at a non-extensive instant of time, because there is no next instant after the starting instant in an infinite regression of bisected acts of becoming,[52] is not a cogent rejoinder to Zeno's argument in terms of his own general philosophical position. Whitehead's view that an actual entity is essentially an act of experience is the real key to the whole issue.[53] Zeno's arguments contribute indirectly to the undermining of the conception of a static universe composed of aggregates of non-extensive units of becoming or of inert and immutable substance. If, following Whitehead, we believe in a pluralistic universe, in which change is neither an illusion nor to be fully accounted for under the terms of post-Newtonian cosmology (wherein matter is essentially without internal relations and capable of only accidental external relations), we must conceive of change as a process of supersession. Moreover, to assert the plurality of actual entities is to claim a real diversity of individual acts of experience. And if one grants to Whitehead his general principle of relatedness (and this principle seems intimately bound up with the meaning of 'act of experience'), we must allow that no one of these is entire and sufficient unto itself. Each actual entity is inescapably in some sort of relationship with every other entity. The relational complex of the world is thus both "one" and "many." The upshot is that it will make all the difference from what standpoint the actual entity is viewed.

For in order to analyze the general scheme of relationships which constitute the actual world, and to describe, in particular, the characteristics of space and time, we must take into account the complementarity inherent in becoming. One can either analyze an actual entity from the point of view of its genesis as an *individual* act of experience. Or one can analyze it from the point of view of the extensive relationships of its concrescence. These modes of analysis Whitehead calls "genetic division" and "coordinate division" respectively. The latter mode of analysis is involved in the question as to whether or not the space-time continuum is indefinitely divisible. Therefore the question of the relation between atomicity and continuity reduces to the following: Is it possible to regard the coordinate divisions of an actual entity (corresponding to sub-regions of the basic region) as actual entities in their own right?

In order to understand Whitehead's response, it is necessary to elaborate a little more on his theory of becoming. An actual entity, as an individual unit of experience, presupposes certain relations of extension for its becoming, and this, in turn, governs the elements of pure and of real potentiality which will be admitted into its completion. There are, Whitehead insists, alternatives always available in any concretion of potentialities: "These alternatives are represented," he says, "by the indecision as to the particular quantum of extension to be chosen for the basis of the novel concrescence."[54] This means that the growth of an actual entity must always be *toward* some definite and determinate end. This doctrine (of subjective unity) effectively introduces the notion of purpose and creativity into acts of becoming. It asserts that an actual entity, as a subject of experience, imposes a pre-established harmony or ideal on the processes of its growth. This ideal is a complex eternal object, a pure potentiality, which specifies the final form of the entity. It is a 'final cause', or, in Whitehead's words, a "conceptual aim" which, he says (without intending any connotation of human mental processes), constitutes the "mental pole" of the process of becoming. It is here, in the mental pole, that atomicity ultimately resides: the mental pole, says Whitehead, is "incurably one."[55]

Thus an actual entity, as a unit of experience, must be regarded as possessing both a mental pole and a physical pole. Both poles involve potentiality: the mental pole refers to the pure potentiality of the final form; the physical pole refers to the real potentiality inherent in that which has already come into being. An independent analysis of the physical pole or of the mental pole is not possible. This is because they are complementary aspects of one process.[56] An analysis of the physical pole alone will reveal only the extensional characteristics of the final achievement. Hence Whitehead calls such an analysis a "coordinate analysis," an expression that serves to warn us that here we have only an analysis of potentiality, not actuality.[57] It is only through "genetic analysis" that we can determine whether or not novelty has entered an act of becoming through the mental pole. For it is only in the mental pole that we can find potential freedom in the face of constraining conditions imposed by the settled past.[58] And it is only to the extent that this potentiality for novelty can be neglected that coordinate analysis will result in the determination of definite actual entities.

Hence Whitehead's answer to the question posed above is summed up as follows:

> For many abstractions concerning low-grade actual entities, the coordinate divisions approach the character of being actual entities on the same level as the actual entities from which they are derived. It is thus an empirical question to decide in relation to special topics, whether the distinction between a coordinate division and a true actual entity is, or is not, relevant. In so far as it is not relevant we are dealing with an indefinitely subdivisible extensive universe.[59]

We are now ready to assess Whitehead's contribution to Zenonian problems and to the related problem of the role of the mathematical continuum in physical description. In terms of Whitehead's conception of process, the world is a hierarchy of organisms, or structures of more primitive structures, and so there would seem to be the possibility of an infinite regress at the primitive end of the hierarchy. There would therefore appear, at first glance, to be an opening for a Zenonian paradox couched in terms of indefinite divisibility at the base of the hierarchy. For as one proceeds in the analysis of low-grade physical events, that is, in the direction of increasing primitivity, definiteness of individuality fades.[60] Nevertheless, Whitehead rejects, rightly I think, the notion of an infinite regress in nature. His theory of becoming is consistent with this belief. For even if very primitive organisms possess no high degree of definiteness, the existence of individual character of any sort whatever is the sign of non-divisible unity and this precludes indefinite divisibility in any concrete sense. Nor is it intelligible to speak of individual entities of such a primitive nature that they lack all defining characteristics–such entities would communicate nothing of themselves to the rest of the world, and so, for all purposes, simply would not exist. It is very likely that, as Whitehead maintains, there is at the ground of physical reality only blind reiteration of structures with only a negligible element of originality in the process of becoming. The latter notion is in fact one of the basic assumptions of physics. But this is not equivalent to absence of individuality.

At this point it becomes clear that an important distinction must be maintained between what may be called 'real' and 'artificial' Zenonian problems. This distinction is bound up with the answer to the vexed question as to *why* the abstractions of physics, and their mathematical developments, are so useful in our attempts to understand the order of process. It is just because physics is concerned with primitive organic structures, where the element of originality is negligible, that the analysis of potentiality approaches the analysis of actuality. In other words, at lower levels of the hierarchy of organisms we meet, for all practical purposes, an indefinitely divisible extensive universe which is more or less accurately describable by continuum-centered mathematical theories.

As for real Zenonian problems at this level, there is no opening for paradoxes unless the problems are expressed in terms of the abstractions of physics themselves. In which case, since the abstractions of physics are partly involved with mathematical (i.e. potential) aspects of the extensive regions of actual entities, the paradox can be dealt with by mathematical methods. But then they are essentially artificial problems. This is the case with the use of the infinite series argument, for example, to solve the geometric sequence formulation of the bisection paradox. If the mathematical theory is coherent and consistent in itself and in the use of reinterpreted (tropological) terms, such as 'sum', 'length', and so on, it is scarcely remarkable that "solutions", such as Gruenbaum's resolution of the metrical paradox, can be found. But it requires the addition of a strong metaphysical hypothesis, such as the exact correspondence hypothesis, to give the mathematical solution any meaning, that is to say, any metaphysical significance.

Whitehead's approach to Zeno's paradoxes therefore does not lead to solutions so much as a way of seeing why Zeno's arguments are so puzzling. For after all, it is not as if Zeno has ever convinced his successors of the truth of the Parmenidean dictum that all intuitions of plurality and change are illusions. Zeno reminds us, and Gruenbaum indirectly shows us, that the really puzzling question is not whether continuity exists in nature or even if there is a direct correspondence between the mathematical continuum and the physical continuum. The becoming of continuity is a psychological fact which few deny and which is amply supported by physical investigations. The real difficulty is to explain the very complex relationships between the concept of continuity as developed in potentiality and the concept as it applies to actuality. To take Whitehead's approach is at least to avoid begging the whole question. We do arrive at an answer to Zeno's general philosophical objection to the notion of a changing world which manifests real pluralities. Based upon the notion of the complementary duality between actuality and potentiality, a complementarity which carries over into atomicity and continuity, Whitehead's approach has the great merit of providing a reply into which Zeno can get his philosophical teeth.

8. *Conclusion*

While the foregoing discussion does not pretend to be an exhaustive study of current treatments of all, or even a small part, of the puzzles stemming from Zeno, it nonetheless points to the strong conclusion that a purely mathematical response to Zeno is unlikely ever to be adequate or satisfactory. While I have concentrated on the particular question of whether or not the highly abstract theory of the mathematical real continuum has sufficient metaphysical significance to be employed in a rebuttal of Zeno, my negative conclusion has in fact wider significance. For the mathematical responses which I have examined illustrate what is arguably one of the more pernicious features of scientific explanation, as this is currently understood. Much of scientific explanation is shot through with assumptions about mathematics that have all the makings of a myth. Even Whitehead, who, I am claiming, does not need any mathematical support for his own properly metaphysical response to the arguments of Zeno, succumbs, albeit momentarily, to the temptations of this myth. But Zeno's puzzles demand, when all is said and done, that a stance be taken with respect to age-old questions about the nature of being. Mathematical arguments contribute nothing which can properly be called an explanation, let alone a resolution, of the real difficulties involved. The failure of mathematical arguments in the treatment of Zenonian problems is perhaps an object lesson pointing towards the inevitable failure of mathematical arguments generally, when the issues are essentially metaphysical.

By contrast with the mathematical response to Zeno, Whitehead's metaphysical response does provide something in the way of an explanation. The question which must now be faced is whether or not his explanation is really appropriate. Whitehead's (almost) thoroughgoing metaphysical response to Zeno explicitly evokes a rather complicated and, to most modern eyes, strange (some would even say bizarre) theory of becoming. The solution offered seems, at least in the light of common conceptions of the nature of the physical world, radical in the extreme. However, when the props are pulled on the mathematical underpinnings of philosophical positions, the whole question of what should count as an adequate explanation is thrown wide open. My next concern is to determine whether or not Whitehead's theory of becoming is in fact open to the objection that it goes against the grain not only of what is best in scientific explanation, but also against common sense and generally accepted principles of rational philosophizing.

Chapter Four. On Philosophizing Adequately About Science, Mathematics, and Reality

> It is a well-founded historical
> generalization, that the last thing to
> be discovered in any science is what
> the science is really about.
>
> A. N. Whitehead

1. Science, Scientism, and Truth

There is still a strong movement in the philosophy of science which, at least in spirit, upholds Galileo's famous dictum:

> The true philosophy is written in that great book of nature which lies ever open before our eyes but which no one can read unless he has first learned to understand the language and to know the characters in which it is written. It is written in mathematical language, and the characters are triangles, circles, and other geometric figures.[1]

But even allowing for a considerable expansion and development in Galileo's list of mathematical characters, it is still very much an open question whether or not we are any closer to a "true" philosophy of nature.

It is undeniable that the study of nature has, on account of advances in mathematics, steadily amassed an impressive collection of remarkably reliable systems of knowledge about the physical world. Moreover, were it not for the efficacy of mathematical methods, there are apparently facts about the nature of physical reality, at least in that part of the world which lies outside our direct sensory awareness, which would be forever beyond our intellectual grasp. Science has unquestionably altered our picture of reality. But the skeptic may nonetheless be forgiven for wondering just how seriously he or she should take scientific "pictures," especially when it is obvious that it is not at all clear, either to scientists or to philosophers, just exactly what kind of world they depict.

80

Of special interest, then, is the whole-hearted Galilean-Newtonian point of view, whose estimation of the true cognitive role of science could scarcely be stated more plainly than it has by W. V. Quine. In his words, "The general task which science sets itself is that of specifying how reality 'really' is. . . ."[2] Quine, who is one of the more eloquent advocates of a science-centered approach to philosophy, firmly maintains that the scientific path is the best way to truth. Moreover, the goal of truth is, for him, not fundamentally at odds with the evidence in the history of science that scientific systems are never entirely free from the possibility of future falsification. So he brings out into the open an issue which is of great concern to the critic of the Galilean-Newtonian point of view: the question of the relation between truth and science construed as a body of inherently corrigible theories. In particular, the question to be faced is whether it is reasonable to try to conceive, as Quine puts it, of "an idealized form of scientific language in which sentences are so fashioned as never to vacillate between truth and falsity." Rather than being a reasonable ideal, this notion, that the royal road to truth is by way of science, may amount simply to an invitation to renounce the untidy world for the sake of a relatively tidy method.

This suspicion grows in spite of, or indeed on account of, Quine's adducement of mathematical support for this ideal, for he claims that science grows more perfect in respect to truth-formulation as it becomes ever more mathematical. In his words,

It is significant that scientific discourse does tend toward this ideal, in proportion to the degree of development of the science. Ambiguities and local and epochal biases are diminished. Tense, in particular, gives way to a four dimensional treatment of space-time.[3]

The reference to time in this context is especially interesting in that it points towards what is arguably the fatal flaw in the scientistic view. On Quine's account, which accords with a widely held assumption about the one-to-one correspondence between the mathematical continuum and physical time, there would seem to be a close connection between truth and timelessness. That the connection should have been made in the first place is perhaps not to be wondered at in view of the great success of the mathematical method in science. This success owes not a little to the development of a logically rigorous calculus of the mathematical continuum. But the latter, as a highly abstract conceptual structure, is peculiarly time-free. In consequence, the move to subsume the notions of change and process under the timeless abstractions of the four-dimensional continuum creates acute philosophical difficulties. It is here that the skeptic may focus his or her doubts.

Is it really conceivable, one may ask, that high mathematical abstractions, of a kind apparently antithetical to the concept of the dynamic, are capable of expressing the characteristics of change in any sense which can reasonably be described as 'true' and 'objective'? For in the eyes of the common sense realist at least (and Quine himself seems at times to want to be counted in their number)[4] it is a truism that the objective world is the scene of a dynamic interplay of physical events whose real differences require the postulation of a real time. But it is not easy to see how real time is to be constructed out of the high abstractions of the real number continuum except by arbitrary fiat. The paradoxes of Zeno are always at hand to remind us of the dangers of too direct an identification of time with the continuum. If truth in science is, under a Quinean view, so intimately related with the timelessness of mathematical abstractions, than it is reasonable to wonder whether there is some major incoherence at the base of scientistic estimations of the true significance of the scientific pursuit of truth.

We have here one of the more perplexing puzzles facing the modern monistic materialist. By 'monistic materialist' I am referring, at this point, only to the general characteristic of a shared aim, and not to any particular doctrine about matter. With reference to the most popular variant of materialism, Whitehead succinctly describes this aim thus:

> The strength of the theory of materialistic mechanism has been the demand, that no arbitrary breaks be introduced into nature, to eke out the collapse of an explanation.[5]

The Quinean approach is thus in accord with monistic materialism in not wanting to have to introduce arbitrary breaks into nature: the collapse of explanation is thwarted by making mathematics the glue which bonds the underpinnings of science together. This move, however, if pursued to its logical conclusion, gives to any Quinean inspired doctrine of materialism a peculiar quality of 'thinness'.[6]

In fact, the entire Galilean-Newtonian tradition seems to progress inexorably towards what might be called "mathematical materialism." By this phrase, I mean principally the widespread tendency to ascribe to mathematical abstractions meanings of high ontological import. A particular fault of this version of materialism is that it robs the world of most of its dynamic character. For if the concept of action is, as modern physics would have it, crucial for a full description of physical reality, we are faced here with a rather barren choice. We must either find some means to ascribe to mathematical abstractions, such as points, the character of causal efficacy, or we must assert, with Hume, that nature is devoid of causality altogether.

Either way we seem to end in absurdity. At the very least, mathematical materialism has no place for the notion of motion in any ordinary sense of the word. Thus to opt for the first half of the dilemma is to infect scientific explanation with a kind of absurdity commonly associated with the excessive rationalism of scholastic thinking. I shall have more to say later on this matter. If one opts for the second half of the dilemma, science itself becomes absurd insofar as it pretends to provide answers to the irrespressible "why" of human curiousity. Science, and mathematics by implication, have nothing whatever to do with explanation: they are essentially fictions designed to keep a certain type of intellectual busy.

In sum, the various mathematically governed strands of the Galilean-Newtonian scientistic tradition converge to a view in which, paradoxically, science itself seems not to be taken very seriously. Neither science nor common sense, however, seems able to do without the concepts of causality, action and motion. If the scientistic approach is inherently incapable of producing a plausible ontology which can deal with the fact that reality is shot through with tense-ridden events, this would be a reason enough to reject it entirely. However, this observation evokes the fundamental question of method: if the scientific methodology does not deserve to be the paradigm of philosophical methodology, what, if anything, does? It is an urgent problem in philosophy to find a general mode of philosophizing to counterbalance the excesses of the scientistic mode. It is even more urgent for the common sense realist, given that he or she desires to take science at least partly seriously, while at the same time avoiding, if possible, explicit or implicit appeals to scientistic preconceptions and prejudgments. Hence it is a primary concern of the common sense realist to map out a minimal conceptual ground upon which to stand.

2. Realism and Monistic Materialism

Whatever science is, it is neither purely fictional nor entirely subjective. So whoever takes science seriously would seem to be at least partially committed to some form of realism and materialism. Both these terms, however, are far from having a univocal meaning, so I shall first attempt to outline what I take to be their minimal conceptual content.

To be a 'realist', as I shall use this term, implies having a commitment to some conception of external reality, that is, to a reality which in some sense is independent of cognitive agents, human or otherwise. The meaningfulness of this vague notion is underwritten by, among other things, the very nature of the scientific enterprise. To take this at all seriously is to commit oneself to the existence of an independent process which is just one element of a much wider historical process. We note also that the scientific process has never been a fully autonomous or completely demarcated unity within reality. To take science seriously is to allow the existence of a constantly changing community of practitioners. This observation, which seems scarcely much more than a truism, nevertheless becomes pertinent whenever the realist is presented with views of the kind which Eddington has made famous. His suggestion is that the unexpected and counter-intuitive puzzles which science has uncovered in the foundations of our studies of physical reality require the postulation of two or more realities; one reality belonging to the esoteric world of microphysics and the other to the world of the ordinary observer. Such speculations, which point, so we are told, to the conclusion that there is no "really real" reality, have an air of perverse unreality about them. It is as if the encounter with puzzling phenomena at microphysical levels of the physical world is enough to undermine all confidence in the everyday world of the common objects. What has gone wrong here is that an important fact about explanation *per se* is simply overlooked. For we accord differing degrees of confidence to explanations according to the degree of familiarity which we are prepared to accord to the objects elicited in the explanation. We have confidence in the existence of the explaining scientist and his or her vital organs, perhaps a little less confidence in the existence of the cells which comprise these organs, and still less confidence in the existence of molecules, atoms, nucleii, and so on, which go, so we are told, to make up the cells. That we have so far failed to give a coherent account of the perhaps entirely conjectural esoteric entities at the bottom of the chain is no reason to renounce ordinary meanings of either reality or of explanation itself, for these turn in the end upon what we are prepared to regard, with confidence, as familiar.

To common sense a scientist is one of the more familiar of everyday objects. Moreover, it is inconceivable that real scientists (and who ever seriously doubted the reality of Eddington himself?) would pursue their various experiments upon nature for very long if they did not believe in the external reality of the objects which they set out to discover and study. Furthermore, it is undeniable that science is an important determining factor in human practical and cultural affairs. It is therefore not difficult for common sense to accept the sort of realism which most practising scientists believe in, whatever doubts they may have in their off-duty moments of reflection. The power of science to control physical events in or outside the laboratory, and to effect dramatic (some might say potentially catastrophic) changes in the constitution and organiza-tion of what there is, is evidence enough for the commonsense realist. The rallying cry of the realist might well be modelled upon Whitehead's response to pseudo-problems in philosophy, such as the existence of other minds: of these he is reported to have said: "Hang it all! *Here we are.* We don't go behind that; we begin with it."[7]

In other words, the realist's problem is not how or whether we know that there is an external reality (into which, on some accounts, we have presumably been inexplicably or fortuitously dropped as free-floating consiousnesses), or whether or not it will still be there when we, as individual existences, are no longer conscious. That there is an external reality in some perhaps not-quite-so-ordinary sense of the word must surely be taken as given. The real difficulty is how to make sense of it all in terms of the conceptual tools we have inherited. Or, if these turn out to be inadequate, in terms of whatever else we can come up with. This means that the commonsense realist cannot avoid becoming, again in Whitehead's words, a relentless "critic of abstractions," especially of the abstractions of science.

This brings us to the issue of materialism and, in particular, to the concept of matter. While science may or may not show us how "reality 'really' is," it does aim to show us how matter really is. Despite the overwhelming preoccupation of philosophers of science with the subject of scientific methodology, scientists themselves are undoubtedly preoccupied with the question of the nature of (if not the meaning of the concept of) matter. Thus while it is reasonable to believe that not every realist need be a materialist, a realist who takes science seriously is well on the way to becoming something of the kind. But this point may not be universally acknowledged as obvious, so I will try to state my position more plainly.

Since science occupies itself with the study of the properties and law-like behavior of forms, structures of forms, and transformations of matter, however uncertain it may be as to what it is really talking about, the realist who takes science seriously is obliged to take matter seriously. In other words, his or her problem is not whether there is such a thing as matter, but rather which of the multifarious matter-related concepts, properties, laws, and so on, are indispensable to an adequate and satisfying description and explanation of how things really are in the world of ordinary as well as of scientific experience. To the extent to which the realist is inclined to take seriously the monistic materialistic programme of science, which eschews the notion of mind as something to be set over against matter, to that extent the realist is something of a materialist. But it must at once be acknowledged that the latter is an extremely vague and easily misconstrued term. It may be possible and desirable to rescue it from obsolescence with a sort of minimalist definition: a materialist is one who takes science seriously enough to hold that the chief concern of science is, in some general sense, to reveal as much as possible about the nature of matter so as to be able to give a coherent account of nature in the widest possible variety of mani-festations, both in the physical and the mental spheres.

This quasi-definition of materialism does not, however, get us very far. The trouble is that in its development throughout history, the concept of matter has gradually lost many, if not most, of its traditional connotations. There have been a number of responses to the resulting problematic of 'matter'. One of the most popular of contemporary moves has been to take the extreme view which, in effect, denies that the term 'matter' "really" refers to anything at all in external reality. Indeed, the term 'matter', under this view, is entirely dispensable; it is, we are told, 'structure' that really counts. But here the problematic of 'matter' has actually being evaded, not resolved.

There is, in fact, extreme difficulty in conceiving of science as the study of formal structures, and only of structures. Without gainsaying the obvious fact that scientists often appear as if they were only engaged in the study of structure, and of structures of structures, the claim that there exists nothing *but* structure is virtually unintelligible, at least if 'structure' means only the formal (e.g. logico-mathematical) expressions of structure. And the latter idea seems to be intended in the claim that theoretical terms, which the scientist uses to refer to specific instantiations of matter, are only linguistic devices which stand in for more cumbersome formal expressions in the conceptual structure. To reduce 'matter' to 'structure' in this way only evokes the question: "structure of what?" The answer, "structure of formal mathematical concepts or entities" is no answer–it merely describes the nature of a particular mode of expression. One is still left dangling over an ontological void, suspended, as it were, by a kind of miraculous mathematico-metaphysical sky-hook.[8]

It is therefore not an insignificant fact that, in practice, scientists stubbornly refuse to talk about instantiations of matter as if they were merely talking a certain kind of fiction. They insist on speaking about instances of matter as real existents and appeal to criteria only part of which involve spatio-temporal locatability. For there is another important aspect of matter which has gained prominence through advances in science itself, namely, the aspect of activity. It seems that matter cannot be fully described without using terms like 'interaction' and its cognates. This consideration is not so easily taken care of under the purely structural view.

I have already, in the first chapter, touched upon this subject. The upshot of my previous discussion is that for all that the study of structure may be indispensable to the investigation of matter, there is nothing in the end to study which does not first presuppose that there is something that matters in the most general sense of the word. That is to say, to associate the term 'matter' with the term 'interaction', while maintaining at the same time that science is not a complete fiction, is to put oneself under the obligation to make some attempt at ontological elucidation of the processes involved. For modern physics has raised into prominence a primary puzzle which bears upon our most fundamental conceptions of physical processes, and, in particular, of our conceptions of 'substance', 'matter' and 'existence'.

At the ground of physical reality, if modern physics is in any way correct, things can be regarded as substantial only insofar as those things will somehow matter (i.e. make some sort of discernable difference) to other things. The "mattering" of matter is, furthermore, very much dependent upon the natures of the entities involved. And these natures cannot be precisely specified in mathematico-physical terms because the things are only more or less exactly specifiable in respect to place and time. In a word, significant differences are not completely reducible to mathematically describable spatio-temporal differences.

Thus, while most connotations of 'stuff' have gone by the board, there is nevertheless a sense in which the substantiality of matter seems never to be quite lost. However far from substance (in the traditional sense of permanently enduring rigid, inactive corpuscles) some of the more ephemeral entities of microphysics may be, they remain substantial in their capacity to interact with some other definite and distinguishable representatives of matter. For example, an electromagnetic field is matter in the sense that it possesses the capability for making some difference to certain determinate representatives of matter, such as electrons, but no discernible difference to gravitons (supposing there are any). And this surely is an important, if not the crucial criterion for being real, for what lacks the capacity to make or register differences has little claim to be called either 'substantial' or 'real'.

I have suggested earlier that both modern science and common sense point the realist towards a kind of monistic materialism, where this term refers to the basic requirement that matter and mind be conceived in a univocal manner. But it must be acknowledged that there may be too many pitfalls lurking in the term 'materialism', which stem from incoherent and confused conceptions of matter as well as from the variety of uses to which the term is put. Used without qualification, the term is virtually meaningless, or worse. For it elicits notions that are wholly antithetical to the extreme subtlety with which the topic of matter needs to be handled.

Perhaps it is for some such reason that Western philosophy has not given monistic materialism much of a hearing. But whatever the reasons, doctrines of monistic materialism have not generally been regarded by professional philosophers, as worthy of serious discussion.[9] It is more than a little ironical, then, that so much current philosophical discourse should implicitly appeal to and be dependent upon the metaphysically suspect doctrines of materialism which grew out of the Galilean-Newtonian reorganization of science. These doctrines, which may be gathered loosely under the heading of scientific materialism, do not comprise a systematic and coherent doctrine of materialism. Nevertheless, they have crept, as it were, through the back door of philosophy by way of ordinary language. Evolved under the single-minded pursuit of pragmatic and theoretico-empirical successes and largely indifferent to the metaphysical incoherence within the basic conceptual framework, scientific materialism has had an inordinate influence on the development of philosophy. It has greatly affected decisions not only about which problems in philosophy are worthy of study but also, and perhaps more importantly, about how the problems themselves ought to be formulated.[10]

One unfortunate consequence for our general understanding of the physical world is that the deliverances of common sense have been deemed to be wholly subordinate to the scientific view, despite the fact that science frequently, if often only tacitly, appeals to the inadequate and uncriticized metaphysical doctrines of scientific materialism. This means that the elucidation of the extremely complex relation between common sense, scientific theories, and ordinary language is a crucial worry for the common sense realist in any attempt to estimate how seriously science is to be taken. For it is clear that common sense is not a static condition, nor a state arrived at by purely conventional or arbitrary routes. It evolves only more or less in tandem with science, whose more revolutionary discoveries eventually become embedded in the language of everyday life, yet usually not without a significant time-lag. On the other hand, the interpretation of scientific theory is dependent not only upon the celebrated objectivity of the scientific mind but upon the subjective philosophical tastes of the expositors of science. Moreover, the language of interpretation is affected, probably quite deeply affected, by the metaphysical presuppositions which any language contains in its basic vocabulary and structure. And the latter is of course the repository of many of the norms which help to decide what is or is not common sense.

It is one of the more simplistic and pernicious of modern myths that science is unequivocally superior to common sense. This is not to deny the manifest superiority of the scientific appraoch in getting at the way things really are in *some* more or less clearly definable regions of human cognitive activity. But for the commonsense realist the prudent course, I am contending, begins with a critical suspension of common scientistic assumptions. In the interpretations of formal scientific theory, common sense must seek for more fundamental guidelines. This obligation cannot be escaped by assuming that science is in some way a refinement of common sense. This in fact is a good example of a scientistic preconception which begs many important questions.[11] A better estimation of the relation between them will start by taking note of their interdependence. Science and common sense grow together in mutual dependence and with reciprocal influence, each, as it were, lifting the other a notch at a time up the metaphysical ladder.

In order to support this view, and also to set the stage for further discussion of the topic of scientific explanation, a few remarks of a methodological nature now seem to be called for.

3. *On Modes of Philosophizing*

The reasons why monistic materialism has not been taken very seriously by Western philosophy, while science is taken very seriously indeed, would make a fascinating study in the history of philosophy. The natural tendency of scientists is to adopt a realistic stance, yet the temptation to take an idealist position appears to have been almost irresistible to many influential philosophers of science. This is the case even with those philosophers who might otherwise be expected to have a zealous interest in defending a realist philosophy.[12]

To the commonsense realist of the sort under consideration, any idealist view that seems to be based, if only tacitly, on notions that presuppose disembodied minds, or free-floating consciousnesses, is extremely problematic, not to say downright queer. The debate between realism and idealism always has a somewhat artifical flavour, for the issue could never be resolved by a clear choice between contrary views. The idealist position is itself a realistic position, being parasitic on an even more fundamental realist assumption. This is because a philosophical assertion of any kind may be viewed in general as a response to some sort of problem, an attempt to elucidate or to explain something about "what there is". So however much like a dream one might hold the world to be, or however eloquently one might argue that our sole contact with it is through the medium of minds, at least one crucial assumption predominates: there is something that just *is*. In fact, there is usually one more key assumption involved: it is usually assumed that what there is can be accounted for or described, at least in principle, in a rational manner. So preconceptions about the nature of mind always come into play, usually in a covert way, to shore up the idealist's arguments. In particular, the putative cogency of idealist arguments depends upon the presupposition that mind, whatever it is, is in some sense the touchstone of rationality. While all philosophy, not to mention science, begins with an assumption that mind is somehow intimately connected to the rational aspect of the world, the idealist view skips over the crucial question of what to make of all the evidence, scientific and otherwise, that mind seems explicable in terms only of the functioning of organisms. In other words, the idealist view tends not to take science very seriously at all. It thus begs most of the interesting questions about the meaning of rationality and of the relation between various schemes of thought and the order of the world.

It is not surprising, therefore, that the idealist view, despite its great popularity, has not been notably successful in giving an account of scientific knowledge.[13] It is not, however, my intention to pursue here the ongoing debate between realsim and idealism. Instead, my more limited aim is to argue, somewhat indirectly, that this putative dichotomy does not present a real difficulty, at any rate not one which can be described as a problem of simple choice between competing alternatives. It rather presents a challenge to reconcile important notions, many of which also come in apparent dichotomies. In what follows, I shall suggest how the commonsense realist may with assurance, if not with complete confidence, go about his philosophical business. Since this involves some reference to the concerns of mainstream philosophy, if only in order to outline an alternative to more standard approaches, a rough sketch of the present philosophical landscape is needed.

Fortunately, some of Richard Rorty's writings are at hand to help us discern two philosophical landmarks, or perhaps better, benchmarks. In his critique of the central concerns of Western philosophy, Rorty locates the source of its impetus in the epistemologically-centered quest for justification and certainty in knowledge. According to the Western philosophical tradition, he says, the paradigm of human activity is founded in the act of knowing, which includes the aim to establish "justified true belief, or better yet, beliefs so intrinsically persuasive as to make justification unnecessary."[14] Hence a considerable amount of philosophical effort is directed towards finding the means to fulfil the Kantian task of rendering all knowledge claims commensurable, thus establishing once and for all an accurate mirroring or reproduction of the world. The overall picture of Western philosophy which Rorty sketches for us is of a rather obsessive process of continual construction-demolition-reconstruction governed by the single-minded pursuit of an ideal, perfectly unified, conceptual structure. Under this view, any cognitive edifice which falls even a little short of the ideal deserves to be summarily demolished. Rorty describes the situation thus:

> Successive philosophical revolutions within this mainstream have been produced by philosophers excited by new cognitive feats–e.g. the rediscovery of Aristotle, Galilean mechanics, the development of self-conscious historiography in the nineteenth century, Darwinian biology, mathematical logic. . . . A 'mainstream' Western philosopher typically says: Now that such-and-such a line of inquiry has had such a stunning success, let us reshape all enquiry, and all of culture, on its model, thereby permitting objectivity and rationality to prevail in areas previously obscured by convention, superstition, and the lack of a proper epistemological understanding of man's ability accurately to represent nature.[15]

Such an approach to philosophy Rorty calls "systematic." The programme is characterized by an attitude of confrontation, and by the clash of rival claims to the possession of the objectively correct plans for epistemological reconstruction.

Yet it is clear that there is much of value to be found in most philosophical systems which have occupied the minds and interests of powerful intellects throughout the history of philosophy. Whatever one's attitude towards the expression of details and the development of central ideas, mere survival within the corpus of the tradition seems to be sufficient reason to look for useful insights in apparently conflicting conceptual systems. Moreover, the limitations of particular central doctrines often turn out to be more instructive than destructive of understanding.

Consider an example of particular interest to the commonsense realist who is concerned to reconcile his or her position with the historically robust insights of idealist philosophy. Certain epistemological considerations, which stem from Kant, are not to be dismissed lightly. There is an important truth in the claim that we can come to know reality (in any sense of 'know' which requires that what is known be communicable) only through the medium of inherited conceptual frameworks. These, as it were, stand between us and the way things really are. This concession, when juxtaposed with an acceptance of the validity of certain deliverances of modern physics, is often adduced as sufficient reason for the realist to concede defeat and gracefully abandon the realist view altogether. For it is frequently argued that the more startling aspects of modern science point toward the final triumph of idealism. The claim is that to take science seriously is to admit that since so many, if not all, commonsense attributes of reality have gone by the board in the quantum world, there is nothing recognizable left of the realist's world. Coupled with the more startling deliverances of relativity theory, quantum theory has shown, it is said, that microphysical reality (where reality is thought in any case to be founded) bears no resemblance to the manifestly causal and substantial world of the realist. What is real is mere abstract conceptual structure.

But such arguments illustrate perhaps only how strong a grip the systematic approach to philosophy has within the philosophy of science. For underlying this view is a confused tangle of metaphysical presuppositions about the nature of the world-order, as science reveals this order to be. These include debatable preconceptions about the role of the mathematical method in revealing ontological truths about this order. I have already suggested, in my general remarks about matter and substance, that modern physics may be interpreted as providing important support for a realist view of these concepts. Also, many current interpretations of physics are highly suspect by virtue of their adherence to the Galilean-Newtonian desire to mathematize the world. It therefore appears that we have here a clear example of how the success of the mathematical method can be thought to be a deciding factor in what is essentially a metaphysical debate.

The idealist view is indeed naturally sympathetic to the view that it is possible to reconstruct the world from a unified mathematico-physical description of matter with all the apodictic certainty which mathematics is thought to have. So the possibility arises that the idealist position may owe its surrealistic aspects to a complete misunderstanding of the implications for philosophy of mathematico-physical theory. A more cautious, as well as a more realistic view, is that what is happening at the sub-quantal level of reality is at present beyond the capacity of ordinary language, and hence of standard philosophical language, to describe. We are faced with a lack of appropriate and adequate conceptual frameworks, rather than a proof of the absence of some sort of external reality. For the Kantian insight cuts both ways: if conceptual frameworks stand between us and the external world, one can no more prove the unreality of the world than one can prove its reality.

It is worth noting that the oft-remarked incommensurability of classical and quantum physics is relevant here. A currently influential interpretation of this situation is that it is not only not possible to speak of sub-quantal events unambiguously and completely in the language of classical physics, it is, in principle, not possible to devise another language which will serve us better. This view, which stems from Niels Bohr, cannot simply be ignored since at the very least it is germane to the question of how seriously we should take the findings of science, as well as how we might best speak of them. So I will return to this problem in the next chapter. At the moment, I wish only to point out that the systematic mathematico-physical approach seems incapable of handling this important philsophical problem.

A related problem, perhaps a generalization of it, centers on the strong tendency of the systematic epistemological approach to prejudge the crucial issue of the meaning of 'order.' For what is involved is a fundamental ontological point: namely, whether or not we may safely assume that we understand the concept of order sufficiently well to extrapolate from the instances of order as revealed by physical science to meanings which have any direct bearing on order in the world at large. Once again, we find that current conceptions of order are shot through with assumptions which stem from the barren ontological viewpoint of mathematico-physical materialism.

The above remarks reveal just some of the difficulties involved in the consideration of the commensurability of knowledge systems. It is not easy to see how such matters can be treated adequately without first having made explicit one's ontological commitments. The notion of commensurability itself is thrown into doubt once it is recognized that apparently radically competitive cognitive systems may not indicate faults or limitations in one or the other system. What may be needed is not some sweeping epistemological reform but a recognition of fundamental ontological divisions or levels of order in reality.

But if for reasons such as these the commonsense realist is not disposed to be sympathetic to systematic philosophy, he or she is unlikely to be much happier in having to settle for what Rorty holds out as the alternative. In direct contrast to the systematic approach to philosophy is the approach which rejects the very notion of a systematic view. On Rorty's account this approach to philosophy, which he calls "edifying" philosophy, self-consiously and intentionally places itself outside the mainstream. It is skeptical about and reacts against systematic philosophy and the notion of ideally commensurable knowledge claims. However, this position immediately raises a difficulty for itself, one which is connected with a concept which seems inseparable from that of the very activity of doing philosophy.

However one interprets the overall responsibilities of the philosopher, the obligation to strive for rational expression must surely rank very high among them. Yet it is not easy to see how rationality can be served by a denial of the usefulness of having views while at the same time holding this view about having views. Furthermore, to attempt to make intelligible, coherent, and cogent remarks about the way things are in the world is unavoidably and inevitably to evoke certain standards of rationality and consistency. On the face of it, a consistent edifying philosophy, under Rorty's interpretation at least, would seem to be bent upon reducing philosophy to the exchange of unrelated (according to standard notions of rational discourse) utterances–to intentional doggerel, in other words. This is of course not what Rorty has in mind.

Two of the most celebrated practitioners of this mode of philosophizing are, in his view, Wittgenstein and Heidegger. They succeed just because they understand so well the true nature of philosophy–that is, that it is primarily conversation. As Rorty puts it, in philosophizing

> We might just be *saying something*–participating in a conversation rather than contributing to an enquiry. Perhaps saying things is not always saying how things are. Perhaps saying *that* is itself not a case of saying how things are. Both men suggest we see people as saying things, better or worse things.[16]

But the last phrase of the last sentence brings out, at least for the realist, a non-trivial puzzle. How is one to make any sense of the terms 'better' and 'worse' without having already made some prior commitment to a view about the way things are and perhaps even about the way that things ought to be? Even if the meanings of 'better' and 'worse' are considered to stem ultimately from purely arbitrary and conventional decisions, we are no further ahead. As long as something has been said which is not meant to be taken in a purely frivolous spirit, even if only the *manner* of saying it is understood to exemplify rational discourse, then views which say *something* about the way things really are have, at least indirectly, entered the conversation.

But such observations are not intended to dismiss Rorty's claims for edifying philosophy. Philosophy in a more ideal world than this one would be more like conversation than a battleground for conflicting views about the truest or most objective of the many possible cognitive systems which the human cognitive agent has devised or is capable of devising. Much philosophy, under the systematic view, has been carried on as if in some future brighter philosophical climate the unruliness of words could, at least in principle, finally be tamed into an orderly march of logico-mathematical symbols and algorithms. All the evidence points, however, to the opposite conclusion; that is, to the indispensability of words for the communication of concepts which can only be expressed, if they can be expressed at all, with the groping inexactness of words. And of words there will almost certainly never be a last one. So the commonsense realist should have no difficulty in endorsing Rorty's concluding observations: "Edifying philosophers can never end philosophy, but they can help prevent it from attaining the secure path of science."[17]

Yet this remark is clearly not the last word either; in fact, it seems to present the realist with a dilemma. If justice is to be done to the insights of philosophy and of science, then to attempt to fit philosophical activity exclusively into one or other of the above-mentioned modes is, for the commonsense realist at least, a futile exercise. As for the question of the true significance of science, and the question of its proper scope, neither systematic philosophy nor edifying philosophy is likely to serve the realist at all well. Even to consider the subject-matter of science is, as I have maintained, to put oneself under the obligation to take some concepts, such as matter, with great seriousness. A general concept of this sort, and this includes the concept of rationality itself, never comes as an isolated individual entity, which can be analyzed in complete independence of other key concepts. Without some over-reaching view, which draws the tangle of evolved and evolving meanings of key concepts together into some more or less comprehensive whole, one can not do much more than try to keep a tidy house. But perhaps a more precise metaphor would be that of removing sweepings from under one carpet to conceal them under another.

4. *Philosophy and Evolutionary Materialism*

One thing that emerges clearly from the foregoing discussion is that commonsense realism, insofar as it takes science even a little seriously, would be well-advised to determine at the outset which scientific concepts are most significant for philosophy. Some evidently deserve to be taken more seriously than others. The concept of matter is such a one; the concept of evolution is another. Such concepts may be regarded as privileged in the sense that it is difficult to imagine them ever becoming completely meaningless or obsolete. Their role in philosophy is indirect: they force upon the scientifically concerned realist the necessity to make ontological commitments. To see why this is so, let us consider some of the implications of taking the concepts of matter and evolution seriously.

While the concept of matter presents great difficulties to a purely edifying or conversational approach to philosophy, the concept of evolution presents a different, but equally awkward, set of difficulties for the purely systematic approach to philosophy. And if modern science is generally right, the two concepts are intimately related. For if the term 'matter' refers in some general way to what there is, the term 'evolution' refers to the general mode of organization of matter. It seems that 'what there is' does not come in discrete and independent lumps of amorphous 'stuff': it comes in distinguishable forms possessing in varying degree the marks and traces of synchronic and diachronic organization.

The intimate connection between the concept of matter and the concept of evolution has only comparatively recently been recognized, partly on account of spectacular advances in molecular biology. These tend to close whatever gap might remain from the historic tendency to divide the so-called inorganic and organic worlds into two distinct realms. The concept of evolution, which incidently, does not originate with Darwin but which attained new significance and prominence through his work, is one which few philosophers or scientists would want to reject as meaningless or insignificant insofar as the organization of the forms of matter is concerned. In its full generality, and with due consideration for its implications for monistic materialism (implications of which, incidently, few expositors of the so-called modern synthesis in biology seem to be aware), the concept undermines a favorite picture which Western philosophy has painted of the human organism's place in the scheme of things.

For the concept of evolution renders otiose the 'pre-Copernican' picture of the human animal as the ontological and epistemological culmination of organic existence, a type of being around which lesser beings can be thought to revolve. That is to say, it is difficult under a thoroughgoing evolutionary view to hold fast to the traditional notion of the human animal as the central cognitive agent in the world, or as Rorty puts it, as the essential knower of essences, especially of his own essence.[18] More particularly, there seems little left of the Cartesian picture of the human cognitive engine which, in principle at least, is capable of producing work of absolute precision. The ideal of a clear description of an exactly describable world becomes incoherent once the human cognitive agent is seen to be embedded in an essentially evolutionary world. For if it is admitted that the human animal is merely one stage in a more or less continuously evolving chain of organic forms of matter, any notion which suggests that the human organism can be held up as a measure of all things, in some ultimate metaphysical sense, becomes suspect. Regardless of the fact that the human organism seems particularly well-constructed and adapted to play the role of the world's most complex and subtle cognitive agent, the agency itself appears to be distinguishable from that of the so-called lesser animals more in terms of its high degree of efficacy (for which we owe much, if not everything, to the ability to develop symbolic forms of communication) than to the fact that it represents a radically different kind of cognitive functioning.

But here we are touching upon a highly controversial topic. Fortunately it is not vital to this discussion that this issue be definitely settled here in one way or another. It suffices to observe that realistic evolutionary monistic materialism, of the sort which I am advocating, must locate the human cognitive enterprise in an organic field in which it becomes part of what may be called a cosmic cognitive project. For whether or not we interpret the fact as an essential or as an accidental characteristic of the world, all of what there is does come to know itself in a piecemeal manner through its cognizing individuals. Thus matter becomes both self-consciously reflective and cognitively critical, in its more mindful forms of organization, as well as imaginative, creative, and so on. In short, the overall picture of the world which commonsense realism leads to, insofar as it takes matter and evolution seriously, is of a vast self-referential system, with cognitive agents which are forms of process inextricably embedded in a larger process. This picture is wholly antithetical to the Cartesian notion of free-floating intellects. For it is not only difficult but wholly unnecessary to try to fit entities into this world-picture which are only describable as consiousnesses, needing nothing but themselves in order to exist.[19]

Under the evolutionary light, then, the commonsense realist has good reasons to regard the traditional concerns of philosophy, especially of systematic philosophy, as of secondary interest. Thus there are empirically grounded reasons (inasmuch as the concept of evolution has empirical foundations) for agreeing with Rorty that the balance of Western philosophy is badly in need of redress. This must involve, among other things, a reassessment of common assumptions underlying talk about 'truth,' 'objectivity,' and 'necessity.'

Consider, as an important example, the notion of truth. This concept is bound up with the idea of perfect comprehension, of a grasp of things in just the way that they are. But it is difficult to conceive of any one intellect, or even a legion of geographically and temporally extended co-operating intellects, which could perform a paradigm act of truth-utterance in such a manner as to deliver up all that the concept promises. So while one may speak of Truth, which is surely all that there is in just the way that it is, and not a bit less, it is a concept of limited usefulness. Since there is no conceivable cosmic act of cognition which could accomplish the momumental task of grasping the Truth, at least not in any thoroughgoing evolutionary world, one may speak only of partial truths. Furthermore, when the process of understanding must be viewed as part of that which is to be understood, the idealized notion of truth loses even more of its point. There even arises a problematic element in the traditional notion of an individual act of cognition. In short, when seen from the evolutionary perspective, the goal of a final system of justified beliefs is a myth which obscures the possibility that the proper business of philosophy is the search for adequacy of expression rather than for certainty or truth.

Thus the commonsense realist is led to a primary epistemological consideration: that is, that every cognitive enterprise very likely has its own peculiar and finite horizons. That is to say, a properly realistic epistemology should start from the position that the human cognitive enterprise is an endless generation of only more or less adequate conceptual systems, none of which will ever be rescued from incoherence or inadequacy by a happy intervention of some transcendental insight, by some serendipitous discovery of special facts, or through exceptionally astute conceptual analyses.

Granted the essential correctness of these observations, the commonsense realist is faced with an endlessly difficult problem of choice. But it is not the simple and straightforward choice between the alternatives of systematic and edifying philosophy. Something of the character of each mode of philosophizing is worth preserving, but either mode taken alone is bound to turn out to be unsatisfactory. Having conceded at least one crucial point to idealism, that the cognitive process is as much world-making as it is world-taking, the commonsense realist must certainly maintain that one aim of philosophy is to be "edifying", as opposed to something like "objectively and conclusively right." On the other hand, it is unlikely that edification about the nature of matter will be forthcoming unless it is linked more or less explicitly to a world-view. What is indicated, then, is not just the necessity for reconciliation between the rival claims of system and conversation, but also the necessity for ontological commitment. Hence we arrive at the conclusion that a realistic mode of philosophizing is more akin to story-telling than to conversation or to systematic analysis of knowledge or truth claims. And it is perhaps also worth remarking that while this conclusion cannot be accommodated easily within the systematic or edifying modes of philosophizing, it arises naturally out of a story which begins by taking science, and in particular the concepts of matter and evolution, moderately seriously.

5. *Philosophy and the Story*

It is my contention that to do philosophy in a manner compatible with the minimal demands of commonsense realism is to be concerned primarily with whether or not one's conceptual apparatus provides sufficiently solid ground upon which to construct a plausible and adequate story, as opposed to an objectively true, complete, and final account. This entails the rejection of a common belief which is deeply ingrained in Western philosophy, that we shall find in logic the ultimate underpinnings of rational philosophizing. The hard truth is that logic is as much in need of elucidation as is mathematics. Thus it cannot be located at the ground of explanation when part of what we want to determine is which one of the many variants of logical system is implicated in the best story of what there is and how it all hangs together. Short of prejudging the whole issue, it would seem that it is only reasonable to assume that logic has little to do with the former and probably much to do with the latter. That is to say, the topics of logic *per se* need lose none of their great interest for philosophy inasmuch as logic embodies the valuable results of a long history of attempts to clarify and specify the various possibilities of rational connection. The commonsense realist naturally wants his or her stories to be rational and to have a convincingly coherent structure. This means that in some important sense they will always have a logical form. But form is different from content.

One reason why the elucidation of the rational cannot be exhaustively and exclusively carried out in logical terms is the troublesome notion of reference. On what grounds, one might ask, could one hold that the logical structuring of privileged conceptual structures (supposing there are any) should in itself present no difficulties with respect to reference? The traditional belief that the relation between logical truths and Truth itself is some sort of direct correspondence is not as obvious as the number of adherents to this belief might lead one to think. That logical structures may express something about the *way* things (whatever they are) logically hang together in the external world does not entail that the structures are actually present in reality, or, if present, that they are present-without-remainder.

In connection with the problem of reference, H. Putnam suggests that the concept of truth be understood in terms of what is agreed upon by a community of rational beings who are sensitive to the internal constraints of whatever conceptual system they are using. Such a conclusion is supported, as I have suggested above, by considerations which arise in a thoroughgoing evolutionary theory of the world. The main point can be summed up by saying that what Putnam calls the "God's eye point of view" is seriously mistaken. Putnam's own response to this conclusion, which in effect makes truth a problematic concept, is of interest to the commonsense realist. For Putnam suggests that truth is

> some sort of (idealized) rational acceptability–some sort of ideal coherence of our beliefs with each other and with other experiences as *these experiences are themselves represented in our belief system.*[20]

But the main thrust of his argument is directed against the correspondence theory of truth; and the notion of "rational acceptability" is introduced to replace the idea that truth involves some sort of "correspondence with mind-independent or discourse-independent 'states of affairs'".[21] Hence, for him, "rational acceptability" is "in large part" coherence and fit.

This suggestion is certainly relevant to the realist's problems of deciding what an adequate and plausible story might look like. But Putnam's approach steers too closely to the epistemological side of the problem of truth. For it is over the meaning of the elusive notion of "fit" that the real trouble arises. That is to say, it is not logic that presents the stickiest problems–it is the ontological commitments which the conceptual system represents that are the crucial worries.

Thus while Putnam rightly attacks the viewpoint which he calls "metaphysical realism," by showing that the notion of a direct correspondence theory of truth is unacceptable, his own position, which he calls at times "anti-realism" or "internalism," does not face the key ontological question. If we allow that the notion of truth is not completely vacuous, and granted that we deal at best with only partial truths about the world, there seems no escaping the fact that some of these are manifestly better than others. How to resolve the better-or-worse problem is thus one of the major concerns of the philosophical story-teller.

One very important way in which the proponents of the purely logical approach offend mightily against common sense is by ignoring or denying a common feature of ordinary experience: that a feeling of rightness has as much to do with the assertion of truths as does survival of tests for consistency. This means that the telling of stories in philosophy is not all that different from the telling of stories in serious literature. The main difference is that philosophical story-telling deals in large generalities whereas literature is more closely bound to the particular. Doubts about the plausibility and even the coherence of stories which purport to convey truths about complex relationships which transcend particular events can only be resolved by the critical weighing of the respective merits of competing conceptual systems. And final judgment can only be of the kind "more or less adequate," rather than "true" or "false."

The upshot is that in addition to "rational acceptability" one requires something like "reasonable comprehensiveness" and "maximal cogency" before a philosophical story can be deemed satisfactory. A fair amount of coherence seems indispensable but, as every story-teller knows, this criterion is by itself far from being sufficient. For the cogency of any story depends in good part upon whether or not it rings true; this is not something which can be tested by means of a logical or mathematical algorithm. Given the dominating influence of the latter myth, it seems a definite advantage of the story terminology that it reminds us at the outset that in this mode of philosophizing we shall meet no pretence at presenting truth in some apodictic sense of the word. Instead we may just be offered a glimpse (of inescapably uncertain import) into the way things are.

These observations serve to bring out the realist's most acute methodological problem. One's story cannot proceed far, indeed cannot even begin, before one must face the question of what sort of explanation best accords with a truly realistic and just appraisal of the many factors that deserve attention. In the case of the philosophy of mathematics and the natural sciences, the question which concepts are most deserving of trust has usually been answered unhesitatingly in favour of concepts which can be said to possess a high degree of abstraction. But since the notion of "degree of abstraction" is far from clear, and indeed since it is the long-term aim of a story in this field of philosophy to attempt to make it clearer, it seems more prudent to begin the story at a much earlier point. In fact, a notion which is especially in need of examination is that of explanation itself.

Both explanation and description presuppose an existing conceptual structure. There appear to be two broad and general categories under which the organization of concepts has been carried out in philosophy and science. In W. E. Hocking's terminology, explanations (or descriptions) can be classified as either "homeotypal" or "hetero-typal".[22] The contrast between these categories is concisely summarized by Hocking thus: "We must either explain things by what they are or else by what they are not."

More specifically, in order to be classified as homeotypal, explanations or descriptions of one concept must proceed by enlisting the aid of what appear to be similar or cognate concepts. Thus philosophers such as

Whitehead are often described (and criticized) for attempting to account for change in terms of change. This charge arises from the fact that Whitehead's account of process-in-the-large is based on a conception of events which are themselves primary processes. Thus while Whitehead, rightly in Hocking's view, rejects the notion that change can be derived from changelessness, or the fluent from the static, he in the end falls back, says Hocking, on the old metaphysical device of "explaining a phenomenon by an 'essence' of the same sort".[23] The suggestion is that this mode of explanation is inescapably and viciously circular.

By contrast, the mode of "heterotypal" explanation (or description), championed by most scientists and scientistic philosophers, such as Quine, attempts to account for, explain, or describe things in terms of what they manifestly are not.[24] As Hocking neatly sums up the situation,

> What physics has discovered is *the non-fertility of homeotypal explanation:* heat is not motion; but it is better to explain heat by motion than to refer to the calorific principle, for while we have a mystery we get a fertile correspondence, which is part of what we wanted.[25]

The last point is especially pertinent for us. As far as scientific *method* is concerned, it is true that heterotypal explanation has proved itself capable of forming the basis of a remarkably effective programme of conceptual organization. And the mathematical mode of expression has also demonstrated that it provides the best systematic means to pursue the goals of this programme. But method is one thing and the matter to be explained is another. For mystery undeniably envelops the fact that highly abstract mathematical concepts and entities (such as mathematical points) can be somehow connected to, if not be the fundamental explicanda of, complex phenomena in a physical reality whose constitutents show all the signs of having a character which is by no means static and inert.

As I mentioned earlier, this is the point where the realist may focus his or her doubts as to whether science can, in principle, really tell us (in the words of Quine) how "reality 'really' is." Reiterating a question which I broached at the beginning of this chapter, if we are compelled (for want of an alternative, if for no other reason) to regard the mathematical ground of the scientific mode of heterotypal explanation as having ontological significance, are we not being forced into a metaphysical impasse? For the dynamic world of physical activities, motions, forces, influences, and their like seem to have dissolved into a ghostly display of static abstractions.

Indeed we have here reached the crux of what Hocking describes as a "perfectly good dilemma." He succinctly describes the problematic of explanation as follows:

> If homeotypal explanation is empty, heterotypal explanation is absurd.

From the discrete we can get no continuity, from number no
extension, from the point no magnitude, from matter no mind, from
mind no matter, from the static no change. . . . If the point is in truth a
zero of extension, you have on hand precisely nothing and can do
nothing with it.[26]

But I want to argue that the incompatibility of these two modes of
explanation may be only apparent. Clearly the mode of heterotypal
explanation does not lead to complete absurdities, at least not when it is
confined to the sphere of physical science. There is no doubt that this
mode is an effective means to draw empirical observations together into
coherent logico-deductive systems. But, as I have noted earlier, progress
in science has, at least in this century, resulted in increasingly abstruse
and obscure accounts of the nature of the physical, and this obscurity is
often glossed over with *ad hoc* adjustments to the meaning of
explanation.[27] And the reason why such adjustments are doomed to be
nothing other than arbitrary is that the means to interpret the formal
results of systematic investigation are essentially missing from the
mode of heterotypal explanation.

It is clear that this is the case with current attempts to interpret the
results of modern physics. The inability of the heterotypal mode of
scientific explanation to provide a method to interpret the formal
results of scientific investigations has of course been frequently noted.
Moreover, the lack of such means is not always seen as a defect. Such
views are in fact well represented in philosophies which generally go by
the name of naturalism.[28]

The queerness of "naturalistic" beliefs (for they sit side by side with
the tacit assumption that, despite this aspect of untranslatability into
ordinary discourse, scientific knowledge is something which the
ordinary person must take note of if he or she aspires to some
semblance of rationality) has to do with preconceptions about the
meaning of explanation. The important consideration here, which is
usually overlooked, is that in any ordinary sense of the word an
explanation invariably appeals to concepts which can be said to be of a
low order of abstraction. The latter notion can be roughly summed up as
equivalent to a high degree of familiarity. That is to say, such concepts
are much less remote than scientific theoretical concepts from the range
of ordinary human experience.

Thus while the history of science may show the necessity of, or at
least the indispensability of, the scientific mode of heterotypal
explanation, it has not yet demonstrated, and I am contending cannot
under its own terms demonstrate, the sufficiency of this mode. The
point is simply that what emerges from science appears to be at best
only half the whole story. We thus arrive at the question of where and in
what form the other half is to be found.

The scope of an adequate response is in fact so large that what follows is only offered as a rough sketch of the sort of answer which the question demands. Indeed, the remainder of this book can be regarded as an attempt to explore some of the many relevant considerations in more detail.

6. Scientific and Metaphysical Explanation

An important factor in any response to the question of non-scientific explanation is the conception of matter which is being evoked. Let us consider once again the implications of adopting a position of the sort which I have referred to as evolutionary monistic materialism. If it be granted that the concepts of matter and evolution are indispensable to the description of the facts in at least the realm of the organic, the door is opened to that elusive cognate of 'evolution': namely, 'emergence'. For it seems that the concept of evolution cannot even begin to be analyzed before the reference must be made to emergent properties as real factors in a world of process. But the recognition of this point then launches one directly into the contemplation of 'order': whatever this term means, it is far from obvious that it can be exhaustively subsumed under the notion of mathematical law.

This observation is, of course, not a logical conclusion: it all depends upon how one interprets the available evidence. And given the current stream of scientific reports about radically different types of order whose emergence in complex systems provides much of the justification for the use of the term 'complex', it would be unreasonable to complain of lack of evidence.[29] It is therefore not easy to see how or why one should assume that the explanation of order can be carried out in a purely epistemological plane, as must surely be the case if one's ontology is composed effectively of high (mathematical) abstractions. For the concept of emergence is not simply a shorthand form for an admission of ignorance, as is sometimes suggested. This move in effect claims that a statement about emergent properties is merely a statement about the existence of differences whose systematic connection is at present (and probably only temporarily) missing from scientific knowledge.

This sort of response effectively begs the whole question, for it falls back upon the assumption that all manifestations of order in the world can eventually be subsumed under a single system. But this move, in turn, relegates the terms 'evolution' and 'emergence' to the status of vacuous expressions of no real significance for any satisfactory explanation of the way things actually are. In other words, the evidence for the evolution of novel forms of order is merely discounted, and replaced with a promissory note: future progress in science will clear up the illusion that the world is the scene of the emergence of novelty. Thus the failure to take emergence seriously invites the charge that current science, inasmuch as it takes the concept of evolution and of emergent properties seriously, is not itself being taken very seriously.

A more positive, and one might well add more commonsensical, position on the meaning of 'emergence' is to say that 'order' is generic, and that the application of the term 'emergent' to physical (or even mental) characteristics entails the existence of specific levels or types within the genus 'order'. Put another way, to say that certain systems of matter possess emergent properties relative to some other system or systems (either in the diachronic development of an organic species or in the synchronic organization of so-called primitive systems into more complex systems) is to take a major step in the way of ontological commitment. It is, in effect, to admit as a contingent truth about the world that it is inherently layered with respect to types of organizations. And once this step is honestly taken, one's basic epistemological attitude in the issue of explanation seems bound to take on a distinctive colour. This can be summed up in the notion of complementarity: the two apparently conflicting modes of explanation discussed above appear in fact to be reciprocally dependent.

But before pursuing this thought any further, it may be well to reconsider the appropriateness of our terminology. In the light of what I have just said, it appears to be a mistake to use the terms 'homeotypal' and 'heterotypal', with the respective connotations of 'non-scientific' and 'scientific'. For if the world is really intrinsically layered in respect to types of organization, then it seems proper and reasonable to invert the above usage. That is to say, the sort of explanation which is carried on at any one level of order, in the linking, describing and explaining of entities which share the same type of organization, appears best described as 'homeotypal'. On the other hand, the sort of explanation which is then required in order to link and unify the explanations of a whole range of more or less distinct levels of organization might best be designated as 'heterotypal'.[30] This turning of the terminological tables leads, I am claiming, to a more satisfactory way to view explanation *per se*.

Consider the scientific mode of explanation. The history of science bears witness that the most successful instances of scientific explanation occur when attention is confined to the physical aspects of entities which belong to what can be seen as a distinct type of organization. The programme of mechanistic materialism, for example, is in its element when it is dealing with (in Whitehead's useful phrase) "material societies"–that is, with statistical aggregates, as opposed to organized systems, of units of matter. The statistical point of view can treat both the aggregates and the units as if they possess no internal organization.

And it appears that it is just at the point where factors indicative of internal organization become relevant that the mechanistic approach loses its efficacy. Newtonian physics, in particular, begins to decline in importance and usefulness once elements of atomic, sub-atomic or biological organization begin to dominate in the scientist's interests.

When viewed in this light it seems no accident that, given the general tendency of scientific materialism to overlook, or deliberately to ignore, the possibility that order is generic, that the concept of matter should have developed in modern science in just the way it has. There would seem to have been no alternative to its gradual disappearance into a cloud of abstractions, once the mathematical method of Descartes, Galileo, and Newton had commandeered the scientific imagination. For it was not that metaphysical deficiencies went unnoticed. Boscovitch, for instance, put forward arguments, at the end of the eighteenth century, which showed that the Newtonian corpuscularian conceptions of the units of matter, of rigid, impenetrable corpuscles extended in space and enduring permanently in time, was incoherent and incapable of supporting an ultimate explanatory system.[31] These objections went largely unnoticed: method took pre-eminence over metaphysics. The subsequent development of science has been as detrimental to philosophical understanding of matter as it has been instrumental for the pragmatic purposes of its manipulation.[32]

Beginning with Boscovitch's own reduction of material corpuscles to centers of force, the analogical content of the mechanical model of a unit of matter gradually dissolved into the analogical vacuity of mathematical systems. And these are inherently empty of explanatory power in the ordinary sense of the word, because for something to be an explanatory model of anything else it must have *some* analogical content. This is because nothing has been explained unless it can be grasped in terms of *familiar* concepts. But there is nothing really familiar about the notion of, for instance, moving mathematical points. We have here in fact the absurd situation, which is described above in the quotation from Hocking, of attempting to *explain* magnitude in terms of extensionless points, motion in terms of the static, and so on.

At best, mathematical models are second-order analogies in the sense that they are expressive of certain kinds of systematic order or structure. And it is a second-order familiarity in that it presupposes a relatively sophisticated knowledge base. Such models seem therefore best described as "systematic analogies", if they deserve to be described as analogies at all.

What scientific (which I will hereafter call Homeotypal, to distinguish it from Hocking's usage) explanation largely is is not explanation in any ordinary sense of the word but rather something more aptly described as 'conceptual organization of high abstractions'.

The scientific mode of explanation is an impressively effective means to extract details of the systematic relations which exist between the constituents of a given level of world-order. It is, roughly speaking, a method for scanning the multitudinous details of contingent physical events for evidence of a nexus of logical necessity. That the end result of scientific investigation can *only* be a kind of logical nexus, and not an ultimate explanatory system (one, moreover, which can never issue in a linear deductive structure based upon indubitable primitive premises or self-evident truths), is perhaps most evident in the resistance to final definition of key scientific theoretical terms.

It is a strong possibility that the justly lauded explanatory power of science is limited both as to scope and to metaphysical significance, paradoxically by the very factor which gives it its power. In other words, the scientific method seems inherently incapable of fixing the meaning of its terms. Consider, for instance, the development of the concept of mass. With Newton, this concept acquired the connotation of 'quantity of matter'. In Newtonian physics, the concept has three senses according to whether it is used to denote inertial mass, passive gravitational mass, or active gravitational mass. Thus the meaning of the concept is heavily context-dependent. Furthermore, it makes no sense to ask, in respect of Newton's second law of motion, whether it is a definition (of force or mass, since only two of the three quantities involved–mass, force and acceleration–are independently observable) or an empirical statement. The question appears misguided, for it was Newton's special achievement to have shown how these key terms could be systematically related, rather than to have provided the means to resolve problems about the meaning of 'matter' itself.

We seem to have uncovered here the roots of some of our current confusion about explanation as such. For the strength, and weakness, of Newton's method is, as E. McMullin describes it, that it makes "The system as a whole. . . definition, description and explanation, all at once; [the system] is both postulated and empirically (approximately) true."[33] As subsequent developments in physics have illustrated, it does not seem possible to formulate a definition of mass which will be consistent with the many uses of the term.[34] And if it should be the case that such definitions are simply not to be found, then this is one good reason to believe that scientific Homeotypal explanation is only capable of providing at most half of what is needed for a fully rounded explanation of physical phenomena.

The difficult question remains to be discussed how the details of layered Homeotypal explanations are to be fitted into a coherent and comprehensive world-picture. This mode of explanation, properly called Heterotypal, since it involves explanation *across* levels of order, demands the full generality of metaphysical thinking. And this would seem to be possible only when carried out analogically.[35] The foregoing discussion indicates that the main reason why this is so is that explanation in its widest sense involves the task of encompassing within the narrow range of the familiar what in actuality belongs to intrinsically incommensurable types of world-order.

I have already discussed some reasons why the existence of real differences in the emergent properties of complex organizations of matter indicate that order in general is not reducible to a single logical mode of relatedness. If the world is truly heterogeneous with respect to order, the positivistic ideal of a unified, formal (preferably mathematical) theory of world order takes on the character of an unwarranted prejudice. And it is just at this point of positivistic failure that the story-telling element of philosophy comes into its own. For the creation of a fruitful analogy depends in large part upon a fertile imagination, not unlike that of the insightful story-teller, rather than upon the orderly imagination of a system-builder.

It is also just at this point that ontological commitment becomes unavoidable. This is not to suggest that creative imagination which involves ontological commitment cannot and does not appear in the more restricted and positivistic domain of scientific explanation. But it is more often the case that such commitment is seldom spelled out, and, in general, not too deeply held. Scientists, as a rule, are not very concerned with, or have much time for, explicit metaphysical thinking. This means that the ontological content of scientific models will perhaps always turn out to be minimal. Indeed, scientific models frequently serve chiefly as heuristic aids to imagination and calculation.[36]

This means that an ineradicable quality of 'fuzziness' is characteristic of explanation in its fullest sense, if for no other reason than that the metaphysical generalities of the Heterotypal mode can never be made absolutely precise and complete. It is perhaps well to stress that this does not necessarily make Heterotypal explanations inferior to the Homeotypal explanations of science. Apart from the consideration that these two modes of explanation are actually mutually dependent, as I shall subsequently maintain, the scientistic tendency to insist upon the superiority of Homeotypal explanations is at odds with important insights in recent philosophy of science. For the putative clarity and exactness of scientific explanations is never unequivocal in respect to assertions about the way things really are. The view that scientific theories are inherently corrigible, which stems from the work of Kuhn, Popper, and many others, can be adduced as support for the view that scientific explanations are, in their own way, 'fuzzy'. As I have already noted, they can be regarded as systematic analogies, more or less indicative, but not necessarily entirely representative, of the sorts of order which actually exist in our many-layered world.

The question now arises as to whether there are any extant examples of Heterotypal analogies, and if there are, what is special about their nature. To take the latter part of the question first, the key to the success of a Heterotypal analogy would seem to be that element which is indispensable to any analogy: familiarity. To see the importance of this feature, we need only recall some of the considerations of the previous section. Granted the cogency of the commonsense realist-materialist evolutionary view of the world, it follows that it is vital to view mind as something *in* the world. That is to say, mind neither invents the world, nor imposes its structure upon the external world, nor mirrors the things of the external world, and very likely does not even reflect or grasp perfectly the logical structures of the world. This means that it would be a mistake to speak of perception in terms that connote passive reception: instead every act of perception must be viewed as an active response. Thus it is not correspondence between formal attributes of the mind and things-bearing-properties which the analogy-seeker is looking for. Rather, what is sought is a means to express a feeling of rightness. The test of a successful search is the satisfaction of an affirmative recognition that *this* well-known object or situation is akin to *that* hitherto obscure object or situation. The consequence is that our entire conception of the familiar has been enlarged to include regions hitherto closed to understanding.

It is perhaps worth noting also that unfortunate consequences for understanding can just as easily arise in the choice of particular analogies. I have pointed out that the above observations entail a theory of perception utterly opposed to the traditional belief in a sharp distinction between knower and known. The traditional view appears to be based upon a misleading and false analogy, that of a passive receiver gathering, in some mechanical manner, signals from external objects. As useful as such a view might be for some practical purposes, it seems completely detrimental to the philosophical problem of understanding perception, not to mention understanding itself. The connection between mind and world is much more intimate than the common 'picture' of the mind as the mirror of external events suggests. But further exploration of this extremely difficult topic is not possible here. For my present purposes, I wish only to point out how closely understanding is bound up with the establishment of fruitful analogies. Success here seems highly dependent upon the genius of particularly insightful individuals. And the possibility of insight of any kind would seem to be explicable in the end only in terms of there being some sort of *rapport* between nature and our intellectual processes.[37]

It appears useful to distinguish between two broad categories of analogy. These correspond roughly to the modes of explanation which I have designated as Homeotypal and Heterotypal. In the scientific

Homeotypal mode, the kinds of analogy which appear to be most prevalent are, apart from systematic analogies, those which deserve to be called "illustrative analogies": they must be counter-balanced in the essentially metaphysical Heterotypal mode of explanation by what might be called "co-ordinating analogies".[38] It is arguable that much confusion has been generated in the philosophy of nature through the failure to distinguish between these types of analogy. That the prime example of an illustrative analogy, mechanism, has been made to carry an unwarranted metaphysical burden is almost too obvious to mention, were it not for the fact that it still appears, usually in a tacit form, in popular accounts of important recent scientific developments.[39] And when systematic analogies are mistakenly construed as having metaphysical significance, we have an instance of the philosophical sin which Burtt describes as "making a metaphysics out of a method."[40]

The claim that metaphysics calls for co-ordinating analogies does not express a radically new view of metaphysics. This type of analogy has underpinned some of the great metaphysical systems of the past. Most of contemporary philosophy is, however, totally bereft of such analogies, that is, with the outstanding exception of Whitehead's theory of organism. His notion of "organism" is a co-ordinating analogy whose analogical content is capable, Whitehead claims, of linking all the various instances of order in the world. These range from the order exemplified by elementary particles of physics to the order exemplified by extremely complex biological systems. Whether or not Whitehead's co-ordinating analogy will ultimately help make the world a more familiar place for us is, of course, a complicated and controversial matter, for there is an enormous range of factors to be considered. Here I am claiming only that in following Whitehead one at least begins with a balanced approach which gives each type of analogy, and each mode of explanation, its proper due.

For if the foregoing observations are in any way correct, an adequately comprehensive and plausible world-view must be one which reconciles Homeotypal and Heterotypal modes of explanation. These modes must be regarded as complementary. Neither mode can be pursued very far before appeals must be made to evidence or arguments arising from the other mode. Indeed, the plausibility of large generalizing co-ordinations presupposes prior judgments about the reliability of the facts and of the systematic interconnections between the facts of ordinary or specialized domains of experience. In other words, Heterotypal explanation proceeds on the assumption that Homeotypal explanation is capable of indicating something worthy of being included in a world-picture. On the other hand, a multiplicity of accurately described details is of limited interest or importance in the absence of broad co-ordinating generalizations.

I am claiming that a major reason for the present confused state of the non-specialist's understanding of the scientific picture of the world may be traced to the consideration that he or she has been offered (*pace* Quine) only inherently thin descriptions of the way things really are. A properly thick description must be a story whose central character is a co-ordinating analogy which is sufficiently powerful to bridge the inevitable discontinuities between the detailed thin descriptions of scientific theories. But it must be stressed that such discontinuities very likely cannot be demarcated precisely, because of the essential complementarity of the two modes of explanation. The situation can perhaps best be understood in terms of the metaphor of the horizontal and the vertical. Neither of these two concepts can be fully understood in the complete absence of reference to the other. A thick Heterotypal explanation is in danger of becoming an empty shell if it does not allow enough room for the detailed deliverances of thin Homeotypal explanations. On the other hand, thin detailed descriptions require reference to the generalizations of Heterotypal explanation if they are to have any metaphysical body at all.

These considerations profoundly affect the meaning of 'scientific truth'. Any epistemological project which sets out to establish either a pure correspondence or a pure coherence theory of scientific truth seems doomed to failure. Whatever partial truths actually do emerge from our cognitive enterprises, they appear to come about through the careful balancing of the complementary demands of correspondence and coherence. Neither of these terms can be taken too literally. For by 'correspondence' one can only mean something like 'rightness of ontological fit', and by 'coherence' something like 'rightness of mode of rational expression'.

At the beginning of this discussion, I suggested that the common-sense realist's methodological problems centered on the difficulty of resolving the question of the relative ontological status of abstract concepts. My discussion brings out the possibility that the notion of "degree of abstraction" deserves more careful consideration than it normally receives. For what seems to underlie the view that non-scientific ('homeotypal', as they were first designated) explanations are empty is the assumption that all concepts can be regarded as belonging to the same order of abstraction. That is to say, It is as if all concepts could be regarded as members of a single class.[41] Such a move, I am contending, misses an essential point about explanation. In terms of degree of abstraction, there is a world of difference between concepts of a low degree of abstraction, such as those which physicists attach to the more accessible instances of matter (e.g., those which leave tracks in bubble chambers), and the highly abstract mathematical concepts which are involved in their discovery and description. And any attempt to find some direct link between these two conceptual realms, each of which involves abstractions of different degree, is not only presumptuous, it appears wholly mistaken. The chief difference between these two orders of abstraction, a difference which at first glance seems so impressive (and which no doubt inspires some of our wonder at the "remarkable effectiveness of mathematics"), involves a distinction between fundamental metaphysical categories, namely, a distinction between the 'concrete' and the 'abstract'. For it now appears that the sort of explanation that our general problem of the application of mathematics requires is not one which can be conceived in terms of passing from the 'abstract' (i.e., mathematical) to the 'concrete' (e.g., the life-histories of concrete elementary particles) in, as it were, a single leap. Rather the real difficulty can be pinned to our present conceptual poverty. We simply lack the means to speak of abstract concepts in their proper settings (i.e. with regard to the type of order to which they are most suited), and we lack co-ordinating analogies of sufficient depth and breadth to allow us to pass from one level of discourse about the 'abstract' to another in such a way as to do the least violence to the legitimate cognitive claims which can be made at each separate level.

In an obvious sense, all concepts are abstract in that they are always the shadow and never the substance; that is, they are never real concrete entities but always tools designed to capture reality in one of its many aspects. This truism is sometimes expressed with the metaphor that we first must murder the world in order to dissect it. Thus its 'concrete' dynamic character is arrested and embalmed in static 'abstract' conceptual systems. What is so queer about scientistic attempts to explain all of reality in terms of the abstract concepts of mathematics is that all traces of concreteness have vanished from the world in the attempt. In the terms of the present discussion, what has gone wrong is that the fundamental complementarity of the categorial distinction between the 'abstract' and the 'concrete' has been ignored. For while it is a commonplace to say that we cannot get away from the necessity to invent abstract concepts if we are to say anything at all about the concrete world, it is just as important a fact that if we want to say anything substantial about an abstract concept we must in the end go back to the concrete world. And this means, in effect, that we must constantly consult ordinary experience, for this is the source of our important analogies and, in the end, of our most meaningful stories.

Chapter Five. The Model in Physical Science

1. The Problem of Models

A model of a physical theory is, among other things, a means to interpret the formal results of that theory. Thus one of its chief characteristics is its dependence upon concepts which are intelligible by virtue of their familiarity, that is, their intimate connection with ordinary experience. But the notion that a specific formal (e.g., mathematical) theory might possess such a thing as a model which is capable of conveying knowledge about significant aspects of physical reality has become especially problematical in the light of developments in modern science. The picture which modern science now presents to its students is clear in only one respect: the so-called 'exact' sciences do not, contrary to popular beliefs, present us with unequivocally exact and uncontroversially true pictures of physical reality.

The most intractable aspect of the endeavour to understand recent developments in physics does not lie in the formidable technical language of the formal systems as such. Even though ever more abstruse theories of mathematics are being employed in physics, the real difficulty appears, as it has in the past, in the interpretation of the formal symbolism and in the problem of how to make a just estimate of the significance of the conclusions.[1] In short, the real difficulty in the way of understanding modern science is one of language. I have argued in the previous chapters that the problem of proper choice of language is essentially metaphysical. We cannot escape the fact that some idea of 'reality' must, sooner or later, be appealed to. More often than not this appeal is merely implicit in the language adopted in the description.

Quantum theory is of particular interest in this respect, for it is in the realm of microphysics that the problem of interpretation has arisen in its most acute form. Here one finds references to characteristics of real phenomena which were inconceivable only a relatively short time ago. Such references, however, are usually couched in the language of classical physics. They exist side by side with denials of the existence of any language which can adequately interpret the formal theory.

Furthermore, the theory is widely acclaimed as successful, despite the lack of agreement on whether there exists, even in principle, a model for the formal mathematics. So my first concern is whether or not there is any compelling reason to accept the intriguing, and epistemologically crucial, notion that a physical theory can be satisfactory while being at the same time inherently uninterpretable.

The simplest position on the question of models is that which is taken by many physicists, who maintain that a concept of physical reality is not directly relevant to their working methods. From this point of view, the success of a physical theory is a function of its predictive power. For instance, the physicist A. B. Pippard uses words like 'wave' or 'particle' not to refer to real entities but as "picturesque flourishes employed as a shorthand notation to indicate the sort of observation or mathematical process I am referring to."[2] The theory itself is viewed as "a system of thought . . . which correlates different observations, and which allows future observations to be predicted from present knowledge."[3] Consequently, a model, whether that of particle or of wave, is unnecessary for the formulation of theories in quantum mechanics and for the conveyance of the significance of the theoretical results.

Nevertheless, it is simply not the case that the language of models is dispensable for the physicist. While it is true that the formal structures of physics are a means of foretelling future experience on the basis of present experience, it is not true that the model of the formal theory is essentially irrelevant to the process of prediction. The language of the model serves an important regulative function in actual practice. The role of the model throughout the development of science appears to have been a vital one, if not an indispensable one. The model, as a focus in the formulation of physical ideas, functions not only as a means of describing existing phenomena but also as a reservoir of suggestive hints for the discovery of new phenomena.[4] The model does not simply provide intelligible correlates for the formal symbolism, it also carries in itself a collection of expectations concerning the way in which physical reality will become manifest.[5]

A model is only regarded as a 'good' model for a long as new data agrees with and satisfies the expectations aroused by the model. However, to be useful a model does not have to be applicable to every occasion. The model comes to be regarded as inadequate, if not entirely suspect, when contradictions or conflicts arise which confound the expectations aroused by the model. Such has been the case in the development of quantum physics. Here two models, each adequate for the explanation and prediction of sub-atomic behaviour in certain situations, conflict with each other in special circumstances, such as in the quantum equivalent of Young's interference experiment. It appears to be impossible to describe this experiment without confounding the expectations raised by the concept of wave and the concept of particle.

So it is not that the wave model and the particle model both fail in the task of describing all quantum phenomena, for it is generally understood that every model has inherent limitations.[6] That is, with regard to the use of the particle model and the wave model, it is evident that there are limits to the range of their applicability. In quantum physics, these two models display a fundamental incompatibility in a particular experimental situation where it is not possible to make a clear division between their respective fields of applicability. The overlapping of these fields of applicability gives rise to the problem (and so-called paradox) of wave-particle duality. Hence there is a controversy over which model is the truest model, for it is generally agreed that one cannot have both. On the other hand, others argue that this situation indicates that we must renounce altogether our "classical" attempts to find models for all types of physical events, especially at the sub-atomic level of physics.

The problem of models is not resolved by merely relegating the concept of model to that of a linguistic device or aid to communication between experts. For it is a fact that, however inadequate a hitherto successful model might turn out to be, its partial success means that it has satisfied some of the expectations aroused by certain circumstances. This must surely be evidence that the model has provided us with partial knowledge of some aspect of physical reality.[7] Even if it is argued that the formalism has no direct correlation to physical events, but is merely a logical device for predicting new experiences on the basis of old experiences, the question is begged rather than answered. For if it is admitted that experience is real, whether 'real' refers to an extra-mental reality or to the intra-subjective content of mental processes, the 'real' possesses certain recurring characteristics which the concept of model is designed to express. The success of the formalism in the prediction and explanation of physical phenomena indicates that it has some relation to aspects of actual physical events. The language of the model which is used to interpret the formalism is therefore of considerable philosophical importance. For the more successful the model is, in the sense of interpreting the formalism and providing satisfiable expectations, the more it is regarded as a true description of physical reality. In this respect, it can be the carrier of a large metaphysical substructure, implicitly, if not explicitly, implicated in its claim to having a toe-hold on reality. There is, therefore, no reason either to ignore as irrelevant or to abandon the tradition in science which has accorded, albeit often only tacitly, a significant metaphysical component to its physical models.[8]

Nevertheless, this position has been seriously challenged by an important group of thinkers who base their conclusions on the results of advances in physics rather than on, they claim, philosophical argument.

Associated with the names of Bohr, Heisenberg, and many others, the so-called Copenhagen Interpretation denies that the search for an adequate model of quantum phenomena is anything more than a regressive and nostalgic hankering for some kind of classical deterministic theory. That this is a vain endeavour follows, it is argued, from the fundamental principle behind quantum theory itself. That is to say, the argument against the meaningfulness of the notion of a model in quantum mechanics is based upon the physical principle of the quantum hypothesis. The 'no-model' dictum is thus an integral part of the Copenhagen Interpretation of quantum mechanics. The argument in support of the 'no-model' position is, according to Bohr, a matter of drawing certain epistemological conclusions from the quantum hypothesis. If this argument is correct, it follows that the whole of the microphysical world, or at least that part of it which is governed by the quantum hypothesis, is forever beyond the boundaries of human understanding. For the understanding of physical processes requires the mediation of various kinds of physical models. Since there is abundant experimental evidence for the validity of quantum theory, and thus of the quantum hypothesis, the choice of positions on the question of models is presented as a very stark either-or: either abandon quantum theory as a whole or abandon the desire for a model which will interpret the theory. This position, with its important metaphysical and epistemological consequences, must be examined more closely.

2. The 'No-Model' Argument

One of the most elequent proponents of the Copenhagen Interpretation is Niels Bohr. He maintains that a primary feature of quantum physics is the emergence of a new kind of entity which he calls a quantum phenomenon. The essence of a quantum phenomenon resides in what Bohr calls the 'indivisible' aspect and the 'closed' aspect of the phenomenon. These two features are often illustrated by reference to the electron analogue of Young's interference experiment. In this experiment an electron gun fires a stream of electrons towards a target. The electron beam is intercepted in mid-stream by an interference screen. At the target plate a detection device, usually a photographic emulsion, records the arrival of the electrons. The conflict between the expectations for wave-like behaviour of the electrons and the expectations for particle-like behaviour arises from an examination of the target emulsion. For my purposes, it is sufficient to describe the conflict as the impossibility of reconciling two classical concepts: the interference patterns on the target plate indicate a wave-like motion for the electrons, which cannot be reconciled, on account of the experimental arrangement, with the notion of the electrons behaving as particles. The latter, according to classical principles, must traverse definite 'paths' in space; that is, they must be describable in terms of a well-defined sequence of positions and momenta.[9] This experiment illustrates, according to Bohr, the general conclusion that a quantum phenomenon cannot be broken up into physically well-defined steps; i.e., that it is 'indivisible.' The formalism which describes the phenomenon is therefore not to be thought of as providing, in a classical sense, information about the events interior to the phenomenon. That is to say, once the whole experimental arrangement is specified, the formalism only provides information about the probability of a spot, indicating the arrival of an electron, appearing at any one place on the target plate.

The second aspect of a quantum phenomenon, signified by Bohr's term 'closed,' concerns the fact that something (albeit a non-classical something) happens in the phenomenon. Here, however, Bohr's account is obscure; the term 'closed' appears to refer to a transition from the potential to the actual taking place, even though it is impossible to form an unambiguous description of this happening in terms of individual electron wave-particles.[10]

According to the Copenhagen Interpretation, then, the terms 'wave' and 'particle' are useful merely as devices for descriptive purposes. It must be emphasized that this position is not a positivistic rejection of metaphysical terminology. Rather, it is an epistemological conclusion derived from the fundamental principle of quantum theory, namely, the quantum hypothesis.[11] For Bohr, if one accepts the quantum hypothesis (and there are many empirically verified consequences of the postulate to warrant its full acceptance) one is then forced to change one's ideas concerning basic scientific method. An important principle of classical science is that it is possible to distinguish between the observer and the observed. Bohr denies that a clear distinction can be made between a closed physical system (one which exists in a well-defined state free from external influences) and the observation of it. Furthermore, Bohr maintains that it is impossible, in principle, to describe every aspect of a quantum phenomenon in a classically deterministic way. In other words, there is, for Bohr, a two-fold limitation inherent in the description of any quantum phenomenom.

The conditions of the description, which arise from the indivisibility of the quantum of action,

> . . . not only set a limit to the *extent* of the information obtainable by
> measurements, but they also set a limit to the *meaning* which we may
> attribute to such information.[12]

This insistence upon limitation is related to Bohr's belief that the language used in the description must be classical. Hence the interpretation problem, instead of being a problem of finding a model of physical reality consistent with the formalism, is seen as a problem of description. Briefly, it is the study of "the proper use of words."[13] From this standpoint, the philosophical significance of quantum theory must be seen as purely epistemological, for there is no provision in Bohr's account for a treatment of the ontological problem of what the words, when properly used, really do describe. Indeed, the position would seem to preclude the possibility of any ontological conclusions at all arising from a study of micro-physical behaviour.

The reasoning behind Bohr's position begins with the quantum postulate. This principle, which is symbolized by Planck's quantum of action, "impose upon individual atomic processes an element of discontinuity quite foreign to the fundamental principles of classical physics, according to which all actions may vary in a continuous manner."[14] In quantum physics there is an ineradicable element of atomicity, embodied in Heisenberg's uncertainty relations, which ultimately precludes the conjunction of concepts usually found together in classical theories. In particular, says Bohr, one may no longer refer to the coordination of a causal description with a space-time description. For a causal description assumes the existence of a well-defined physical system (called the state of the system) which is causally connected to its predecessors and to its successors. The notion of the observation of the system involves the presupposition that the state of the system may be co-ordinated in some reference frame without altering that state. But this assumption is not compatible with the quantum postulate. It is a consequence of this postulate that "any observation of atomic phenomena will involve an interaction with the agency of observation not to be neglected."[15] As a result, an unambiguous definition of the state of the system is not possible and so a causal description is likewise impossible.

This conclusion, one notes, is in no way dependent upon arguments concerning the grossness or inaccuracy of measuring tools used at the level of atomic processes. It states merely that the quantum hypothesis implies, via the uncertainty relations, that the measuring apparatus is inevitably part of the whole interaction; that is, of the quantum phenomenon. Hence the concepts of causality and of space-time coordination are regarded by Bohr as complementary. They are mutually exclusive features in the description. Thus, when one wishes to coordinate events in space and time, one cannot expect to have unambiguously defined causal relationships. On the other hand, if one employs the concept of causality, as in the application of laws of conservation of energy and momentum, one must forgo unambiguous specifications of space-time parameters. Complementarity, then, is an expression of the limitations imposed upon the use of classical concepts in quantum descriptions; formally complementarity is implied by the uncertainty relatons.

However, in spite of their inadequacy for quantum descriptions, Bohr believes that the classical concepts are indispensable and irreplaceable. That is to say, the abstractions of physics, such as radiation in free space or the notion of isolated material particles, are such as cannot be expressed in terms other than those of the language of ordinary perception. The argument for the indispensability of classical concepts is thus closely bound up with the idea of complementarity.[16] The linkage is provided, according to Bohr, in the notion of 'definability.' Heisenberg's interpretation of the uncertainty relations (which express "the inevitability of the quantum postulate in the estimation of the possibilities of measurement") is given the further interpretation that they express also the "possibilities of definition." Thus Bohr stresses that uncertainty "equally affects the description of the agency of measurement and of the object."[17] That this leads to the claim for the indispensability of classical concepts is not an easy argument to follow. The main points seem to be these: unambiguous specification of physical quantities requires (and implies the existence of) ideal definition; ideal definition is related to the principle of causality; but causality cannot be considered independently of the quantum postulate. For the quantum postulate places an unavoidable limitation on the claim of causality in physical description. Since this claim can only be completely realized in classical theory, it is only in the latter that we can have unambiguous or ideal definition. That is to say, it is only in the ideal classical theory that the mutual exclusiveness of certain physical concepts, expressed by complementarity, can be resolved.

Even if one grants the validity of the above observations, which revolve about the notion of 'possibility of definition,'[18] as an argument for the indispensability of classical concepts, it seems to lead only to the circular assertion that classical concepts are indispensable because they are used in the description of all physical events. For the main argument still returns to the notion of 'definability,' that is, Bohr is mainly concerned with the need for unambiguity:

> At the same time, however, we must bear in mind that the possibility
> of an *unambiguous* use of these fundamental concepts solely depends
> upon the self-consistency of the classical theories from which they are
> derived and that, therefore, the limits imposed upon the application
> off these concepts are naturally determined by the extent to which we
> may, in our account of the phenomena, disregard the element which is
> foreign to classical theories and symbolized by the quantum of action.[19]

It is difficult to see how Bohr's position amounts to more than the statement that classical concepts are completely and unambiguously applicable to classical systems alone. The absolute indispensability of such concepts, as a consequence of the quantum hypothesis, is not made clear in his writings.

If one turns to other commentators on this peculiar aspect of the Copenhagen Interpretation, one finds the following admittedly "poignant" expression for the paradox of the inadequate but indispensable structure of classical concepts. In the words of von Weizsaecker,

> Classical physics has been superseded by quantum theory; quantum theory is verified by experiments; experiments must be described in terms of classical physics.[20]

The argument used by von Weizsaecker proceeds from Bohr's observation that our descriptions of phenomena are not based upon elementary sense data but upon "the full context of what we usually call reality."[21] Furthermore, this context is described by concepts which "fulfil certain conditions which Bohr took to be characteristic of classical physics.[22]" These concepts will forever dominate our way of expressing our experience of nature because they are inescapably involved in all our methods and instruments for observing it. Hence, for von Weizsaecker, and elucidation of the term 'classical' must involve an examination of the term 'measuring instrument.' For a system to be a measuring instrument, he says, it must

> both be describable in the space and time of our intuition and be describable as something functioning according to the principle of causality. For the first condition ensures that we are able to observe it at all, and the second that we can draw reliable conclusions for its visible properties (like the position of a pointer on a scale) to the invisible or dimly visible properties of the object which we observe by it.[23]

Von Weizsaecker's position is, then, very similar to Bohr's except that, where Bohr attends to the phenomenon, von Weizsaecker attends to the measuring of it. Indeed, he concludes: "a measuring instrument must be described by concepts appropriate to measuring instruments."[24]

This argument does not establish the indispensability of classical concepts but rather points out, once again, limitations upon their use. In the last analysis, the 'indispensability' argument comes to rest upon a psychological presupposition concerning the nature of human thought and perception. For von Weizsaecker concludes: "No further adaptation of our intuitive faculty to quantum theory is needed or possible." In other words, the position is founded upon the belief that the human mind is ineluctably 'classical.' That is, according to von Weizsaecker,

> a mind that observes nature by means of instruments themselves described classically cannot possibly adapt to the actual laws of physics (i.e., the quantum laws) other than by describing nature classically.[25]

Thus von Weizsaecker's position is similar to Bohr's position, which rests on the belief that all our ordinary verbal expressions reflect our customary forms of perception.[26] But this can be countered with the observation that it is also true that our customary forms of perception are strongly conditioned by the language of their expression. The 'no-model' argument is extremely weak at this point, for the abstractions of classical physics are here being accorded an unwarranted and unjustified significance. This move in effect evades, if it does not actually beg, the whole question of models.

At any rate, enough has now been said to conclude that the argument against models in quantum physics is not a direct consequence of the quantum postulate. The arguments do serve to underline the important fact that there are limitations inherent in the abstractions of physics and that a large part of the difficulty in understanding the results of quantum physics comes from ignoring this fact. In short, classical concepts are abstractions applicable to certain physical situations only. In particular, they can be unambiguously applied only to those situations in which the quantum effects can be neglected. The 'no-model' dictum ultimately rests upon the arguable assumption that the processes of human perception and understanding are dependent upon classical concepts for their expression. But this assumption is not self-evident even to strong supporters of the Copenhagen Interpretation.[27] While it is true that the measurements of the physical world are made with instruments described classically, this does not preclude the possibility of there being a model of greater generality than either the wave or the particle models. Such a model may possess features belonging to each of the classical models, but it may also have features which are not reducible to classical concepts. It is the latter which may further our understanding of quantum phenomena.

3. The Concept of Reality in Modern Physics

Reference to one other important principle of the Copenhagen Interpretation, the correspondence principle, will serve to emphasize the point that the problem of models is one of choice of language. The proper role of this principle is a matter still under debate. On the one hand, it is regarded merely as a useful recipe for the calculation of quantum mechanical quantities from their classical counterparts. On the other hand, Bohr considers the concept of correspondence to express the fact that quantum physics is a "rational generalization" of classical physics.[28] Thus the principle is sometimes regarded as a means of providing a bridge between the quantal world and the familiar classical world.[29] However, this view fails to deal with the fact, which Bohr himself emphasized, that classical physical and quantum physics are radically different conceptual structures. As such, they cannot be transmuted one into the other, even in the realm of large quantum numbers. Thus to maintain that the correspondence principle is a bridge between classical and quantum physics is to introduce a semantic confusion into the interpretation problem. For the two theories use essentially different languages.[30]

There seems to be little hope, therefore, that further clarification of the Copenhagen Interpretation will lead to a better understanding of the quantal world. The problem is indeed one of "the proper use of words," but it does not just involve the proper use of "classical" words. Moreover, although it is the most elaborately constructed interpretation of quantum theory, the Copenhagen Interpretation provides no guidance in respect to the choice and analysis of concepts with ontological significance.[31] The importance of the Copenhagen Interpretation for philosophy would seem solely to concern the epistemological dictum that the abstractions of physics have a limited range of applicability. But as for extending our understanding of the significance of the quantum postulate in a re-constructed view of physical reality, the Copenhagen Interpretation leaves everything much as it was before.[32] The discontinuities introduced by the quantum hypothesis into our conception of the physical world are an important aspect of reality which at any interpretation of quantum physics must take into account. This cannot be done if it is maintained, at the same time, that the language of classical physics is indispensable. An observation of Whitehead's is especially pertinent here:

> At any epoch the assumptions of a science are giving way, when they exhibit symptoms of the epicyclic state from which astronomy was rescued in the sixteenth century. Physical science is now exhibiting such symptoms. In order to reconsider its foundations, it must recur to a more concrete view of the character of real things, and must conceive its fundamental notions as abstractions derived from this direct intuition.[33]

The problem is complex, for it is not only the findings of quantum physics which need to be taken into account. A brief survey of some other salient features of modern physics further underlines the need for a new language of models.

Another important modern scientific theory which requires consideration is, of course, the special theory of relativity. This theory forces us to relinquish certain common conceptions of the fundamental nature of space and time. Instead of space and time being independent basic receptacles and continuous manifolds in which events take place, space and time have acquired an inter-dependence which is inextricably related to the happenings themselves. For it space-time is not an absolute given, a receptacle in comparison to which all events partake of a secondary or accidental status, then the events themselves become involved in the description of space-time. The language of classical physics, however, presupposes absolute and invariant spatial and temporal separations between point-events. The theory of relativity obliges us to take the relative motion of inertial coordinate frames into account when making such basic measurements: only in everyday experience, where the velocities involved are small compared to that of light, can we safely assume the separation of spatial and temporal characteristics. Thus there is a limitation in a cosmic sense, analogous to the limitation in a micro-cosmic sense which exists in the quantal world, to the use of classical concepts. The boundaries of intelligibility are, as it were, indicated respectively by the velocity of light and the quantum of action. Since these boundaries are wholly inaccessible to human perception, it is perhaps not unreasonable to argue for the indispensability of classical concepts. However, too great an emphasis on sense perception obscures the fact that the fundamental concepts of science are abstractions and that a central problem for the philosophy of science is to make the abstractions cohere in some intelligible system.

This point is further illustrated in the implications of the special theory of relativity for the interpretation of very familiar, but not well understood, macro-events. The experiences of light sensations (or other electromagnetic phenomena, such as radio transmissions) is an everyday occurrence. But the special theory of relativity renders unnecessary and irrelevant the notion of a special medium or 'ether'; that is, there is no evidence of a supporting medium which serves to 'carry' electromagnetic waves as undulations within its 'stuff.' Such a medium, if it existed, would have to have the special status of being at rest in one specific inertial coordinate frame, a prospect which is denied by the invariance principle.[34] Therefore, electromagnetic waves must be thought of as existents in their own right, as occupants of 'empty space' (whatever this now means) which do not need the assistance of some supporting medium.

Not only do electromagnetic waves lack the classical connotation of substantiality, in the sense of existing as vibrations in a stuff-like ether, matter itself has lost its special characteristic of fundamental immutability. The classically distinct concepts of mass and energy are, according to the special theory of relativity, transmutable into one another. The presupposition of classical mechanistic physics, that descriptions of physical phenomena are ultimately reducible to statements about the motions of fundamental bits of indestructible units of matter, is completely vitiated. Energy, once conceived as subsidiary to the concept of matter, has, according to some thinkers, usurped the primary position in the ranks of fundamental physical concepts. There appear to be compelling reasons, which arise from elementary particle physics, for inverting the classical predominance of mass over energy. Larger and even more powerful particle accelerators reveal, instead of a basic substructure of irreducible entitites, a proliferating system of rapidly transmutable entities. Rather than as a classical substance, some physicists conceive of a particle as "energy in a highly concentrated state, prone to explode into massless particles flying off with the speed of light."[35]

Some attempts have been made by physicists to speak of such aspects of modern physics in an ontological manner. For example, the extreme mutability of matter, whereby particles can be created from energy, or annihilated into energy, or transmuted into different particles, is seen by Heisenberg as

the final proof for the unity of matter. All the elementary particles are made of the same substance, which we may call energy or universal matter; they are just different forms in which matter can appear.[36]

Heisenberg's speculations are interesting because they make some concessions to the fact that something indeed happens in a particle phenomenon. He takes the position that modern physics has the means to formulate mathematically a description of these happenings.[37] While accepting the consequence of the quantum postulate according to the dicta of the Copenhagen Interpretation, Heisenberg advances an ontology based explicitly on his understanding of Aristotle's concept of matter and form. Matter, from this standpoint, is regarded as mere 'potentia' until it acquires actuality through form. Heisenberg thus avoids having a classical materialistic ontology, while at the same time maintaining an epistemology in agreement with Bohr's insistence on classical descriptions. For example, in speaking of the happening in the interior of the electron interference experiment, Heisenberg describes the 'particle' in its intermediate stage as mere 'potentia,' without form and so indeterminate. The transition from the potential into the actual occurs in the event of detection; that is, upon the interaction of the object with the measuring device.

The task of modern physics, according to Heisenberg, is to formulate "those natural laws that determine the 'forms' of matter, the elementary particles and their forces."[38] That mathematics is essential to the formulation of these laws follows from Heisenberg's Pythagorean belief that a complete understanding of the unity of matter can be achieved through the establishment of a universal equation of motion for matter. The solutions to such an equation would be the mathematical forms of elementary particles, and from these solutions all possible properties of individual particles would be derivable. Indeed, for Heisenberg, the elementary particles are the mathematical forms themselves, in a sense analogous to the forms of Plato's *Timaeus*, and are manifestations of a universal substance, namely energy.[39]

As interesting as these speculations are, they contain a serious fault. For Heisenberg believes that modern physics justifies an ancient quest, whose first articulation he finds in Anaximander, for an eternal, infinite, ageless substance which in various states and transformations gives rise to ordinary substance. In a word, energy, for Heisenberg, is the universal substance; it is substance in the sense that it is conserved through all its transformations. However, the idea of energy as a substance invokes the conceptual difficulty involved in speaking of a 'substance' which is boundless, endless, and altogether lacking in determinate qualities.[40] While it is true that modern physics expresses energy measurements as definite magnitudes, in contrast to the classical mode of expressing only differences in levels of energy, all other notions traditionally associated with the concept of substance have vanished. Modern physics has rendered the concept of a 'stuff-like' substratum meaningless, at least at the basic levels of the physical world, so its invocation at the most basic level of all merely introduces conceptual confusion. The tendency to appeal to traditional notions connected with the concept of substance is the first obstacle to be overcome in the search for new approaches.

4. *Summary*

The problem of models, as modern physics has forcefully reminded us, is a problem of language. The widely held opinion that quantum physics has obliged us to retain classical concepts for all physical description, even at sub-atomic levels where they do not properly apply, is not an inescapable consequence of the quantum postulate. Nevertheless, the language used by even the most philosophically minded physicists contains notions which are, in the end, at variance with the results of physics itself. The notion of substance, for instance, is one which must acquire a different meaning if it is to be compatible with the theories of relativity and of quantum mechanics. These theories have enormous consequences for the whole structure of scientific Fortunately, the language of physicists is also rich in suggestive hints as to what will serve as the appropriate replacements for classical concepts. For example, in noting the lack of a clear distinction to be made between the concept of matter and force in particle physics, Heisenberg remarks that "each elementary particle not only is producing some forces and is acted upon by forces, but it is at the same time representing a certain field of force."[42] At the same time, the concept of 'field of force' is undergoing a change of meaning to that of 'field of interaction.'[43] In short, whether we use the language of 'particle' or 'field,' the distinguishing feature in the use of both terms is 'interaction.'[44] One thus discovers a radical shift taking place in the physicist's conceptual framework, despite the continued use of classical words and phrases. A 'particle,' for instance, is regarded as a centre of action and activity. Instead of its motion being conceived as a secondary characteristic of its matter, abstracted from the more basic concepts of force and mass, it *is* its motion in some sense which requires an elucidation not possible in an exclusively classical language. That is to say, physical science has not yet evolved a language capable of expressing the nature of the activity underlying the apparent solidity of the world. A new or revised language of models must express the idea that the fundamental entities of the physical world are essentially structures of activity in a continual process of interaction, creation and annihilation. Nothing is served toward this end by the postulation of yet another variation in the age-old quest for some fundamental 'stuff' whose coalascences in various forms make up the matter of the world. The real question is whether the concept of a physical organism, clearly implicit in the language which refers to structures of activity and their interactions, is a feasible solution to the problem of models. The answer to this question depends, as Whitehead notes, on whether it is possible to "define an organism without recurrence to the concept of matter in simple location."[45]

Chapter Six.
The Model of Organism in Physical Science

1. The Concept of Organism

In the previous chapters I have indicated reasons why physics and philosophy, not to mention common sense, have forced upon us the need to reformulate our entire conception of the nature of the physical world. In the following passage Whitehead summarizes succinctly and vividly some main points which must be considered in any attempt to construct a new conceptual framework:

> Modern physics has abandoned the doctrine of Simple Location. The physical things which we term stars, planets, lumps of matter, molecules, electrons, protons, quanta of energy, are each to be conceived as modifications of conditions within space-time, extending throughout its whole range. There is a focal region, which in common speech is where the thing is. But its influence streams away from it with finite velocity throughout the utmost recesses of space and time. . . . For physics, the thing itself is what it does, and what it does is this divergent stream of influence. Again the focal region cannot be separated from the external stream. It obstinately refuses to be conceived as an instantaneous fact. It is a state of agitation, only differing from the so-called external stream by its superior dominance within the focal region. Also we are puzzled how to express exactly the existence of these physical things at any definite moment of time. For at every instantaneous point-event, within or without the focal region, the modification to be ascribed to this thing is antecedent to, or successive to, the corresponding modification introduced by that thing at another point-event. Thus if we endeavor to conceive a complete instance of the existence of the physical thing in question, we cannot confine ourselves to one part of space or to one moment of time. The physical thing is a certain coordination of spaces and times and of conditions in those spaces at those times; this coordination illustrating one exemplification of a certain general rule, expressible in terms of mathematical relations.[1]

Whitehead believes that the proper description of the (classically) 'insubstantial' ground of all physical things requires some form of Platonic doctrine. But he is careful to point out that a "complete existence" cannot be conceived simply as the composition of mathematical formulae. One can hardly put too much emphasis upon the word "expressible" in the above passage. As Whitehead puts the point, the facts of existence "illustrate" mathematical formulae; that is, mathematical patterns are evident in the order manifested by real physical events.[2] But the components of events possess qualitative as well as quantitative elements. That is to say, the formulae express the relations and patterns which are realized in the 'states of agitation', but they should not be confused with the activity itself. In short, one must remain alert to the vital difference between the symbol and the thing symbolized. The natural desire to find the simplest account seems often to result in the assumption that the abstract concept is identical with the concrete fact. But this is to commit what Whitehead aptly calls the Fallacy of Misplaced Concreteness. In the present context, one would commit this fallacy by asserting that the unique particularity of an event is capable of being completely expressed in terms of concepts whose very usefulness is grounded in their complete generality or absence of particularity. We thus arrive at one of the most urgent problems of philosophy of science: how to speak about the particularity and its formal relations without implying that the world reduces in the last analysis to a mere conglomeration of symbols.

In present-day microphysical thinking, the most fundamental physical things are the so-called elementary particles. However, the term 'particle' is used with a broad spectrum of meanings. It is regarded by some thinkers as merely a form of shorthand notation referring to certain kinds of observations and the mathematical expressions relating to them.[3] In other contexts, the term is used to refer to a composite system of lesser particles.[4] Here and elsewhere the term 'particle' is certainly of practical value in the description of those physical things which, for the purposes at hand, can be regarded as completely located at their focal regions. In these circumstances, the abstract notion of an instantaneous point-event is useful. But the usefulness of the term 'particle' breaks down at the point where the influences which "stream away from it," or, for that matter, which enter into it, must be taken into account. Here, the concept of particle needs to be replaced with a concept which is capable of encompassing the activities of an entity the essence of whose character is the capacity for interaction with similar entities.

The familiar concept of organism seems to meet this requirement best. It possesses many features which are appropriate to the description of phenomena in micro-physics. While it might be objected that there are aspects of this concept which are wholly incompatible with the description of material happenings at atomic or subatomic levels of the physical world, this objection overlooks an important aspect of the role of the model in physics. Any model in physical science has both positive and negative correlations with actual events. A model is never rejected solely on the grounds that it possesses features which have no correlates in actual experience.[5] The real question is whether or not the model of physical organism provides sufficient positive correlation between actual events and formal expressions to have a significant descriptive or explanatory value.

One immediate obstacle to understanding the notion of physical organism must first be dealt with. The concept of physical organism, as used here, must be distinguished from the common (i.e., classical) conception of a physico-chemical composition of fundamentally inert substances. In the present state of ordinary language, many forms of speech are thoroughly permeated with the concepts of the pervasive cosmology of scientific materialism. In this view of the world, even life itself is conceived as ultimately reducible to the random motions and accidental collisions of lifeless bits of permanent, rigid units of characterless matter.[6] The concept of a physical thing "which obstinately refuses to be conceived as an instantaneous fact," a thing not only extended in space and time but which also possesses identifiable individual characteristics, is simply not compatible with any form of scientific materialism.

A micro-physical entity is analogous to a biological organism in the sense that its existence is not precisely localizable. This follows from the meaning of the term 'activity': an event which is pure activity seems incapable of analysis either solely in terms of internal relations or solely in terms of external relations. Like a biological organism, it must be a complex amalgam of both. Hence it is Whitehead's view, as we have seen in the discussion of his response to Zeno,[7] that the denial of instantaneous punctiform events leads to a completely non-classical conception of an event as a "becoming." And he shows us that if we allow this point, it very much depends upon the circumstances of how an event is viewed whether or not we can consider an event to be comprised of instantaneous or punctiform parts. In brief, to the extent that we insist upon the event having a character of its own we are speaking of a spatio-temporally extended existent.

An event which is pure activity possesses, like a biological organism, a regulated structure. Incorporated in this structure there are probably hierarchies of lesser but still regulated structures which partly account for the nature of the whole entity. But the event-organism will always be more than the sum of these parts, however far this analysis is carried out. For mere combination of parts does not explain the fundamental feature of the whole, namely, its function. In this respect, the analogy between physical organism and biological organism seems most complete. In a word, the physical organism, like its biological counterpart, "does not live where its body is."[8] A physical organism, like a biological organism, is essentially a functioning entity. Its dynamical characteristics are fundamentally different from those of a Newtonian particle of matter, an entity which essentially is isolated from the rest of the world.[9] Indeed, what *is* known about primitive physical organisms concerns only their interactions with other organisms; those particles which do not interact with other particles have, for the physicist, a dubious claim to existence.[10]

The concept of the physical organism as a mode of functioning is, in sub-atomic physics, implied in the emphasis placed upon what the particle does; that is, how it acts and is acted upon. These considerations evoke certain descriptive terms which have hitherto been restricted to the description of living organism. For example, the physical organism can be said to "experience" or "feel" the functionings of other such organisms.[11] This does not gratuitously introduce into the realm of the purely physical a term which only properly belongs to the realm of the biological. It is worth stressing that the use of the term 'feeling' does not imply, for instance, that the physical organism is being endowed with something akin to life.[12] The concept of feeling is intrinsic to the general notion of selective interactions between patterns of structured activity. Feeling, in other words, is what is meant by the functioning of one organism upon another, or upon itself. For if a particle is not a rigid, permanent unit of matter floating, as it were, in the container of space-time, its integrity as a distinct entity must, in some sense, be dependent upon the environmental influences to which it is subject. Furthermore, its present being must, in some way, be a function of its past being and a factor in its future being. The explanation of this relationship thus requires a theory about the transmission and inheritance of definite physical characteristics within an all-pervasive flux of activity.[13]

Again, it is not possible to separate the concept of functioning, even at the most primitive physical levels, from all considerations of purpose and selectivity, as is the case with the Newtonian cosmology. Potential influences in a given environment are neither equally nor similarly effective. In being acted upon, a particular organism is selective of what it shall feel, unlike a bit of Newtonian matter whose experience is merely that of submission to external forces.[14] On the other hand, in exerting its own special influences, the physical organism can be said to be functioning toward some end, namely that which produces that effect which is dependent upon its own peculiar character.[15]

Many organicistic terms, in addition to that of feeling, may be useful in the description of the transmission of and reception of influences even at the most basic levels of the physical world. But it must be stressed that the use of the term organism does not necessarily introduce a version of anthropomorphism into physical description nor does it entail a doctrine of vitalism.[16] Some concepts in ordinary usage which are often associated with the term 'feeling' very likely do not apply at the physical level of description. For example, that a physical organism 'feels' does not entail the existence of mental processes in the sub-atomic world.[17] The features of the familiar concept of organism which are germane to descriptions at purely physical levels will become clearer after further exploration of the physical requirements which a model of sub-atomic phenomena must satisfy. While it is beyond the scope of this study to explore these in detail, certain general features of the model of organism can be outlined.

2. Substantiality and Matter

The phrase 'an organism does not live where its body is' signifies the enormous conceptual gap which exists between the concept of a particle as an organism and the concept of a classical particle. Nevertheless, there are features of the classical concept which are still relevant to the organic concept but which are in need of reinterpretation. Two such features are the notions of individuality and of endurance of character. These features are deeply implicated in any account of order which assumes the existence of enduring regularities exemplified by distinguishable individuals. The question which classical physics attempted to answer with the doctrine of mechanistic materialism remains unresolved. If matter, once conceived as fundamentally comprised of solid perduring configurations of "stuff," is really only to be described in terms of transient and interacting structures of activity, how is it possible to speak of those features which are, in any sense of the word, permanent? This question in effect demands that one's fundamental assumptions about the nature of the physical world, and in particular, of space and time, be made explicit.

Under the organic view, it is entirely mistaken to try to conceive of time as something prior to events. And indeed there appear to be insurmountable difficulties in any attempt to conceive time or space (or space-time) in a manner which makes of them receptacles in which events unfold. But the denial of the latter view, and the rejection of the common conception of time that it is somehow absolutely independent from the contingent happenings of the world, faces us with the problem of how to make sense of the ordinary word 'permanent'. Behind the innocent-sounding question posed above there lie a host of deep puzzles.

In the theory of organism, the most basic assumption is that the world is process. At the basis of physical existence there is, in Whitehead's view, an interrelated plurality of primitive organisms, or actual entities. To refer to the fundamental character of this plurality is to refer to a complex of external and internal relationships. Furthermore, every relationship is capable of significant change. For it is a fundamental assumption of this theory that both change and time are to be taken very seriously indeed.

In Whitehead's view we shall only begin to make sense of time when we view it as a characteristic of process. Furthermore, an adequate theory of time will be one in which time has an atomistic character. That is to say, we need an "epochal" theory of time. For it is Whitehead's view that time comes into being in discrete amounts or epochs ("arrests"). As a consequence, the term 'permanent' takes on an entirely uncommon and radically new meaning. For the standard definition of the permanent as something that lasts indefinitely *through* time is, under the organic view, without sense. Since this point has important implications for my subsequent discussion of the notion of order, I shall first attempt to sketch briefly some reasons why Whitehead is justified in proposing his complex theory.

At issue is how one should go about taking time seriously. One does not take time seriously, Whitehead points out, if one "*either* conceives of a complete totality of all existence, *or* conceives of a multiplicity of actual entities such that each of them is a complete fact, 'requiring nothing but itself in order to exist, God only excepted'."[18] The repeated use of the term 'complete' in the above remarks is highly significant. Whitehead explicitly denies the connection between time and completeness. He is saying, in effect, that neither the world itself, if it is conceived as One, nor any of its individual creatures, if the world is conceived as Many, can be regarded as complete without doing violence to the whole notion of time.

To see why this is a reasonable view we must refer to Whitehead's developed theory of organism in which the world is held to be built up from actual entities. Each of these is essentially an act of becoming embedded within an interrelated community of such acts. Since all talk about what there is and how it is related to everything else must ultimately refer to this community, we must speak of space and time in terms which refer to the community of acts of becoming. Moreover, it is not enough merely to assume mutual relatedness within this community in order to arrive at a coherent conception of a changing temporal world. As Whitehead points out,

Time requires incompleteness. A mere system of mutually prehensive occasions is compatible with the concept of a static timeless world.

Each occasion is temporal because it is incomplete. Nor is there any system of occasions which is complete; there is no one well-defined entity which is the actual world.[19]

The point is that if we are disposed to rest content with a mere system of mutual relatedness we do so at the risk of renouncing the dynamic aspects of the world. Process is not just system, it is dynamic system. Hence the assumption of change means that we must speak in terms of the becoming of system or systems of mutual relatedness. However, there arises here a danger of falling into a trap which lies parallel to the completely static view. If we lean too much towards the dynamic view by postulating becoming as completely continuous, we end with a conception of becoming as an entirely unbroken process of changing relations which is at odds with the notion of becoming itself. For the world is now over-endowed with change: indeed it is nothing but change, and it is thus extremely hard to see how we could derive an adequate conception of time from this basis. This is because to take time seriously is to recognize not only the existence of changing differences, it is to presuppose the existence of persistent regularities in the midst of flux. But if becoming cannot be completely continuous, no more can it be complete. For if we attempt to conceive of the world as comprised of completed acts of becoming, the ongoingness of process is again arrested in a static set of unchanging conditions. We arrive at a conception of a world from which all significant differences have been erased. And as I have argued earlier,[20] such a world might just as well not be, for all the difference it could make to any creature capable of cognition. In other words, to take this route seems to lead either to incoherence or to a denial of time and change.

The upshot is that the notion of becoming cannot be forced into a setting which relies solely upon either the notions of pure continuity or of pure atomicity. We thus arrive back at a point which I have argued is central to this whole study. An adequate treatment of becoming depends upon finding a delicate balance between the complementary elements of atomicity and continuity. As I have argued previously , it is one of the major strengths of Whitehead's theory of becoming that he achieves this balance. Hence there is good reason for him to assert that there is a becoming of continuity but no continuity of becoming. It follows that time, as a derivative of becoming, inescapably possesses an element of discontinuity.

Granted that Whitehead is correct, and that it is just as wrongheaded to try to conceive of becoming as entirely continuous as it is to try to conceive of acts of becoming as punctiform, we thus arrive at the need for an epochal theory of time. That is to say, we must try to make sense of the common notion of change through time in terms of "supersession" of discrete acts of becoming. This means that our deep belief, which is central to our everyday existence as well as to the rational pursuit of science, that there are certain things that are permanent in time, cannot be adequately described in terms of everlastingness. The latter notion is misleadingly evocative of the idea that change is essentially the continual replacement of one set of external relations by other such sets. What is permanent in the order of the world must be explained in terms of the recurrence of definite characteristics within incomplete processes of organization or concretion. This conclusion, which seems to impose a paradoxical demand that we explain fundamental processes in terms of things which change and yet remain the same, is nevertheless easily understood in terms of the analogy of wave motion. For a wave form is just such an entity and, moreover, one whose every completion is also a beginning.

Indeed, Whitehead finds much support for his general views of becoming, as well as the means to describe and explain endurance amid a flux of activity, in a concept which is as old as science itself; that is, in the concept of periodicity.[21] The concept of periodicity first acquired importance with the very birth of science. It is at the core of the revolutionary musical theory of Pythagoras, a theory which linked not only the acoustical but also the aesthetic nature of musical sound to a mathematical structure. As science has extended its investigations into regions ever more remote from the normal range of human perception, the concept has continued to gain in importance. In particular, it appears to be indispensable in the investigations into the structure of processes underlying the erstwhile solidity of matter.[22] It is significant that the ubiquitousness of the concept of periodicity becomes most evident at the sub-atomic level. For it is at the level of basic physical entities that the problem of explaining non-material endurance becomes most acute. The notion of rhythmical variation as the basis of non-material structures of activity satisfies an essential requirement of a theory of the physical: it makes it possible to speak without contradiction of a substantial entity as changing and yet remaining the same.

At the most elementary level of physical processes, there are entities which are substantial in the sense of being recognizable as individuals with definite and determinate characteristics. The possibility of recognition is dependent upon the existence of characteristics which, if they do not belong to a static timeless entity, must be periodically repeated. In other words, recognition presupposes regular repetition of certain distinctive features. The process of the world cannot consist solely of random variation. For if variation is random, that is, not subject to any manner of control or principle of order, there is, *ipso facto*, no repeated groupings of recognizable elements in its process. Hence the physical organism, considered as a fundamental individual exemplifying a particular order within the general flux of the world (or, in other words, as a substantial primitive entity), can be conceived as essentially a rhythmical patterned form of activity.

The notion of periodicity is capable of accommodating another intrinsic requirement of an organic theory. Such a theory must contain the means to account for evolutionary change as well as the continued existence of particular species of individuals. Put another way, an evolutionary theory must provide the means to explain the possibility of the emergence of novelty within a given species. The notion of periodicity appears to be capable of accommodating such theoretical considerations at the level of primitive physical processes. The concept also appears to be compatible with either an abrupt or gradual alteration of a given structure which may take place when its components are rearranged, or added to, or annihilated, either as a result of interaction with other structures or in response to internal pressures for change.

There are possibly many different basic forms of activity, as indicated by the physicist's continually amended list of elementary particles. The primitive forms of activity, it may be conjectured, are the constitutents of more complex entities. Thus various combinations of primitive physical organisms, according to the nature of the constituents, could explain the existence of the special individuality of a composite entity. This notion is also compatible with the observation that definite patterns of activity in the form of elementary particles permit alteration by other patterns of activity only in a selective manner. That is to say, the stability of a given physical organism, as part of a complex of interrelated structures of activity, depends not only upon its internal constitution but also upon its environment. Hence it is not difficult to accommodate the notion that certain elementary particles, regarded as organisms, are inherently more stable than others, and that more or less violent interactions with other organisms are needed in order to alter their structure.

It also follows from the notion of physical organism that there is no reason to expect to find absolute stability in any species of physical organism, however primitive. That physical substance consists ultimately of more or less stable rhythmical patterns of activity is a notion compatible with the existence of inherent mutability in the basic processes of the world. This is perhaps the most remarkable result of modern physics. Theoretical and empirical findings indicate not only that all matter is subject to violent and spectacular transformations but also that the laws which govern the behavior of matter no longer have a claim to absolute immutability.[23]

The organic view, in summary, is that matter is essentially activity regulated into different types of patterns; these are capable of analysis into less complex patterns. This view provides the means to account not only for the variety and various complexities of micro-physical entities, but also of satisfying common sense with regard to the notion of substance. The classical concept of matter is especially attractive to common sense because the world of ordinary sense perception manifestly consists of bits and pieces of more or less solid and permanent substances. Some of these are evidently more rigid and inert than others. Indeed, the classical concept of matter is an idealization of this common sense idea of matter. However, to conceive of substance in terms of patterns of activity does not contradict ordinary sensory experience of the manifest solidity of the physical world. For the solidity of a thing is related to its individual integrity; that is, it is solid to the extent that it refuses to accept the imposition of another form upon its present form. The notion of interactivity, therefore, can be invoked in explication of 'substantiality'. In brief, those physical organisms, or their composites, which display reistance to pressures for change (and all organisms are subject to such pressures since, as Whitehead rightly stresses, no single organism can be entire and sufficient unto itself) are the most substantial. Again, it is likely that individual characteristics of physical organisms are an indication of various degrees of substantiality. For individual characteristics, such as the charge of an electron, are essentially modes of interaction.[24] That is to say, each characteristic is indicative of how the organism will behave in a given environment. Weakly interacting physical organisms, such as the neutrino, seem to deserve to be classified among the least substantial.[25] At any rate, it is sufficient to note here that the concept of physical organism does not violate but rather elucidates common sense experience of the solidity of the world.

In taking up the question of the nature of the internal constitution of physical organisms, one is faced with the difficulty of describing activity without referring to some material substratun. The description seems only to be possible if given in terms of the forms of the activity. It is here that the account of the role which mathematics plays in our knowledge of the physical world begins.

As has been mentioned above, in order that recognition of individual character be possible, there must be distinct and enduring forms within pattern which are capable of being recognized. This factor introduces the need for a theory concerning the forms of activity, a need which Whitehead strives to face squarely. Whitehead's cosmology is firmly grounded in a theory of forms, reminiscent of the Platonic doctrine but differing in enough important aspects to deserve a different name. This theory he calls the theory of eternal objects.[26] What Whitehead continually stresses in his own theory is the importance of conceiving these forms of activity in such a way so as not to put undue stress upon either half of a traditional duality. For it is a recurrent problem in philosophy as to whether the Platonic forms are immanent or transcendent.[27] The forms of activity must be regarded as immanent because a thing can only be what it is in some definite and determinate sense if there exist definiteness and determinateness within the elements which make up its structure. The regularities in a physical organism, regarded as the composition of primitive forms of activity, require the existence of forms of order which transcend the events themselves.

To summarize, the theory of physical organism accounts for the manifest order of events by postulating the existence of recognizable enduring individuals (organisms) amid an underlying flux of activity . This requires, in turn, through the mediation of the concept of periodicity (which is the means of avoiding an ultimate appeal to some kind of traditional materialistic doctrine), the postulation of a doctrine of forms. These Whitehead calls eternal objects in order to secure his conception of their undualized nature (i.e., their complementary immanence and transcendence) from possible intrusion of unintended traditional meanings. The pattern in the structured activity of a physical organism is ultimately explicable in terms of the periodic repetition of fundamental forms of activity, or eternal objects. Hence a Whiteheadian account of the role of mathematics in physical knowledge is related to Pythagoreanism, for among the eternal objects are those which are specifically mathematical in character.

The concept of periodicity illustrates not only how persistence of individual character can exist in a flux of unceasing activity. It also indicates how one can begin to explain the relation of mathematical systems to this flux. It is true that, in one sense, mathematics consists of structures of timeless and universal truths, abstracted from all particulars of transitory events. But, as Whitehead maintains, the regularity between and within events is only explicable if there exists some kind of underlying regularity which controls the potentially infinite accidents of change. This underlying regularity must ultimately be accounted for in the realm of eternal objects. Thus mathematics, in so far as it applies to the flux of events, ultimately refers to certain patterns of eternal objects as immanent in the flux. Mathematics is capable of expressing the properties and behavioral characteristics of very elementary physical phenomena, as well as more complex compositions of these, because of the periodic repetition of patterns of eternal objects in the composition of basic physical entities. This explanation rests, of course, upon the assumption that there *is* order underlying the flux of events. Or, in Whitehead's words, that there is "a systematic framework permeating all relevant fact," an assumption which makes it possible to speak of knowledge of the physical world.[28] The systematic framework, which mathematics is capable of exploring, is the structured and interconnected realm of eternal objects.

It will be worth concluding this part of the discussion by once again considering the conceptual gap between the organic and the classical conceptions of the nature of fundamental physical events. If the most primitive of physical organisms are to be thought of as rhythmical repetitions of patterns of eternal objects, then it follows that there can be no such thing as an instantaneously existing physical organism. For a finite temporal duration, according to Whitehead's epochal theory of time, comes into being with the "complete" pattern of activity which is the organism. But the complete realization of a definite pattern is never instantaneous. This means that, while it may be possible to conceive of a temporal duration smaller than that required for the realization of a certain individual organism, the organism is, strictly speaking, non-existent in the divided duration.

Thus the classical abstract concept of nature-at-an-instant (the notion of the world as the sum-total of instantaneous configurations of matter), however useful for practical purposes in scientific pursuits (e.g. in physical situations where Newtonian mechanics is applicable), is philosophically meaningless. The model of organism is wholly antithetical to the model of particle in this respect. For the particle in the classical cosmology manifests its existence over durations of time as the totality of an infinite sequence of instantaneous punctiform existences. The gulf between the classical and organic views of the world is so wide at this point that is affects the formulation of all philosophical problems.[29] This warrants the postulation of a general principle of space and time which precludes the existence of instantaneous events.[30] From the standpoint of the model of organism, certain erstwhile paradoxes of quantum theory, such as the puzzle of wave-particle duality, no longer arise. The model of organism is compatible with the principle of uncertainty, for the physical organism does not have properties, such as velocity or position, which can be thought to exist instantaneously.[31] In short, those aspects of a particle which are wave-like, or those aspects of a wave-packet which are particle-like, can be regarded as those characteristics of a physical organism which happen to be accessible in a particular mode of observation.

3. Whitehead's Theory of Primates

In the development of Whitehead's theory of organism, the discoveries of quantum mechanics seem, among the many influences from physics, to have been the least important.[32] Whitehead found in early quantum theory illustration of and justification for ideas already present in his theory of organism. His theory of primates, therefore, must be viewed as an illustration of the theory of organism rather than as a contribution to the interpretation of quantum mechanics. Indeed, most of his observations about quantum theory must be viewed in the context of Bohr's model of the atom.[33] Thus there is no Whiteheadean interpretation of quantum theory in the sense of an account which is relevant to the details of the present formal theory.[34] Nevertheless, Whitehead's conjectures concerning the behaviour of atomic phenomena are fully in accord with the essence of quantum theory, which resides in the quantum hypothesis, and are thus interesting and important for the light they throw upon the general concept of physical organism. To provide this illumination is, in fact, the sole aim of Whitehead's discussion of the theory of primates.[35]

Whitehead's theory of primates postulates a primary genus of organism which consists of (possibly many) distinct species of primates. It is a characteristic of primates that they are not decomposable into subordinate organisms. Moreover, the primate, as a concrete event in nature, must be distinguished from the primate as known in physical science. For the latter is an abstraction of a kind peculiar to that discipline; that is to say, what is known about the primate in physics is not necessarily all that there is to be known. From the standpoint of physical science,

> we are not thinking of what a primate is in itself, as a pattern arising from the prehension of the concrete aspects (of the immediate past); nor are we thinking of what a primate is for its environment, in respect to its concrete aspects prehended therein. We are thinking of these various aspects merely in so far as their effects on patterns and on locomotion are expressible in spatio-temporal terms.[36]

Thus while the primate for physical thought illustrates important properties of the primate *per se*, namely, the spatio-temporal characteristics of an ordered and complex regularity, the difference between the two conceptions of primate is of vital philosophical significance if one is not to confuse the abstraction with the actual event.

These observations provide a timely reminder of a main tenet in Whitehead's epistemology: There are limitations inherent in any mode of knowing. It is precisely on account of the order which underlies basic physical processes that physics is able to use mathematics to express certain characteristics of these processes. Order, for Whitehead, is synonymous with interrelatedness and is a precondition of knowledge: "If anything out of relationship, then complete ignorance as to it."[37] But the expressions of physics are limited to those characteristics of physical processes which are amenable to mathematical formulations. For Whitehead, mathematical abstractions are only applicable to those aspects of physical reality which are concerned with general relations of extension. In particular, the simplest and most accessible forms of these relations are realized in spatio-temporal relations.[38] Furthermore, Whitehead inverts the Kantian doctrine of space and time as *a priori* conditions of experience, maintaining instead that space and time are abstractions derived from experience.[39] This emphasizes the necessity of keeping in mind the distinction between the abstract concept and the concrete event in the discussion of the nature of primates. In other words, the study of the primate in physics may only reveal one type of a variety of relationships which are possible in the constitution of a physical organism.

Whitehead introduces the theory of primates with the observation that "there are certain indications in modern physics that for the role of corpuscular organisms at the base of the physical field, we require vibratory entities."[40] In keeping with the distinction between concrete events and abstractions, he uses the term 'vibration' when an abstract entity is under consideration, reserving the term 'reiteration' for a concrete event. Thus a 'vibratory entity' is an *abstract* notion, analogous to the physicist's conception of a stationary electromagnetic wave. The actual electromagnetic field, for Whitehead, is composed of a multitude of rhythmical repetitions or 'reiterations' of concrete events. The abstract entities, as opposed to the concrete events, are what concern the physicist: for him they are vibratory patterns regulated by Maxwell's laws. In the following discussion, unless otherwise specified, the term 'primate' refers to the physicist's abstract 'vibratory entity'.

Whitehead distinguishes between two sorts of vibrations. These are vibratory organic deformations ("vibratory change of pattern") and vibratory locomotions ("vibratory locomotion of the given pattern as one whole").[41] The first type of vibration concerns the internal consitution of the primate. It can be conceived as analogous to the form of a standing wave in a stretched string. A more complicated example, discussed by Whitehead, depicts the hypothetical constitution of a primate as "stationary vibrations of the electromagnetic field of definite frequency (resulting in) a vibratory spherical nucleus satisfying one set of conditions and a virbratory external field satisfying another set of conditions."[42] A primate is thus what it is according to the mode of composition of contrasting basic forms, just as a tune is what it is according to the composition and arrangement of contrasting notes and silences. And just as a tune requires a definite lapse of time for its complete unfolding, so does a vibratory pattern require a definite duration for its complete realization. Thus there is associated with each primate a definite quantum of time.

In referring to the entities talked about in physics Whitehead suggests that a proton (and perhaps an electron) "would be an association of [basic vibratory primates], superposed on each other, with their frequencies and spatial dimensions so arranged as to promote the stability of the complex organism. . . ."[43] It is tempting to see in this suggestion an adumbration of de Broglie's wave-packet model of the electron. Whether or not this is the case, [44] the notion of wave-packet is helpful in understanding the notion of a primate. In short, a primate can be conceived as a superposition of basic electromagnetic vibratory entities. As such, it provides a means to solve a difficult problem, in the description of atomic phenomena, of how to account for stability amid ceaseless change. Whitehead's concept of primate is well-suited to meet this difficulty. He points out that certain associations of "basic vibratory entities" are likely to be more stable than others, and that stable associations may become unstable in unfavourable environments. [45] The details of this notion are not as important as the underlying idea of association for the sake of stability of endurance. For a physical organism must be ultimately conceived as an organism of organisms; that is, as an association of lesser organisms or primates. [46]

While Whitehead's speculations about primates are avowedly tentative and intended to be recast in the light of developments in physics, they nevertheless provide a general conceptual framework with considerable unifying power. The concept of organism, in its extended sense, is applicable to all levels of scientific description, from the purely physical to the biological. The traditional attempt to account for biological phenomena in terms of physico-chemical concepts has been converted into the attempt to determine the extent to which the biological notion of organism applies to the physical organism.

Whitehead offers a unified system of thought which is based upon the concept of organizations within structured organizations, beginning at the very basis of physical reality and extending upwards into increasingly complex structures. One may conceive of this structure of structures as a hierarchy of organisms with a base level of purely physical (i.e. material or 'non-living') organism underlying all complex organic (i.e. 'living') organisms. The various levels can be distinguished, although not necessarily in any exact sense, by the degree of complexity of organization within its members. In Whitehead's view, this hierarchy of organisms is characterized by various degrees of "organic unity." That is to say, there is not just one order of unity within the hierarchy nor is there a uniform change in the order of unity as one progresses through the various levels of the hierarchy. At the most primitive level there are

> basic organisms whose ingredients are merely aspects of eternal objects. There are also organisms of organisms. Suppose for the moment, and for the sake of simplicity, we assume, without any evidence, that electrons and hydrogen nucleii are such basic organisms. Then the atoms, and the molecules, are organisms of a higher type, which also represent a compact definite organic unity. But when we come to the larger aggregations of matter, the organic unity fades into the background. . . . It is there; but the pattern is vague and indecisive. It is a mere aggregation of effects. When we come to living beings, the

definiteness of pattern is recovered, and the organic character again rises into prominence.[47] The value of Whitehead's theory of primates lies in the insights which it contributes to the understanding of the lower levels of the hierarchy of organisms.

But here the question arises as to whether Whitehead's conception of the world as a hierarchy of organisms is consistent with his stipulation that a primary organism must be one which is not analyzable in terms of subordinate organism. This concerns the status of the electromagnetic field in the hierarchy of organisms. It is not clear in the description of primates that, at lower levels of the hierarchy, one is not reintroducing concepts properly belonging to a materialistic ontology. Some attention must now be given to the question whether the theory of primates entails the assumption of a 'stuff-like' entity, under the guise of the term 'field', at the base of concrete reality.

4. The Hierarchy of Organisms

At the lowest level of the hierarchy of organisms one is concerned with physical phenomena having minimal claim to substantiality. The existence of field phenomena has given rise to the possibility of physical reality being grounded in entities which have a very nebulous claim to physical existence. An example of such an entity is an occurence of an electromagnetic field, which perhaps deserves the name 'empty event'. Following the acceptance of Maxwell's theory in the late nineteenth century, the notion of an electromagnetic field as an entity pervading the whole of space and time acquired great importance in physics. The subsequent repudiation of the concept of the ether, as the undulating medium or 'carrier' of electromagnetic waves, left philosophy and science with the problem of describing energetic occurences of an electromagnetic nature which take place in what appears to be a total vacuum: hence the 'emptiness' of such events.

For Whitehead, an empty event is one which occurs in empty space "where the word 'empty' means devoid of electrons, or protons, or of any other form of electric charge."[48] Nevertheless, the term 'empty event' is not empty of meaning. From the standpoint of the hierarchy of organisms, the term can be understood to refer to a basic primitive organism or primate. This conclusion emerges from Whitehead's analysis of the concept.

An empy event has three roles to play in physics: (i) Since there is no corner of space which is not pervaded by the electromagnetic fields, every empty event is "the actual scene of an adventure of energy, either as its *habitat* or as the locus of a particular stream of energy. . . . This is because the presence of a field is synonymous with the presence of energetic occurences. Thus this type of empty event approaches the character of an occupied event, with important differences to be explained below. (ii) An empty event plays the role of "a necessary link in the pattern of transmission, by which the character of every event receives some modification from the character of every other event." (iii) An empty event is "the repository of a possibility, as to what would happen to an electric charge, either by way of deformation or of locomotion, if it should have happened to be there."[49] The second and third roles of an empty event, in Whitehead's account, illustrate his theory's general principle of relativity, which asserts the interlocked nature of all events. In other words, there are no spatial or temporal references to any event which can be made completely independent of the complex network of events which make up the world.

The three roles of an empty event are all characterized by Whitehead as displaying "deficiency. . . . of individuality of intrinsic content."[50] Lack of individuality is especially characteristic of the second and third roles. However, the emptiness of an event is an abstract notion referring to the type of role played by a certain entity, and to its method of detection. In contrast, an occupied event, such as an electron, has a determinate individuality in the sense that it retains definite identifiable characteristics as it progresses through a variety of interactions, such as a path in a bubble chamber. One mark of its individuality is, of course, its charge.[51] The absence of such marks of individuality characterizes the emptiness of an event.

To refer to a *habitat* or locus of energy, as Whitehead reminds us, is to refer to an abstraction and not to "an individual discrimination of an individual bit of energy. . . ."[52] For energy is a quantitative measure of the activity and not the activity itself.[53] As for the actual content of the empty event:

> An empty event is something in itself, but it fails to realize a stable individuality of content. So far as its content is concerned, the empty event is one realized element in a general scheme of organized activity.[54]

But stability of content at very basic levels of physical activity requires, as we have seen, the postulate of the reiteration of forms of activity as the constituents of a definite pattern. It might therefore be objected that a difficulty with the concept of empty event arises in connection with the requirement that identifiable entities have some stability of content. For how can an event lacking stability of content be regarded as an entity? Whitehead's answer involves the idea that the degree of individuality is related to the number of individual identifiable characteristics. For example, referring to the situation "when the empty event is the scene of the transmission of a definite train of recurrent wave-forms," he ascribes to the event a certain measure of individuality. However,

> it is individuality without the faintest capture of originality: for it is merely a permanence arising solely from the implication of the event in a larger scheme of patterning.[55]

The reference to "a larger scheme of patterning" gives rise to the question as to whether Whitehead is violating the definition of a primate, which is defined as an entity which cannot be decomposed into subordinate organisms. There is a difficulty in viewing empty events as the building blocks, as it were, of more stable organisms having higher individuality of content. For then there appears to be no reason why the hierarchy should be closed at its lower end. That is, the hierarchy would seem to be fundamentally open-ended, with the possibility that there are primitive organisms even more primitive than those currently recognized. Nevertheless, Whitehead does not envisage an infinite regress of primates.[56] The concept of infinite regress is, in fact, logical rather than metaphysical.

The difficulty is resolved by attending to the meaning of the term 'nature'. The world must be understood as the world as it is and not as a hypothetical or possible world. Whitehead makes this important distinction by stressing that nature, as it is known to us, is nature which pertains only to one cosmic epoch. Each cosmic epoch possesses its own general characterisitcs and this current epoch Whitehead describes as one characterized by "electronic and protonic actual entities, and by yet more ultimate actual entities which can be dimly discerned in the quanta of energy."[57] Thus the term 'empty event' can be understood as referring to primitive organisms which have a low degree of individuality in the sense that they are constituents of more substantial events.

In any given cosmic epoch, certain types of primitive organisms dominate and give that epoch its special character, but they need not be regarded as the absolute and immutable constituents of all physical matter. Therefore, the hierarchy of organisms can be regarded as open-ended in the sense that the building blocks of matter are capable of being analyzed into more primitive entities. But the hierarchy is also closed in a practical sense, for the detection of these primitive organisms becomes ever more difficult. Moreover, what is detected is very much contingent upon the general character of the current cosmic epoch. While Whitehead's emphasis upon the electromagnetic nature of this epoch may be mistaken, his theory appears to be in accord with the experience of particle physicists who, in delving deeper into the substratum of particle events, find particles which are, on the whole, increasingly insubstantial, as measured by individual lifetimes and the difficulties of detection.[58]

It seems that the analysis of primitive physical organisms, which shades into obscurity as degree of individuality diminishses, indicates an indistinct boundary between the actual and the potential. The difficulty in distinguishing the actual from the potential is perhaps reflected by the ambiguity in the terms 'field' and 'particle' as they are used in sub-nuclear physics.[59] While a clear conception of the structure of primitive physical organisms awaits future developments in physics, it seems safe to say that the most primitive organisms are basically receivers and transmitters, having little individuality of their own and merely contributing, by participating in the composition of higher organisms, to the individuality of others.[60]

In the theory of organism, the term 'actual occasion' designates a fundamental entity: the world is made up of actual occasions. An actual occasion is a whole concrete entity, the complete pattern of an organism is realized in a definite quantum of time. Referring to what has been discussed above in terms of empty events, Whitehead describes "the actual occasions in so-called 'empty space'" as occupying the lowest grade among four grades of actual occasions in the actual world. In the next highest grade there are objects such as electrons: these objects are "actual occasions which are moments in the life-histories of enduring non-living objects."[61] He also provides a means to further clarify the notion of individuality in the lower levels of the hierarchy. Compared to organisms of the next highest grade, the organisms at the lowest level lack individuality in the sense of failing to contribute to the spatialization of the world.[62] An electron, which does contribute to the spatialization of the world, is, in the language of the theory of organism, a *society* of "electronic occasions." In other words, the question of degrees of individuality which are evident in the hierarchy of organisms is related to the nature of complex societies of actual occasions. But for my purposes, it is sufficient to note that the concept allows one to reach the important conclusion that a field has as much claim to physical reality as other, more substantial, physical organisms. Even the most nebulous and short-lived fields of elementary particle physics can be accommodated within the hierarchy of organisms without invoking the aid of substance-oriented concepts.

Some of the details of Whitehead's conjectures about the nature of primates are very likely not in full accordance with recent developments in physics.[63] So it is worth noting again that his main intention is to provide an alternative organic view of physical events. Central to the general characteristics of the hierarchy of organisms are the following:
(i) The primary physical organism (or primate of physics) must be regarded as an abstraction and not as the whole organism.
(ii) The abstractions of physics involve the extensional relationships of the whole organism. These are only some among the many possible

relationships involved in the complete organism. They are the organism's physical characteristics, and are essentially spatio-temporal because, according to Whitehead, these are the relationships which mathematics is most capable of expressing.[64]

(iii) The endurance of a primate as an insubstantial but determinate entity with a unique life-history requires a non-classical explanation. The entity is to be seen as a pattern of activity attaining individuality by means of the reiteration of transcendent forms of activity.

(iv) The stability of a primate is also non-classical. It depends on the kinds of associations into which the primate enters.

(v) The motion of a primate does not, as is the case with classical particles, involve reference to absolute space-time coordinate systems. Rather, the motion of a primate is a derivative concept, dependent upon the more fundamental spatio-temporal relations of the primate. A primate moves by the process of changing its relations with the whole process of the world.[65]

Given the general principle of relativity, which asserts that no individual pattern can be regarded as entirely independent of all others, the full description of the motions of primates is bound to be very complicated.[66] Indeed, all the features of primary organisms invoke a complex interweaving of related concepts, instead of the enlistment of a few select simple concepts. The organic view is thus entirely at odds with the pervasive but misconceived hope that science will eventually provide us with a simple account of the world. The physicist's own investigations into the nature of the physical continually undermine this hope.[67]

It has been mentioned in the previous chapter that there is a tendency among physicists to elevate energy to the status of universal substance. From the standpoint of the theory of organism, energy is merely a measurement of the degree of activity in a given event. That is, the amount of energy in any event must somehow be related to the capacity of that entity to affect the endurance and stability of other entities. If one grants that a primary organism is extended over a finite duration, it then seems reasonable to replace the concept of its energy with one which also takes the duration required for the realization of the complete organism into account. This is, in fact, just what is specified by the uncertainty relations of quantum mechanics, where the product of energy and the corresponding interval of time is called the "action" of the event. The concept of energy is only independent of the concept of time in a classical context wherein events are regarded as instantaneous and punctiform. The theory of organism thus agrees with the interpretation of the uncertainty relations, which asserts that the action of an event is quantized. The organic view of the world is generally well-adapted to the modern physicist's conception of the world in which sub-atomic events display properties with a quantized rather than a continuous character.

To sum up, the processes of the physical world cannot be regarded as either fundamentally atomic or fundamentally continuous, but must always be considered as a complex amalgam of both. Much of physics proceeds on the assumption that nature is continuous in the sense that there is a continuous activity measured by a continuous flow of energy at any point in space-time. But it has recently come to recognize that there are significant breaks in the continuous flow.[68] Nature is also atomic in the sense that the action of each individual in the whole process is neither instantaneous nor punctiform. The abstractions of physics have not, at least until comparatively recently, attended to the element of atomicity in nature but rather have concentrated upon the element of continuity. For all that the view of nature as a continuous flux of energy has been, and will continue to be, fruitful in the practice of physics, it has been detrimental to progress in philosophy. The concept of action is more relevant to the philosophy of science.

For action, along with energy, is transmitted according to regular patterns. This brings us to the notion of natural law, a notion which is of great interest to both science and philosophy of science. It should come as no surprise that the organic view requires a radical reassessment of the traditional conception of natural law. In order to obtain some understanding of the Whiteheadian view, we must first explore in a little more detail his ideas about spatio-temporal extensiveness, for this is the ground of description of physical events and of their lawful behaviour.

5. The Extensive Continuum

The nature of the extensional relations and, in particular, of the properties of continuity existing in the physical world is governed by general properties of the extensive continuum. An account of this notion is perhaps best introduced by a quotation from Kant in which Whitehead emphasizes certain phrases which express his own conception of space and time. Kant observes that there is no part of space or time

> that is not itself again a space or a time. Space consists of spaces only, time of times. Points and moments are only limits, mere places of limitations, and as places presupposing always those intuitions which they are meant to limit or to determine. Mere places or parts that might be given before space or time, could never be compounded into space and time.[69]

Whitehead observes that he is in complete agreement with this view if

Kant's phrase 'time and space' is replaced with his own term 'extensive continuum'; the latter, he believes, is an expression more in accord with the basic metaphysical characteristic of the physical world. This contrasts with Descartes' contention that the primary attribute of physical bodies is extension. Rather, Whitehead maintains, "the primary relationship of physical occasions is extensive connection. This ultimate relationship is *sui generis*, and cannot be defined or explained."[70] However, it is possible to describe the formal properties of extensive connection, whose relationships are those "of whole to part, and of overlapping so as to possess common parts, and of contact, and of other relationships derived from these primary relationships."[71] The property of measurability is not included in the fundamental properties of extensive connection. Indeed, it is Whitehead's opinion that the properties of measure are contingent upon the particular nature of any given cosmic epoch.[72] Since the physical notion of measure is associated with the practical application of the theory of the real mathematical continuum, it appears at first glance that the mathematical continuum will not be found to display characteristics having profound metaphysical significance. This becomes more evident as one examines the notion of extensiveness. It is unlikely, given that space and time are derivative aspects of becoming, that the general relationships of extension can, in themselves, determine specific facts about space and time.[73]

The concept of the extensive continuum expresses the physical interconnectedness of the world of actual entities as realized atoms of becoming. In accordance with the general principle of relativity, which denies that the plurality of the world consists of mere undifferentiated multiplicity, it expresses the "solidarity" of the world:

> This solidarity embraces not only the coordinate divisions within each atomic actuality, but also exhibits the coordinate divisions of all atomic actualities from each other in one scheme of relationship.[74]

In short, the extensive continuum is the ground of all the physical relationships between the actual entities which make up the world. The importance of this notion, as far as physical science is concerned, is not to be underestimated:

> There are no important physical relationships outside the extensive scheme. To be an actual occasion in the physical world means that the entity in question is a relatum in this scheme of extensive connection. In this epoch the scheme defines what is physically actual.[75]

The extensive continum does not *determine* the becoming of novel entities; rather it *conditions* this process: "there is always a contingency left open for immediate decision."[76] This element of contingency belongs to the mental pole of the becoming of a novel entity and can only be ignored in primitive organisms. Thus, the extensive continuum, or systematic scheme of extensive relationships, is only potentially infinitely divisible.

As far as the actual world is concerned, the role of the extensive continuum is then that of limitation. Or, in terms of the language of organisms, the extensive continuum limits or governs the ingression of pure potentiality in the creation of novel entities. But creativity arises from the eternal objects belonging to the conceptual aim or mental pole of the novel entity. Thus Whitehead distinguishes between two species of eternal object. One species, called the objective species, appears solely in the physical pole of the entity. The other species, called the subjective species, appears in the subjective form of the concrescence; that is, this species provides the ideal form and possibly the element of originality in the becoming of the entity. It is the objective species of eternal object with which physical science is concerned. For physical science aims to study the morphological structure of the world. That is to say, it is concerned only with eternal objects of the objective species in their functions as the real potentialities which underlie the becoming of novel entities.

Eternal objects of the objective species, then, to the extent that they function in the relationships of the extensive continuum, determine the physical properties and, in particular, the geometrical characteristics of the world. For the definitions of straight line, or of point, or of any other geometrical entity presuppose the relations of extension which are prevalent in the cosmic epoch in question. As Whitehead puts it:

> The order of nature, prevalent in the cosmic epoch in question, exhibits itself as a morphological scheme involving eternal objects of the objective species. The most fundamental elements in this scheme are those eternal objects in terms of which the general principles of coordinate division itself are expressed. These eternal objects express the theory of extension in its most general aspect. In this theory the notion of the atomicity of actual entities, each with its concrescent privacy, has been entirely eliminated. We are left with a theory of extensive connection, of whole and part, of points, lines, and surfaces and of straightness and flatness.[78]

Scientific measurements, then, deal only with the type of eternal objects of the objective species which are included in the relations of extension currently dominant in the cosmic epoch under consideration.[79] Hence Whitehead refers to certain fundamental notions of physical science as "arbitrary factors in the order of nature": as examples, he cites the electromagnetic laws, the four-dimensional property of the spatio-temporal continuum, the axioms of geometry, the fact of measurability, and "even the mere dimensional character of the continuum."[80]

Mathematics, as applied in physical science, expresses the order of the world which is revealed in the functioning of eternal objects of the objective species. Therefore, the character of such mathematics is necessary only to the extent that the patterned relations between eternal objects is necessary. Otherwise, there is an unavoidable element of contingency in the theories of mathematics in so far as they really apply to the actual workings of nature. That is to say, mathematics is only capable of expressing metaphysical truths, in the fullest sense of the word, through the expression of the purest properties of the relations of extensive connection. These aspects of mathematics, and only these, can be of the most general metaphysical character. However, a truly metaphysical expression, according to Whitehead, is rarely, if ever, achieved.[81] Hence the attempt to describe the degree of truth or certainty of an applied mathematical theory is never free from important qualifications. These will be explored in more detail in the next two chapters.

To return to the problem of the nature of continuity in the physical world; it is clear now that the problem cannot be given a simple answer. In the first place, there is no *a priori* reason why the full (i.e., non-denumerably infinite) continuity of the mathematical continuum should have a counter-part in nature. That the physical continuum is potentially infinitely divisible follows from Whitehead's description of the extensive continuum as the ground of real potentiality for the creative advance of nature. Regarded from this point of view, it is an abstraction referring only to the physical poles of actual entities. It is expressed mathematically through eternal objects of the objective species. But these can only convey features belonging to the *potential* divisibility of entities, which as atoms of experience, are indivisible.[82]

There is yet another important point which must be kept in mind. The question of the involvement in physical reality of the real continuum, or of any other mathematical structure for that matter, invokes considerations of necessity and contingency which are inextricably intertwined. For the successful application of a mathematical pattern in natural science indicates necessary characteristics of the physical world only to the extent that the pattern represents the order actually present in the realm of eternal objects. On the other hand, that order, as exemplified in the mathematical structure, must be understood to contain an element of contingency in the sense that the eternal objects so revealed are probably expressive only of a certain type of order prevalent in the current cosmic epoch. That is to say, they are not necessarily expressive of pure metaphysical truth, which is the ultimate meaning of necessity. For there is an ineradicable element of contingency in the expression of physical laws themselves.

In summary, there is no simple answer to the problem of the nature of physical continuity because it is not possible to distinguish clearly between the elements of the mathematical theory which are necessary and those which are contingent. To see this, one must attend to the most general types of relationship which appear in applied mathematics: one must consider the notion of natural law.

6. The Laws of Nature

Many laws of natural science concern the conditions and constraints under which physical quantities manifest their connections. The mathematical continuum is, at present, indispensable in physical science as the means of measuring and expressing the relations between physical quantities. The problem of the role of the mathematical continuum in natural science is thus intimately bound up with the concept of natural law. So an examination of the general notion of a physical law will round off the discussion of physical continuity.

At this point it is worth recalling the distinction between pure and applied mathematics. The former is free to develop according to its own accepted standards, creating and following rules independently of all physical or metaphysical considerations. But the attempt to characterize applied mathematics as a form of knowledge, and to answer questions about the adequacy and aptness of mathematical theories in physical description, unavoidably invokes metaphysical considerations. Any discussion of the mathematical continuum which includes reference to reality sooner or later illustrates this point. An early observation of Whitehead's expresses clearly the main difficulty:

> Now, owing to the necessary inexactness of measurement, it is impossible to discriminate directly whether any kind of continuous physical quantity possesses the compactness of the series of rationals or the continuity of the series of real numbers. In calculations the latter hypothesis is made because of its mathematical simplicity. But the assumption has certainly no a priori grounds in its favor and it is not very easy to see how to base it upon experience.[83]

Nevertheless, the successful application of the entire real continuum in physics, and the lack of a demonstrably viable denumerable alternative theory, is said to provide sufficient grounds for the existence of a correspondence between the mathematical continuum and the physical continuum.[84] That this is a questionable position is evident in Whitehead's hint that the adoption of the hypothesis of full physical continuity is for the purpose of "mathematical simplicity."

It is appropriate to expand upon this point in the context of Newtonian mechanics. For the development of this theory is intimately bound up with the development of the calculus, and hence with the growth of the sophisticated concept of a real number. It is a fact that the methods of the calculus inject great simplicity into calculations involving continuous quantities, notwithstanding the sophistication of the theory itself. Newtonian mechanics is a means of studying, for instance, the behaviour of large rigid bodies moving in a gravitational field. The successful application (and so partial or indirect empirical verification) of its laws lends support to the contention that the physical quantities which conform to them must exhibit properties which correspond to the formal properties of the mathematical entities used in their expression.

A typical question one might ask in this context is why Newton's laws of motion should be applicable to the description of the 'slow' motion of a rigid material body in the presence of other material bodies. More specifically, what is the significance of the fact that the first and second laws of motion, as expressed in terms of a system of differential equations with real number space and time variables, describe and predict the behaviour of a solid enduring material body? Does this fact not imply that the characteristics of the whole real continuum are intimately involved in the spatio-temporal characteristics of the physical world? It is not a sufficient answer, for the purpose of this discussion, to respond that the Newtonian theory provides an inaccurate description of this aspect of reality. That is, the Einsteinian theory has superseded the Newtonian theory in that the latter is regarded as a good approximation to a true description only if the velocities of the motions under consideration are small compared with the velocity of light. To meet this objection, one need only redirect one's attention to the more sophisticated theory and a similar question can be asked. In other words, in so far as the formal structure of the physical theory relies upon some continuum-related aspect of the calculus, it is not unreasonable to regard the mathematical theory as reflecting accurately real physical characteristics. However, the matter takes on an entirely new appearance if the concept of natural law is examined in the light of the theory of organism.

A physical organism, in Whitehead's estimation, is generally not an actual entity but is a type of nexus of actual entities, that is, a society. There are various grades of organism in the hierarchy of organisms, and a specific level in the hierarchy is characterized by the relative degree of internal organization of its members. A material body, which is an aggregate of highly organized societies of physical organisms, possesses little in the way of internal organization; it consists chiefly of a multitude of uncoordinated individuals. Its characteristics, therefore, are not those of an individual but rather are the average results of a plurality of individual characteristics. For example, the mass of a rigid body is the sum of the mass-effects of all the molecules in its composition, and the centre of mass of the body is the average of all the mass-effects with regard to their relative positions.[85] Thus Newtonian theory does not concern itself with the rigid body as such, but rather with the average of a multitude of abstract quantities which are integrated into a single characteristic; the latter is termed the mass of the material body. The process of averaging is done by means of the calculus, that is, by means of the theory of integration. This theory is a mathematical device designed to extract unique values from summation processes. These are basically ideal limits of approximating methods which stem from ordinary arithmetic. The application of the calculus in Newtonian mechanics assumes that the simplification introduced into the approximating processes will not appreciably affect the validity of the results. In other words, Newtonian mechanics is essentially a statistical theory which employs the theory of a limit of a real variable as a means to simplify calculations.

Classical physics is that branch of physical science which, in the language of organisms, occupies itself primarily with material societies. These societies, whether they be solid material bodies, gases or liquids, are characterized by a low degree of organic unity. The laws governing the behaviour of such societies are fundamentally statistical.[86] Thus classical physics cannot adequately describe the ultimate nature of physical organisms, for its laws are of the sort exemplified in Newtonian mechanics. They "blur and obliterate the individual characters of the individual organisms."[87] It is a feature of Whitehead's conception of the hierarchy of organisms that at levels both above and below the level of material societies, the degree of organic unity is considerably greater. Hence, one might expect a different account of the nature of the relevant laws of physics or of biology which apply at atomic or organic levels respectively.

While organisms belonging to quantum levels or biological levels of the hierarchy of organisms do possess a high degree of organic unity, a further complication arises in the case of physical organisms. This follows from the elementary observation that there are enormous practical difficulties in any attempt to follow the life-histories of individual physical organisms, such as electrons. Furthermore, at the quantum level of the hierarchy there are, as the uncertainty relations explicitly indicate, facts about the life-histories of particles which cannot be expressed completely and without ambiguity. The expression of a physical organism's spatio-temporal characteristics is constrained both by practical and by theoretical limits of observation.

It can be argued, therefore, that the expression of the behavioural characteristics of fundamental physical organisms cannot avoid having some statistical component. This component is, of course, different from that of Newtonian physics.[88] But both components contain a common element: the methodological suppression of individual circumstances in the interest of the expression of the most general character of a collection of entities of a certain species.[89] In a certain sense, then, all laws of nature can be described as statistical. But there is a reason for their non-universality which lies deeper than the above observations suggest. For an organic view of nature entails an organic conception of natural law. According to the ontological principle, the reason for the existence of a particular characteristic of the world must be looked for in the nature of the actual entities which make up the world. As Whitehead puts it, "The laws of nature are derived from the characters of the societies dominating the environment." Moreover, "in any one epoch there are a definite set of dominant societies in certain ordered interconnections."[90] Therefore, to postulate the universality of any law of nature would be to assume the eternal survival and unlimited effectiveness of certain types of order within the entire structure of the hierarchy of organisms. But, as we have seen, the very notion of everlastingness is fraught with dubious assumptions. It seems much more reasonable to regard eternal survival of systematic organization as highly unlikely, as Whitehead does. One must allow for an element of contingency in every type of necessary law.

To sum up the discussion so far, the search for laws in natural science is the search for characteristics of the physical world which can be expressed in terms of a systematic framework of concepts. But the concept of order, as it applies to the permanent characteristics of organic behaviour, does not mean absolute order. Rather, it means order relative to a particular society in the hierarchy of organisms.[91] A law of nature ultimately refers to a certain social order pertaining to one level in the hierarchy of organisms, for social order is the only order that there is. In brief, natural laws emanate from within social structure rather than being imposed upon the material of the world from without.[92] Rather than expressing some everlasting or universal characteristic of the world, a natural law expresses, in a more-or-less manner, the behavioural characteristics of a certain type of society.

Turning now to the description of the necessity which is evident in these behavioural characteristics, Whitehead maintains that this is governed by the "dominant ideal" of the systematic organization of the society in question. This is a complex eternal object which, as an ideal in the becoming of the particular structured pattern of relationships, gives to the society its definite and determinate character. So an elucidation of natural law in terms of the concept of society depends first upon an understanding of how such ideal objects are to be conceived as contributing to order.

A society is not an autonomous entity. The order of the society is only partially accounted for by its "defining characteristic". This specifies its internal organization; but the wider background which permits the continued existence of the society must also be taken into account. In general, the order of a society must be described in terms of the complex interweaving of influences which make up the whole world. For the individual members of the society belong as well to a more general society. In Whitehead's words,

In proportion to its importance, this background must contribute
those general characters which the more special character of the
society presupposes for its members.[93]

As for the general status of the defining characteristic, it is ultimately
expressive of purpose or value:

A society does not in any sense create the complex of eternal objects
which constitutes the defining characteristic. It only elicits that
complex into importance for its members, and secures the reproduction of its membership.[94]

The aspect of value, as will be seen in a later exploration of the concept
of necessity itself, is a fundamental characteristic of the theory of
organism.

A second fundamental feature of the hierarchy of organisms
emerges at this point. This is summed up in Whitehead's description of
the world as made up of "organisms of organisms." In other words,

The environment, together with the society in question, must form a
large society in respect to some more general characters than those
defining the society from which we started. Thus we arrive at the
principle that every society requires a social background, of which it is
itself a part. In reference to any given society, the world of actual
entities is to be conceived as forming a background in layers of social
order, the defining characteristics becoming wider and more general as
we widen the background.[95]

All natural laws, then, refer to the specific characteristics of
ordered societies which belong to a particular epoch, but not necessarily
to all possible epochs. The attempt to discover the most general natural
laws is the attempt to reveal the basic characteristics of the widest
society in existence in the current epoch. However, as Whitehead points
out, it is not possible to describe societies of the widest possible
character. For such societies would be those whose "defining
characteristics . . . .[can] safely be ascribed to all actual entities which
have been or may be."[96] That this should be the case follows from what
we mean by metaphysical description. That is, the closer one gets to the
comtemplation of general principles governing the behaviour of all
existing things, the harder it becomes to observe their operation. For
the wider the field of application of a general principle the more
difficult it is to discover contrasts which would allow one to state that
here the principle in question applies but *there* it does not.

In terms of the hierarchy of organisms, the widest society in this
cosmic epoch is that of pure extension. This society does contain
relations of a pure metaphysical character. However, in Whitehead's
opinion, definite knowledge of this society is not possible. After
extension, the next order of society, in terms of increasing specialization
(that is, in terms of decreasing generality), is the geometric society.

Beyond the geometric society, proceeding further in the direction of greater complexity of order, one finally reaches a society which is accessible from the standpoint of physical science. Whitehead refers to it as the electromagnetic society.[97] The term 'electromagnetic society' is probably inappropriate, in view of recent developments in physics which indicate the existence of various kinds of fields. However, a precise characterization of this level of the hierarchy is not vital to this discussion. The essential point for us is that the social organizations which are known to physicists do not involve the most general features of order in the world.

A natural law, then, regarded as the expression of the kind of behaviour prevalent among the members of a certain species of organism, is, of course, limited in its field of applicability. There is a yet deeper aspect of non-universality in the organic conception of natural law. This emerges from the observation that a pattern of behaviour need not necessarily be firmly fixed in the sense that behaviour of the appropriate type of entity can never deviate from that pattern. Since the pattern itself is dependent upon the survival of a certain type of society for its continued existence, it is dependent upon the survival of the defining characteristic which governs the behaviour of the members of that society. But the defining characteristic has no meaningful existence apart from the existence of the type of society which it defines. Thus there is a complementary duality inherent in the very notion of a law, a reciprocity which is evident in Whitehead's description:

> The causal laws which dominate a social environment are the product of the defining characteristic of that society. But the society is only efficient through its individual members. Thus in a society, the members can only exist by reason of the laws which dominate the society, and the laws only come into being by reason of the analogous characters of the members of the society.[98]

In summary, causal laws are not expressive of pure necessity. The discussion of the nature of particular natural law cannot avoid referring, at least tacitly, to a certain type of society which is assumed to dominate a particular part of the environment. This means that the hierarchy of organisms, when regarded in its full generality, incorporates a hierarchy of causal laws, some more general than others, but none capable of claiming an *a priori* necessity. In short, the theory of organism is completely antithetical to the doctrine that natural science is capable of discovering absolute universal and immutable laws governing the behaviour of physical phenomena.

Turning once again to the question about the nature of the statistical component in physical laws, it is not surprising, given the above considerations, that the statistical factor is so prevalent. The factor of necessity in any natural law depends upon the continued existence of the defining characteristic of a certain type of society. But this characteristic is an ideal, and an ideal need not always be completely obeyed in the actual processes of the formation of the nexus of a society. There is always an element of disorder linked to any element of actual order. For the organization of some entities into a particualr ordered structure is not the organization of all entitites into the same structure. The particular order of a given society always emerges from the relative chaos or disoder of its background. Furthermore, there is no reason to believe that ideal order is attained in any society. A plurality of entities ordered into a plurality of different structures must, in some cases, interfere or compete with one another. In a word, order invokes its complement, disorder. Hence Whitehead regards the statistical component of exact science as essentially unavoidable.[99] The degree of necessity exemplified by a particular physical law is, therefore, related to the degree to which the dominant ideal of the society under consideration is in fact dominant and not subject to instances of failure.[100] This is one reason why it is not possible, in principle, to unravel completely the contingent element from the necessary element in the application of mathematics to physics.

The organic view of the physical world thus casts new light on the problem of the nature of the physical continuum with respect to the mathematical continuum. Clearly, it cannot be of high metaphysical significance that the expression of some physical laws relies on the differential and integral calculus, for example, and thus upon the theory of real numbers. For these laws cannot claim universal necessity, and the means of expressing them becomes just that: a device for articulating the consequences of physical hypotheses. That these devices *do* work is, or course, still significant and in need of further elucidation. But there is ample reason to regard their successful application in physical problems as the *partial* expression of dominant defining characteristics of certain types of society rather than the *complete* expression of an element of necessity in the physical event under consideration.

The organic point of view entails a reassessment of other age-old questions about the metaphysical status of mathematical entities, such as those of geometry. Much of physical science involves measurement of physical quantities. Moreover, measurement, as Whitehead stresses, presupposes a congruence-definition. But there are competing definitions of congruence in any geometric society. So the resolution of the question of the nature of the geometrical character of the world is not a logical matter. For the geometric society is embedded in the wider society of pure extension and is, for any given epoch, a society contingent upon the particular nature of the relations of extension which predominate in that epoch. In short, the geometrical character of the world can only be decided upon by empirical means, if it can be decided at all. There is, from this point of view, no ground upon which to base a claim to *a priori* necessity for any mathematical concept with regard to its metaphysical truth. This conclusion can also be reached from an examination of the necessary, as opposed to the contingent, aspect of natural laws.

Chapter Seven.
Mathematics and Necessity

1. Uniformity and Necessity

I have argued explicitly in the first chapter and more indirectly in subsequent chapters that we shall not get far in our attempts to elucidate the connection between the rational and the empirical if we fail to take account of their inherent complementarity. This consideration is usually ignored in positivistic thinking which identifies the rational with logic and mathematics. Yet the faith of positivism in logic and mathematics is not wholly ungrounded: it is, in effect, a declaration that the world evidences order of a certain fundamental kind. Indeed, any belief in the cognitive efficacy of mathematics and, for that matter, natural science, presupposes the existence of a pervasive uniformity underlying the (at times apparently chaotic) onrush of events. The trouble is that positivistic philosophy has been too hasty in supposing that this uniformity may be exclusively accounted for in logico-mathematical terms.

Whitehead explicitly asserts that some principle of uniformity is assumed by any rational system of knowledge of the physical world. The need for a principle of uniformity, says Whitehead, is demanded by a consideration of "the character of our knowledge in general, and of our knowledge of nature in particular. . . ."[1] In fact, the aim to elucidate this principle might be said to be one of the main motivations for his entire work. This aim receives its most general expression in the description of the metaphysical task which is central to understanding the human rational enterprise. It is perhaps best expressed at the beginning of his masterful essay on speculative philosophy in *Process and Reality.* Here Whitehead forcefully states that in order for a philosophic enterprise to be successful, it must intergrate its empirical with its rational aspects. This means that it must be 'applicable' and 'adequate' on the empirical side, and 'coherent' and 'logical' on the rational side. Furthermore,

> The adequacy of the scheme over every item does not mean adequacy over such items as *happen* to have been considered. It means that the texture of observed experience, as illustrating the philosophic scheme,

is such that *all* related experience must exhibit the same texture. Thus the philosophic scheme should be 'necessary,' in the sense of bearing in itself its own warrant of universality throughout all experience, provided that we confine ourselves to that which communicates with immediate matter of fact. But what does not so communicate is unknowable, and the unknowable is unknown; and so this universality defined by 'communication' can suffice.[2]

This passage expresses Whitehead's deep commitment to a very broad conception of rationality, which incorporates what amounts to a general principle of relativity. One of Whitehead's most memorable expressions of his commitment to a radical empiricism appears in his comments on the view that modern relativity theory lends support to the idealist position.[3] He notes that Berkeley's argument, that the objects of sense-perception must be essentially personal to the observer, excludes space and time from its purview. In other words, prior to the modern theory of relativity, the facts of space and time were believed to be common to all observers. However, if Berkeley's argument is to be allowed at all, the facts of space and time can no longer be held as exceptions to the argument. Thus idealism is strengthened and

The realist is now left hugging the multiplication table as the sole common fact untouched by each immediate expression of mind. But the multiplication table is no good to a realist. It shuts him up with Plato's ideas, out of space and out of time, which is just where he does not want to be–poor man, like Wordsworth and the rest of us, he wants to hear the throstle sing.[4]

The last sentence concisely summarizes much of what is wrong with the point of view which I have previously designated as mathematical materialism. The over-riding concern of rational philosophy should be, as Whitehead vividly reminds us, the problem of how to keep the multiplication table, and all the many "necessities" of mathematical thinking, without sacrificing other, equally important, facts and experiences. And one of the more salient of these must surely be the fact that the world as a whole exhibits deep underlying uniformities.

Whitehead's apt observation about the priority of communication with respect to knowledge indicates that a natural way to begin to attempt to elucidate the uniformity underlying all facts and experiences is to examine the puzzle of our definite but limited knowledge of the patterned regularities within the contingency of physical events. In fact, Whitehead's early discussions of necessity revolve about the epistemological difficulties which arise in the attempt to understand the character of scientific knowledge. Since his final position on the nature of eternal objects (as the ultimate factors of necessity in the explanation of uniformity) seems a natural out-growth from his earlier thoughts on the subject of uniformity, it may be useful to take a brief look at some of these.

A salient feature of Whitehead's early philosophy of science is his concern with the meaning of perception. This is because he defines 'nature' as that which is the terminus of perception. Natural science is, under this view, definitely restricted in respect of its subject-matter; its proper domain is delimited by those entities that can be derived ultimately (perhaps by means of some limiting process) from entities disclosed in sense awareness.[5] Hence Whitehead's early thoughts about the uniformity of nature contain many observations that might, at first glance, indicate that Whitehead views philosophy of science as primarily concerned with epistemological problems.[6] To some extent this is true, but nevertheless Whitehead's early views on the philosophy of science are not confined to an analysis and critique of prevailing conceptions. Whitehead developed a physical theory of relativity which must be regarded as a major contribution to science as well as to the philosophy of science. This theory, in contrast to Einstein's, is based upon a theory of "events" and "objects," about which I shall say a little more later. For Whitehead holds that the work of Einstein and Minkowski does not lead directly to a new and better world-view but rather indicates the necessity for a radical reassessment and reinterpretation of many of the traditional fundamental concepts of science, especially time, space, matter, and measurement. And this in turn calls for a general theory of relatedness which does not appeal solely to mathematics in order to secure its cogency and intelligibility.[7]

It is an essential characteristic of Whitehead's approach to the theory of relativity that it attempts to accord with the direct deliverances of sense-awareness. Moreover, he insists throughout that an acceptable theory must pay due respect to the existence of uniformity at the base of all experiences. A major reason for this insistence is Whitehead's sensitivity to the failure of traditional theories of relatedness. The latter generally attempt to describe events (i.e., spatio-temporal happenings) in terms of substance-attribute relations. But this programme inescapably involves, as Locke, Berkeley, and Hume demonstrated, a muddle about the place in nature of primary and secondary qualities. Whitehead sees a large part of this muddle as arising from the attempt to account for perceptual experience by using only two-termed relationships. This approach induces a view of the world wherein universals located in the observer's mind somehow qualify particulars 'out there.'[8]

Taking a contrary view, Whitehead holds that the problems of perception cannot be solved unless we include a third term in every account of perception; namely, the "percipient event." This view leads to a doctrine of general relatedness which involves many-termed relations. By this means Whitehead hopes to be able to resolve some of the difficulties involved in the attempt to bring the transmission theories of modern science into harmony with ordinary descriptions of natural events. For here we want to say that the qualities perceived in events are somehow inherent in the events and are not mere psychic additions, having no counterparts in external reality.

Thus in place of the traditional two-termed theory of perception Whitehead makes the perceiver a full participant in the process of apprehension. As he puts it,

> our awareness of nature consists of the projection of sense-objects–such as colours, shades, sounds, smells, touches, bodily feeling–into a spatio-temporal continuum either within or without our bodies.[9]

The assumption of a dominant spatio-temporal continuum is thus vital to Whitehead's account of perception. For without such an assumption, he argues, we should not be able to discriminate reality from dream. That we are manifestly able to do this points in the end to the uniformity of space-time. For the act of discrimination cannot be effected if the apprehended dominant space-time continuum is not determined in its totality.[10]

Whitehead also argues that the predominance of the principle of uniformity is a consequence of what he calls the "significance of events." Given that events constitute the entire structure of the world, and that "there is no such entity as a bare event," they must be mutually significant in the sense of belonging to a vast interrelated complex of events. The nature of this complex is such that "Each event essentially signifies the whole structure."[11] Furthermore, in sense-awareness, both objects and events are disclosed, where events are the transient happenings of the physical world and objects are the factors which do not pass. There is a fundamental reciprocity in the manifestation of objects and events:

> An event signifies objects in mutual relations. The particular objects and their particular relations belong to the sphere of contingency; but the event is essentially a 'field,' in the sense that without related objects there can be no event. On the other hand related objects signify events, and without such events there are no such objects.[12]

The epistemological consequence of this reciprocity between the necessary and the contingent aspects of events is that it is never enough to attend only to the relations between contingent events in order to understand the necessities within the contingency of experience. We cannot even *conceive* of events in complete independence of non-transient factors of necessity.

Support for the view that there must be uniform significance if there is to be any knowledge of nature at all seems not too hard to come by. It is, in fact, a fundamental assumption of natural science that the range of knowledge always extends beyond the immediate sensory data, i.e., knowledge of an event *presupposes* that the relationships which sense-awareness discerns in the actual event extend in fact beyond the perceptual field.[13] Hence Whitehead distinguishes between discerned entities and discernible entities. Entities of the first kind are perceived directly in sense-awareness, but entities of the second kind are known only through their relationships with discerned entities. Natural science, as a matter of fact, is chiefly concerned with discernible entities, for what is perceived in sense-awareness is only a small part of its subject-matter. In brief, the doctrine of significance leads to the conclusion that discernibles are known solely by means of relations implicated in discerned entities and, for this to be possible, the relations between the discerned and the discernible must be uniform. Thus systematic relationships are implicated in all our partial knowledge of concrete events.

It is only with the aid of an assumption of this kind that we can tackle, with any hope of success, the epistemological puzzle of how it comes about that our knowledge of the world extends beyond the immediate perceptual field. In the absence of a principle of uniformity, Whitehead points out, "there is simply nothing to talk about." The functioning of the principle of uniformity is perhaps most obvious, he observes, in "our knowledge of the geometrical character of events inside an opaque material object."[14] On the other hand, without such a principle "we should have no reason to believe that there is an interior to the earth, or any lapse of time applying to it."[15]

One particular consequence of the principle of uniformity is that there must exist systematic spatio-temporal relationships between events. An elucidation of this point, however, is not possible here for it involves the tricky and controversial question of what to make of the existence, according to the epochal theory of time, of multiple space-time systems.[16] But in whatever manner the intricacies of the theory of space-time are eventually explained, it seems clear that some sort of doctrine of uniformity will be involved.

The chief point of interest for us is that the theory of eternal objects has its roots deep in Whitehead's early and justified conviction that a rational natural science always employs a principle asserting the systematic and uniform relatedness of actual events of the world. While the early Whitehead explicitly dissociates his philosophy of science (defined as "the philosophy of the thing perceived") from a "meta-physics of reality" ("of which the scope embraces the perceiver and the perceived"),[17] there is nonetheless a strong thread running from the early non-metaphysical to the later metaphysical theory. In particular, "objects" reappear as "eternal objects." But now the developed theory extends much further than an attempt to account for the coherence of nature as known in perception. It even goes well beyond the aim to explain the rationality of science, and in particular of its rational (i.e. logical and mathematical) modes of expression. For Whitehead believes that we need such entities in order to satisfy the broader demands which he designates as the "hope of rationalism,"[18] the hope that envisages a coherent account of the world in which nothing that deserves consideration be left out for the sake of expediency.

It is perhaps on account of his early explorations of the topic of uniformity that the later Whitehead does not linger very long over the vexed question of whether or not the theory of eternal objects is really cogent and necessary. Rather, his main concern is to explain *how* eternal objects are to be viewed as taking part in the actual events of the real world whose processes are, at levels studied in natural science, "obstinately indifferent to mind."[19] But there is undoubtedly a problematical as well as an illuminating side to the theory of eternal objects. Granted that the only real things of the world are actual entities, one might ask, for instance, what is one to make of the 'actuality' (i.e. the capacity for acting in the world) of eternal objects? Again, it seems that the 'eternality' of eternal objects is, for many philosophers, a major obstacle in the way of taking Whitehead's metaphysics seriously.[20] Part of the problem may arise from the adjective 'eternal.' Perhaps this is an unfortunate choice of terminology, for it is is certainly misleading in so far as it evokes the ordinary meaning of 'temporal limitlessness.' I will return to this point in the next section.

To sum up these preliminary remarks, there are good grounds for Whitehead's early conviction that the unquestionable existence of our systematic knowledge of the world, however imperfect that may be, attests to some sort of uniform texture underlying events. Furthermore, he provides some reason to think that the exploration of the nature of this uniform texture leads ineluctably to the postulation of non-transient factors of necessity within uniformity. In the next section I will discuss some general considerations that bear on the question of the cogency of the theory of eternal objects. I will then proceed to a more detailed discussion of how they enter into the explanation of mathematics.

2. The Theory of Eternal Objects

In Whitehead's philosophy of science, the counter-parts of eternal objects are simply called 'objects.' The theory of events and objects is developed from the point of view of the limited aims of natural science. But, as I have already noted, there exists a reciprocity between objects and events similar to that which exists between the fully developed metaphysical concepts of eternal objects and actual entities. About objects, Whitehead makes the interesting observation that they might have been called 'recognita.' Whereas events are the things that come and go in the flux of nature, objects are the entities which allow for the possibility of knowledge of the flux.[21]

We also note that the term 'recognita' is not meant to imply that knowledge through the mediation of objects requires a previous knowledge of the objects themselves. For events are not successions of instantaneous happenings. Rather, they occur in extended durations:

> An object is recognized within the present duration of its perception. For this present duration includes antecedent and subsequent durations; and the recognition of the object in the present is essentially a comparison of the object in the antecedents and subsequents within the present, though memory may also be a factor in the recognition.[22]

So it is reasonable to ask whether objects may be regarded simply as relative permanences within events, rather than as absolute permanences. Whitehead unequivocally rejects this notion. Objects may be regarded as "qualities of events," or the permanent characteristics of a duration; events may be regarded as the relations between objects. So a distinction must be maintained between objects and events: "We live through events, and they pass; but whatever is repeated is *necessarily* an entity of another type."[23]

The essential point, found throughout Whitehead's speculations about physical reality, is that nature must be viewed as composed of two fundamentally different types of entity which are intimately related to one another.[24] This reciprocity is at the basis of Whitehead's rejection of the more familiar terms 'universal' and 'particular.' The traditional relationship between these terms he describes as follows:

> The notion of a universal is of that which can enter into the description of many particulars; whereas the notion of a particular is that it is described by universals, and does not itself enter into the description of any other particular.[25]

This traditional notion of particular thus runs counter to Whitehead's fundamental doctrine of the relatedness of all events in the world; that is, of the general principle of relativity. In direct contrast he asserts that, in the theory of organism, the meanings of the terms 'universal' and 'particular' are interdependent:

> Every so-called 'universal' is particular in the sense of being just what it is, diverse from everything else; and every so-called 'particular' is universal in the sense of entering into the constitutions of other actual entities.[26]

This passage adumbrates the basic character of the theory of eternal objects and actual entities.

It therefore cannot be too strongly emphasized that the analysis of eternal objects cannot be carried out as if they belonged to a realm of completely autonomous entities. I have maintained throughout this study that an acute awareness of the complementarity between certain fundamental concepts is characteristic of Whitehead's whole approach. Interdependent dual concepts have been of primary significance in the above discussion of atomicity and continuity, and of those aspects of necessity and contingency which are invoked in the analysis of physical law.[27] I am maintaining that the theory of eternal objects can only be understood in this light. Unlike knowledge of the independent realm of Platonic forms, whatever knowledge we obtain of the permanent, recognizable characters of the flux of events is always flavoured by the contingent. For it is knowledge of the universal as it happens to be disclosed in the particulars of the actual events under consideration.

This point brings us to the question of what to make of the adjective 'eternal.' Events pass, but eternal objects remain. But in what sense? There is never any doubt apparent in Whitehead's references to their eternality; however, the term must be interpreted with care. We have seen, in the discussion of his epochal theory of time,[28] that the term 'permanent' is far from having the ordinary meaning. It would thus be entirely mistaken to conflate 'eternal' with 'temporal limitlessness.' In fact the proper conception appears in the third category of explanation, as given in the categoreal scheme. Whitehead asserts that "there are no novel eternal objects."[29] One might say, then, that 'eternality' for Whitehead means "non-evolutionary."

However, the theory of organism is a thoroughgoing evolutionary theory of nature which maintains, for instance, that the laws of nature are subject to change, none being privileged in respect to permanence. So the question naturally arises as to whether eternal objects, as the forms of definiteness within the patterns of events, might not also be evolutionary in some sense.

The answer turns on whether or not there are good reasons for accepting Whitehead's unequivocal distinction between the two types of fundamental entity. It is essential to Whitehead's theory that an actual entity is that which becomes and which, in the course of becoming, ineluctably perishes. The question then is, can actual entities, considered in isolation from the theory of eternal objects, provide, despite their inherent transience, sufficient reason in themselves for the existence and persistence of definite character and for the endurance of order? A well-known affirmative answer has been given to this question by Everett W. Hall.[30] Hall argues that we can account for identity, permanence, universality, abstraction, and potentiality without needing to create a special type of entity to perform these functions. In support of this view he suggests that Whitehead's fundamental distinction between eternal objects and actual entities amounts to the commission of a 'bifurcation' fallacy. But this criticism, I believe, is not a serious one, for it miscontrues the nature of Whitehead's use of dualisms. The essential point is that these are always complementary, that is, fundamentally unbifurcated.

The argument that the functions which are performed by eternal objects can be accounted for by actual entities alone amounts to the assertion that structures of activity can be regarded as the *relatively* permanent reenactment of determinant and definite characteristics. Hence it would seem to follow that we have no need for eternal objects: relative permanence does not require the postulation of "eternal" or non-evolutionary forms of activity. But to take this approach is to ignore a fundamental feature of Whitehead's theory of organism. It does not appear possible to give a coherent conception of becoming in terms that refer exclusively to the reenactment or the repetition of relatively permanent structures of activity.

The point turns on the meaning of 'order.' It is true that structures of activity exemplify forms of order; moreover, order is not static, given once for all. Specific instances of order are always subject to change. Accordingly, under the Whiteheadian view, they *should* only be conceived as relatively permanent. But order, for Whitehead, is primarily a generic term. We must not forget that at the core of Whitehead's aim to elucidate process is the paramount and laudable urge to throw light upon the notion of order *per se*. He is not merely concerned to explain and account for the endurance and evolution of particular types of order.

Therefore the discussion cannot be restricted solely to topics that pertain exclusively to eternal objects and actual entities. An adequate treatment of this problem must range in the end over a domain broad enough to include the concept of creativity. For if one believes, as Whitehead does, that it is unintelligible to say that the ultimate ground of order is simply chaos, or disorder, one is led to postulate a ground of ordering. Thus the theory of organism presupposes a ground or matrix for the world which can be called a self-differentiating activity. Or, in Whitehead's words, the theory

> requires an underlying activity–a substantial activity–expressing itself in individual embodiments, and evolving in achievements of organism.[31]

In short, the "underlying eternal energy," coalesces into definite drops of individual experience, or 'units of value.'

Whitehead's emphasis on 'individuality' and 'value' is thus an essential part of his theory of organism.[32] This means that the problem of the eternality of eternal objects can be regarded as a special instance of a more general question: can the manifestation and evolution of various types of order be entirely accounted for in terms of undirected, valueless or random changes in preexisting value-neutral structures of activity?

In Whitehead's opinion, an affirmative answer is only consistent with the simultaneous assertion of a doctrine akin to mechanistic materialism: for him this is entirely unacceptable. Such a doctrine asserts that all entities of the world, from the microcosmic to the cosmic, "blindly run."[33] And it is certainly inconceivable that an actual entity, as a structured form of pure activity, could be adequately, let alone completely, described by the phrase: it blindly runs. Each actual occasion exemplifies not only definite physical characteristics and qualities but also an individual unit of value in the sense that its becoming is always directed toward some end, namely, its definite character. Only instantaneous punctiform events totally lack definite character. Thus while it is likely that, at primitive levels of the hierarchy of organisms, there is mere transmission of purely physical characteristics, the general doctrine of transmission requires an indispensable factor of creativity. Hence the complementary duality of physical pole and of mental pole requires that a distinction be made, in the realm of eternal objects, between objects belonging to the objective and the subjective species. Eternal objects are necessary, therefore, not only to account for the existence of definiteness, permanence, and universality of physical characteristics but also as ideals or norms for the achievement of actuality, i.e., of value.[34]

It seems clear that, in the latter role, eternal objects must certainly transcend events, for to maintain otherwise is unintelligible. This is because an eternal object in its normative role as an ideal for the act of becoming cannot be completely and coherently comprehended as a mere abstraction derived from that becoming. In sum, while it may be argued that some forms of definiteness may be entirely immanent in actual events, it does not seem possible to account for all their functions in this way.

But it is only possible here to touch on a few of the many, and probably irresolvable, problems which are raised in any discussion which bears on the meaning of order. One reason why this problem is so immensely difficult is that the question of the nature of the underlying activity, the ground of all ordering, inevitably elicits notions which pertain to the concept of God. This concept, in other words, lies at the terminus of every attempt to give a rational account of the world. Moreover, as Whitehead points out, "no reason can be given for the nature of God, because that nature is the ground of rationality."[35]

Thus granting Whitehead's point that it is not possible to describe God in terms of more basic metaphysical categories, we see that the explanation of rationality is far from being a rational enterprise in the standard sense of the word. Put another way, it indicates that there is not as clear a line dividing rational philosophy from theology as some modern philosophers would have us believe. For it is reasonable to hold that the concept of God must necessarily be incorporated into our explanatory story once it is admitted that the world is the interplay of an ordered structure of events.[36] The recognition of order, that is, of the manifest existence of evolving interrelated structures of activity, entails the existence of a Principle of Concretion to account for the existence of individual instances of order. Since these involve, in Whitehead's view, the concretion of pure potentialities, which belong to the realm of eternal objects, the latter must somehow be intimately related to the ground of rationality. What Whitehead is saying, in effect, is that once we deny the existence of non-contingent forms of definiteness, we bring the intelligibility and significance of all our strong "rational" beliefs in an ordered world into question.

But a proper treatment of the large and difficult question of the status of eternal objects in respect to the ground of rationality is well beyond the scope of this essay. A few more observations of a general nature must suffice. I have stressed that the complementary duality of eternal objects and actual entities reflects Whitehead's complete committment to an unbifurcated world of complimentary dualisms. It is part of his refusal to separate, in the final analysis, the general concepts of order and disorder, of the achievement of value and the frustration of value, and ultimately of good and evil, that must account in part for his insistence upon the theory of eternal objects. Therefore, to attempt to dispense with the difficulties concerning eternal objects by banishing them completely would be to rewrite the theory of organism. What resulted might well be another worthwhile theory of organism, but it would not be Whiteheadian in spirit.[37]

It is perhaps worth observing that if the realm of eternal objects were conceived as capable of evolution, it is difficult to see what would be gained thereby. Whitehead's whole rationalistic enterprise would become much more complicated without any apparent gain in explanatory power. We would now need a theory about the processes of evolution within the realm of possibility which would supplement the theory of the processes of evolution within the realm of actuality. But there appears to be no compelling need for such a theory. So, while there is no evidence that an evolutionary doctrine is required in the theory of eternal objects, the postulate of the 'eternality' of eternal objects can be held simply by appealing to the principle of Occam's razor. Indeed, this may help to explain Whitehead's use of the adjective 'eternal.'

3. The Nature of Mathematics and Logic

Whitehead's most detailed discussion of the realm of eternal objects appears in the chapter entitled 'Abstraction' in *Science and the Modern World*. As the title suggests, an elucidation of eternal objects is related to an elucidation of the notion of abstraction. In the following discussion, I shall concentrate chiefly upon the aspect of necessity which exists in the realm, although it soon becomes evident that this cannot be described without reference to factors of contingency. This is because the abstract ultimately derives its meaning from its connection with the concrete.

It should first be emphasized that Whitehead uses the term 'realm' in preference to the term 'multiplicity' when he speaks of the totality of eternal objects. For he wishes to underline the interconnectedness of that totality. Indeed, the term 'realm,' if interpreted in this sense, expresses the fundamental characteristic of eternal objects: the realm consists of interrelated patterns of eternal objects, where each pattern has its own determinate status with respect to other patterns of eternal objects.[38] It is this property which is invoked in the attempt to describe logic and mathematics as interrelated, but only more or less distinguishable, systems of knowledge.

The systematic mutual relatedness of eternal objects is a consequence, Whitehead believes, of the nature of possibility itself. Therefore, an essential feature of his description of the realm of eternal objects is his conception of possibility. For Whitehead, to say that a certain possibility is implicated in the actualization of an event is to say much more than that a certain quality is predicated of that event. In other words, to assert that an event exhibits a particular characteristic is to make some sort of assertion of how that event is distinguishable from other events, or, what amounts to the same thing, of how that event is related to other events. To put it briefly, possibility is indicative of the how of relationship in actualization. Therefore, the analysis of relatedness must be closely linked to that of possibility: furthermore, relatedness means systematic relatedness. This is because

> ... a relationship is a fact which concerns all the implicated relata, and cannot be isolated as if involving only one of the relata. Accordingly, there is a general fact of systematic mutual relatedness which is inherent in the character of possibility.[39]

This link between possibility and systematic relatedness in the realm of eternal objects is a consequence of a fundamental presupposition of Whitehead's approach. It is not merely a secondary aspect, perhaps dispensable, of a purely descriptive exploration of the nature of the realm. An eternal object is, in the first instance, a possibility for an actualization. Now the actualization of possibility is a definite achievement of value. The achievement of a definite value entails the existence of alternative potential ideals which are connected to that particular value in some systematic manner. Put another way, the systematic mutual relatedness of actual entities, which is accounted for by the general principle of relativity, must be reflected in a systematic mutual relatedness of potential entities. For this reason, Whitehead describes the realm of eternal objects as a realm of "alternative interconnected entities" which "is disclosed by all the untrue propositions which can be predicated significantly of [an actual] occasion."[40]

It is, therefore, essential to Whitehead's account of the nature of eternal objects that every eternal object must be related in a *determinate* systematic manner to every other eternal object. For his insistence on the presence of value in the becoming of actual entities is fundamental to his metaphysical position. This aspect of determinateness invokes, like most fundamental concepts in Whitehead's thought, a meaningful dual concept: indeterminateness. That is to say, there must be an element of indeterminateness, with regard to any eternal object, in the manner of its involvement in the becoming of actual entities. By virtue of the interrelatedness of all potentialities, and once again in accordance with the general principle of relativity, every eternal object must be related systematically to every actual occasion. One is led, therefore, to the need for a special term which will encompass the complexity of the relationship between potentiality and actuality. For Whitehead this term is 'ingression': "Each eternal object has its own proper connection with each such occasion, which I term its mode of ingression into that occasion."[41] This means that, in the analysis of the realm of eternal objects, one may adopt alternative standpoints which concentrate either upon the internal relations or the external relations of the objects.

The internal relations of an eternal object necessarily refer to its determinate status in the entire realm of eternal objects. For the notion of internal relations, as Whitehead points out, is the notion that a certain entity acquires its definiteness only by possessing a definite set of relationships with other entities of the same kind.[42] On the other hand, any one eternal object, regarded from the standpoint of a given act of realization, possesses a degree of relevance with respect to that particular occasion. There is, in other words, a spectrum of relevance for each eternal object, ranging from total inclusion in to total exclusion from the occasion. This means that each eternal object is involved in a 'selective limitation' in the actual course of events. When the eternal object is regarded from the standpoint of this limitation, its external relations are being considered.

The internal relations of an eternal object, consisting of its determinate relatedness to every other eternal object, are, therefore, linked to its external relations through the factor of selective limitation which exists in the becoming of definite and determinate individuals. So Whitehead describes the general relationship between the potential and the actual thus:

> The actual occasion . . . synthesises in itself every eternal object; and, in so doing, it includes the *complete* determinate relatedness of [an eternal object] A to every other eternal object, or set of eternal objects. This synthesis is a limitation of realisation but *not* of content. Each relationship preserves its inherent self-identify.[43]

Hence the eternal objects which are synthesized in an actual event can be regarded as both 'connected' and 'disconnected' with respect to that event. For this reason, Whitehead distinguishes between the 'relational essence' and the 'individual essence' of an eternal object.

These two notions are also central to an analysis of the general characteristics of process. I have already emphasized the importance of Whitehead's fundamental distinction between abstract entities and concrete entities (e.g., objects and events). For an entity to be abstract means that it transcends actuality. But:

> An eternal object, considered as an abstract entity, cannot be divorced from its reference to other eternal objects, and from its reference to actuality generally; though it is disconnected from its actual modes of ingression into definite actual occasions.[44]

From the standpoint of its external relations, an eternal object is what makes an actual occasion what it is. This aspect of the object is its individual essence, that is, its contribution to the definite and unique quality of the occasion.[45] On the other hand, from the standpoint of its internal relations, an eternal object is considered in terms of its relational essence.[46] The latter notion is the key to Whitehead's attempt to explain the existence of finite systems of knowledge.

If mathematics is to be regarded as knowledge, it is knowledge of the abstract pattens which are realized in the becoming of events. That is to say, it is knowledge of abstractness of a certain kind. The relational essence of an eternal object is the means to describe the abstractness of an eternal object. An important aspect of this description of the nature of abstract patterns is that they are limited in scope. Now the scope of an eternal object consists of its definite relationships to other eternal objects. It is clear that there must be limitations inherent in this scope because determinate relations must include definite alternatives. This follows from the consideration that some but not all of an eternal object's determinate relationships can be relevant in the becoming of a given actual entity.[47] Thus there must exist alternative routes within the overall connectedness of the entire realm of eternal objects.

The existence of limited relationships within the boundless realm of possibilities is also required to explain the limitations exemplified in the finiteness of our knowledge of various aspects of the world. The notion can therefore be defended on epistemological grounds;[48] i.e., Whitehead wants to account for the fact that it is possible to know something without having to know everything.[49]

The epistemological significance of the concept of relational essence is summed up in two metaphysical principles. They are:

> (i) . . . the relationships of any eternal object A, considered as constitutive of A, merely involve other eternal objects as bare relata without reference to their individual essences, and (ii) . . . the divisibility of the general relationships of A into a multiplicity of finite relationships of A stands therefore in the essence of that eternal object.[50]

These principles, as Whitehead stresses, are metaphysical in the sense of being absolute presuppositions, required by the fact that systems of knowledge are always limited in scope. These principles provide, in effect, the ground of a Whiteheadian description of the foundations of mathematics and logic.

In brief, the notion of relational essence specifies the *how* of interrelatedness in the realm of eternal objects. But because of the systematic relatedness of the whole scheme, the relational essence of any one definite eternal object must be implicated in the relational essences of all other eternal objects. This means that the realm is describable as a complex interrelatedness of patterns of limited scope. Whitehead's concept of the 'relational essence' of an eternal object is thus difficult and somewhat obscure; nevertheless, such a concept appears to be necessary in order to account for the ineluctably complex character of the subject-matter. That is to say, the concept provides the means to explain the power of logico-mathematical systems to relate certain complex patterns of entities by means of logico-deductive chains of reasoning.

The significance for logic of the relational essence of an eternal object is summed up as follows:

> [The] relational essence is determinable by reference to that object alone, and does not require reference to any other objects, except those which are specifically involved in the individual essence when that object is complex. . . . The meaning of the words 'any' and 'some' springs from this principle–that is to say, the meaning of the 'variable' in logic. The whole principle is that a particular determination can be made of the *how* of some definite relationship of a definite eternal object A to a definite finite number n of other eternal objects, *without* any determination of the other n objects . . . except that they have, each

of them, the requisite status to play their respective parts in that multiple relationship.[51]

In other words, the generality of 'any' in a logical pattern follows from the generality inherent in the relational essence of an object. This generality is that which is exemplified in the non-particularity of mathematics and logic. For, as Whitehead emphasizes, "the relational essence of an eternal object is not unique to that object."[52] Here we have a means to account for the success of the algebraic method in mathematics. The method is, as he vividly puts it, "the reduction of accident [i. e., the contingent] to the ghost-like charater of the real variable."[53]

One can say, therefore, that the relationships between eternal objects are 'logical' in so far as they exhibit complete generality in their relata. The degree of generality depends upon the complexity of the eternal objects involved. One is thus led back to the distinction between the individual essence and the relational essence of an object. For this distinction helps to provide a distinction between logic and mathematics, although the distinction cannot, in practice, be made clear-cut. Logical patterns, as opposed to mathematical patterns, express the relational essences of eternal objects and the general scheme of relatedness which these entail. But to the extent that one is concerned with the individual essences of complex eternal objects, to that extent the logical relationships become more mathematical. The notion of complex eternal object is, therefore, an important one in this description and will be elaborated further below. For the moment, however, it is sufficient to think of such an object as a relation of relations. Its individual essence, then, would be that particular *kind* of relationship which can, say, be identified as belonging to a particular system or branch of mathematics, or mathematical logic.

That mathematics is essentially logic, in a rather crude summary of the tenets of logicism, is true in the following sense. Mathematics is the study of patterned relationships between eternal objects, and the latter are internally related in a scheme which contains all possible relationships. The general connectedness of this scheme is what is meant by logical connectedness. Furthermore, in accordance with the general principle of relativity, the relational essence of any one eternal object is connected in a determinate manner to the relational essence of all other eternal objects.[54] Relational essences are only abstract patterns, more or less divorced from the individual essences of eternal objects in relationships. The divorce is partial because a complex eternal object, as a relation of relations, must have an individual essence. Thus the distinction between logic and mathematics cannot be made precise because the distinction between relational essence and individual essence, at least with respect to complex eternal objects, cannot be made precise. This does not point to an inadequacy in Whitehead's account. On the contrary, current developments informal systems of mathematics and logic indicate the absence of any clear division between their domains. The patterns of logic are more general than those of mathematics, but they are not absolutely general. They are general in the sense that they are capable of including a broader range of eternal objects as relata; however, the inclusion is always "subject to the proviso that these relata have the requisite relational essences."[55] One can roughly characterize this distinction by saying that to concentrate upon the relationships between complex objects is to do mathematics; to perform a deeper analysis of more basic types of relationships is to do logic. The difference between logic and mathematics, then, is a difference of degree of complexity in types of relationship, but not one of difference in kind.

To sum up, the systematic relatedness in the realm of eternal objects is central to Whitehead's general metaphysical position: it expresses his intuition that experience shows the world to be a process which includes 'value' as one of its primary aspects. Whitehead insists that his account of the nature of the realm of eternal objects is pure metaphysical description. The justification for such description arises solely from an examination of the account in the light of experience.[56] For instance, the metaphysical property of relational essence is required by an important epistemological consideration. It is a fact that our knowledge of the world is always piecemeal: even in mathematics and logic we are dealing with systems of finite or limited scope. The description of the entire realm of eternal objects as analyzable into a structure of relational essences leads to an explanation of how there can be 'finite' logico-mathematical systems. Such systems are characterized by more or less complete generality. This is true of mathematics by virtue of its freedom from the need to consider particular instances in the exploration of patterned structures within concrete events. But this freedom is not a freedom from particularity altogether. For the abstractions of mathematics and logic lead to the establishment of knowledge of the real physical world. It is this connection with the concrete which, finally, gives credence to the claim that mathematics is a form of knowledge.

4. Mathematical Knowledge

Mathematics is a special form of knowledge in that it is knowledge of the necessary relationships which are exemplified in the processes of the world. That it is also the most abstract form of all knowledge does not mean that it is certain knowledge.[57] For certainty requires, among other things, complete expression of the relevant features of the objects under consideration. It is not possible to claim certain knowledge of an event without at the same time claiming that *all* the relevant factors are known with certainty. In particular, the completeness of mathematical abstractions is subject, in so far as mathematics is applicable to actual events, to qualifications which depend upon factors of contingency.

In the previous chapter I explored that aspect of contingency which deals with the specific nature of the current epoch. This is the first limitation on the generality of factors of necessity. It is with reference to this particular aspect of contingency that Whitehead observes,

> The generality of mathematics is the most complete generality consistent with the community of occasions which constitutes our metaphysical situation.[58]

Now we shall see that the 'necessary' patterns of applied mathematics are never free from contingency. That is to say, not even the purely abstract mathematical expressions which apparently fully describe certain aspects of concrete events can be regarded as stating necessary truths about those events.

The concept of 'abstraction' is complicated by the fact that it is used with reference both to necessity and to contingency. The term is used to refer to those elements of the actual processes of the world which are, in some sense, transcendent and permanent. On the other hand, the term is used to emphasize the other-worldiness of entities which play the role, if they have any role to play in the world at all, of pure possibility. Thus a clear distinction should be made evident in any use of the term. Whitehead's description of the 'connectedness' and the 'disconnected-ness' of eternal objects is a means to elucidate this distinction, the need for which is reinforced if one examines the application of mathematical reasoning in natural science.

Mathematical reasoning, in so far as it is directly concerned with reality, attempts to express the most general conditions exemplified in particular occasions. The process is described by Whitehead as follows:

> The discovery of mathematics is the discovery that the totality of these general abstract conditions, which are concurrently applicable to the relationships among the entities of any one concrete occasion, are themselves inter-connected in the manner of a pattern with a key to it. . . .
>
> The key to the patterns means this fact:–that from a select set of those general conditions, exemplified in any one and the same occasion, a pattern involving an infinite variety of other such conditions, are exemplified in the same occasion, can be developed by the pure exercise of abstract logic.[59]

The passage alludes to abstract characteristics of the realm of necessity which were discussed in the last section. The problem now is to explain how a select set of fundamental conditions, observed in (and abstracted from) concrete reality, is connected to their status as abstract entities in the realm of necessity. For here is the core of the answer to the question why mathematics works.

Mathematics, according to Whitehead, works in the following way. Once the general set of basic conditions is discovered, mathematics allows us to penetrate into the interconnectedness of the actual occasions which constitute the world. This is what he means by the term 'understanding': it is comprehension of the 'reasonable togetherness' (i.e., ordered interrelatedness) exemplified in actual processes. The power of mathematics lies in its capacity to assist thought to "penetrate into every occasion of fact, so that by comprehending its key conditions, the whole complex of its pattern of conditions lies open before it."[60]

Now the characterization of mathematics as abstract knowledge of the world entails reference not only to the selection of a special set of general conditions which pertain to a given physical phenomenon. It also entails reference to the route taken by the penetration of understanding. For each mathematical abstraction can claim only limited application to concrete physical phenomena. A description of the routes of penetration thus requires further exploration of the connectedness and the disconnectedness of eternal objects. This will lead to the main reason for maintaining a fundamental distinction between two meanings of the term 'abstract.'

The account hinges upon a classification of eternal objects into two broad categories: simple and complex. A complex eternal object is one which can be analyzed into simple eternal objects: it consists of a "definite finite relationship involving the definite eternal objects of a limited set of such objects."[61] An eternal object which cannot be so analyzed, is called a simple eternal object. This classification of eternal objects allows Whitehead to speak of the realm as hierarchically organized. To illustrate this organization, he considers a definite set of simple eternal objects and some relationship between them. The latter is again an eternal object, but of a degree of complexity higher than that of the simple components. Proceeding thus, he constructs relations of relations, moving with each successive combination up into one higher grade of complexity. Whitehead calls such a construction, which consists of "the successive stages of a definite progress towards some assigned mode of abstraction from the realm of possibility," an 'abstractive hierarchy.'[62]

The hierarchy so conceived may be either finite or infinite, independent of whether the base of the hierarchy (the set of simple eternal objects) is finite or infinite. The abstractive hierarchy is finite if it stops at some definite grade of complexity; it is infinite if it does not. Hence, we have one meaning for the term 'abstraction.' The construction of an abstractive hierarchy is what Whitehead calls "abstraction from possibility."[63] In fact, he observes that this use of the term 'abstract' is the closest in meaning to that which is intended when a system of knowledge is described as having a high degree of abstraction. What is meant is that the system illustrates an "elaborate logical construction."[64] When seen from this point of view, the characterization of mathematics as merely a matter of rule-following obtains partial justification. The description is true with the qualification that we are here speaking of formal mathematics. There are indeed unlimited possibilities for making elaborate logical constructions in the realm of possibility. In terms of what mathematicians actually do, this description is fairly accurate, although it begs the question of the nature of the thought processes involved in the creation of formal systems. But as a characterization of the contribution which mathematics brings to knowledge in general, it is quite inadequate.

There is a second interpretation of the term 'abstraction' which is vital for a complete account of the nature of mathematics: there is also abstraction from actuality. Here, the selection of the most general conditions manifested in a particular occasion is the singling out of certain complex eternal objects. The investigation of the patterns of relationship among "general abstract conditions" is the analysis of these objects. The analysis of a complex eternal object also involves analysis within the realm of possibility. However, it is analysis of a significantly different kind from that already discussed. The analysis of a complex eternal object begins with the object at the vertex of an abstractive hierarchy. That is, it is regarded as the sole member of the grade of maximum complexity of an abstractive hierarchy.[65] The analysis now proceeds in the opposite direction from that discussed in the first mode of abstraction. Stages of decreasing complexity are passed through until a base group of simple eternal objects is reached.

Both modes of analysis have in common the analysis of the realm of eternal objects in complete abstraction from actuality. But there is an important difference between them which directly affects the characterization of mathematics as knowledge. There is no reason to believe that the second mode of analysis, even if it should perchance have begun with a complex eternal object actually present in a real event, will inevitably reveal the formal structure of the events under consideration. This interpretation of 'abstractness' thus bears upon the whole question of the adequacy of any piece of applied mathematics. This is because the abstractive hierarchy constructed upon the base group of simple eternal objects, which are derived from the complex eternal object, is always *infinite*. In order to emphasize this point, Whitehead calls this kind of hierarchy an 'associated abstractive hierarchy.' That this type of hierarchy is infinite follows from the general principle of relativity. For the complex eternal object under consideration is an abstract condition ingredient in some actual occasion. Being involved in a particular process of becoming, it is connected to the settled world of interrelated actual entities and the systematically related world of ideal possibilities. More specifically, it is connected to the entire realm of eternal objects, which contains an infinite multitude of interconnected possibilities. Thus from the point of view of applied mathematics, it follows that the variety of possible abstract constructions consequent upon the analysis of the general conditions of certain kinds of particular occasions, is endless.[66] Furthermore, if the analysis of just one complex eternal object leads to an infinite associated abstractive hierarchy, the analysis of many interrelated complex eternal objects (which would, one supposes, normally exist in practice), would lead to a possible inexhaustively complicated network of abstract patterns implicated in any piece of applied mathematics.

There is yet another observation which bears upon the whole question of abstraction. The above description, it must be remembered, applies to a particular type of abstraction which, in so far as applied mathematics is concerned, treats of eternal objects which enter an actual occasion in the physical pole. Hence, we are only speaking of those eternal objects, and their patterns, which belong to the objective species. The subjective forms of occasions, which give them their unique individual values, are left entirely out of the account.

There are many qualifications, therefore, which are indispensable to the proper use of the term 'abstract.' Behind the common usage stands the notion of limitation, of a selection of special features which stand out with more prominence than others. The notion of abstraction implicitly includes a factor of limitation which is significant in the attempt to characterize mathematics as knowledge.[67] But there are more special factors of limitation which can now clearly be seen in the distinction between the two types of abstraction. In the realm of eternal objects, the simplest entities, the simple eternal objects, abstracted from the rest of the realm, are in the sense the least abstract by reason of their simplicity. Thus a complex eternal object is of a higher degree of abstraction, consisting as it does of relations of eternal objects. So mathematics is abstract because it deals with elaborate logical constructions.

The selection of a complex eternal object as one ingredient in a particular occasion is another form of abstraction. Given that the eternal object in question is in fact realized in the actual process, this mode of abstraction is essentially different from the first mode because of the relative proximity of the eternal object to the actual course of events. In this case, the simple eternal objects at the base of the associated abstrative hierarchy are of a higher degree of abstraction than the complex object at the vertex of the hierarchy. In this sense, 'abstract' means remote from the actual event. For the event is what it is by reason of the individual essence of the complex eternal object, which in turn is what it is by reason of the nature of the complex relationship of simple eternal objects, and the relations of relations between them, which are its components.

Pure mathematics and applied mathematics, then, are abstract in different senses of the world. These senses are not entirely unrelated, for they both refer to logical constructions within the realm of possibility. The abstraction of pure mathematics is a reflection of the disconnectedness of eternal objects from actual processes. The abstraction of applied mathematics partakes of the abstraction of pure mathematics in so far as it is an elaborate logical *reconstruction* of the necessary factors within actual events. That these logical constructions lead to infinite abstractive hierarchies, however, means that the purely formal abstract patterns of pure mathematics have a different significance when viewed as abstract patterns within applied mathematics.

The last observation can be expressed in terms which point to an important epistemological conclusion. There is no justification for the common view that, once a mathematical explanation of the structure and regularities of a certain subject-matter is established, a type of certain knowledge has been achieved. For there is no reason to believe that the logical reconstructions of applied mathematics truly represents the actual patterned relationships of the concrete occasions under consideration. Some aspects of the abstract system may, in fact, represent the factors of necessity which are present in a given complex of events. The applicability of mathematics is not an illusion: eternal objects are, as part of their very nature, connected to actual events. But there is no way of knowing whether a given mathematical representation is, in any given respect, an exhaustive or exact description of the necessary features of reality. In the end, the justification for such a belief must rest upon empirical considerations.

To sum up, complex eternal objects, discerned in real events but analyzed in the realm of eternal objects, are capable of revealing possibly infinitely many alternate routes in the realm of necessity. Such routes connect one pattern to another. But the existence of alternate routes, a fundamental feature of the whole interrelated scheme of eternal objects, implies that there may be an unspecifiable number of disconnected eternal objects within the compass of any one systematic application of mathematics. If follows that many of the patterns of such systems will very likely have no counter-parts in actual events. Such patterns merely provide the links, as it were, between more physically significant patterns of the system.[68] From this point of view, then, there is some truth in the description of mathematics as a tool to unravel the consequences of empirical hypotheses.[69]

There is also some truth in the assertation that mathematics comes closer than all other forms of knowledge to the goal of certain truth. For insofar as we are expressing the definite relationships which exist in the realm of eternal objects, we are expressing facts of necessity underlying the order of actual processes. Even here, however, there are limitations in the extent to which a particular formal system can express necessity. As studies in modern logic show us, this *caveat* applies to most mathematical systems. But mathematics does possess a partial claim to certain knowledge by reason of its very abstract nature. In the case of applied mathematics, nevertheless, this element of certainty will always fall short of absolute security. As Whitehead puts it,

> The certainty of mathematics depends upon its complete generality.
> But we can have no *a priori* certainty that we are right in believing that the observed entities in the concrete universe form a particular instance of what falls upon our general reasoning.[70]

In short, mathematics, as knowledge, has as many limitations as do less abstract systems of knowledge, even though they are limitations of different degree and kind.

Chapter Eight.
Aspects of a Whiteheadian Philosophy of Mathematics

V. Lowe reports that as Whitehead developed his own philosophy of science he came to place it more and more in a metaphysical setting: so much that in his later years he often said that he didn't really think there was such a subject as the philosopohy of science.[1] This observation applies *a fortiori* to the philosophy of mathematics. In the foregoing chapters, I have presented reasons in support of my general contention that Whitehead is correct both in his assessment of the shortcomings of traditional philosophy of science and in his choice of a radically revised and explicitly metaphysical approach. I have argued that science itself provides grounds to support Whitehead's view, however heretical this may at first glance seem to be. In this concluding chapter I shall first try to sketch in the salient features of the philosophical landscape which, in my opinion, cannot be overlooked by any philosophy of mathematics which aspires to comprehensiveness and adequacy. I will then briefly outline some important features of the Whiteheadian response.

1. Order, Process and Holism

Sooner or later the philosopher of mathematics must come face to face with the problem of the applicability of mathematics, and hence face to face with the problem of truth and reality. For either mathematics has *some* connection to reality and truth or it has no connection at all. There is no position in between. At present the philosophy of mathematics offers little to help explain how it can be that we have, with considerable assistance from mathematics, acquired an increasingly firm grasp of physical reality. Yet this must surely be *the* central problem in the philosophy of mathematics, for otherwise it is not easy to see why this kind of inquiry should be undertaken in the first place. So if the term 'philosophy' retains any of its ancient connotation of pursuit of wisdom and understanding, it is certainly doubtful if any current approach to the philosophy of mathematics lives up to the name.

One's stance when it comes to trying to explain the applicability of mathematics to the physical world is likely to be distinctively oriented by whether one is inclined to take empirical science more seriously than logic and mathematics, or conversely. It is by no means clear, however, that epistemic priority belongs to one sphere or the other. I have maintained throughout this book that the situation points to a complementarity, not a basic dichotomy, between the realms of the empirical and the rational. To lean more one way than the other is to risk losing one's balance altogether.

A state of unbalance, however, generally prevails. Much current philosophy of science is written as if concepts expressive of the most fundamental characteristic of the empirical are ultimately reducible to the abstract concepts of logic and mathematics. It is as if the concrete world could be placed under a magnifying device with extraordinary powers of resolution, and shown to be comprised of nothing but symbols. Yet abstract representations of the rational, in the form of consistent logical systems, are first and foremost devices for the organization of manifestations of order within the concrete. For scientific explanations presuppose the predictability of concrete events, and this in turn presupposes rational structure, that is to say, concrete order. Current philosophy of science, however, concentrates almost exclusively upon the rational aspect of the world, to the neglect of its concrete aspect. In keeping with its positivistic origins, it does not merely put the cart before the horse; some of its most influential thinkers have argued, in effect, that the cart can actually replace the horse.

There is a certain justice, then, in the fact that modern physics, with its heavy reliance upon mathematics, has contributed no small amount to upsetting the picture of our erstwhile solid Galilean-Newtonian mathematically transparent (at least in principle) world. In particular, research into the nature of the sub-atomic world indicates that matter is permeated with activity, right down to its most fundamental units. But the concept of activity itself cannot be fully captured by static mathematical formalisms, however dependent we are upon them for the discovery and the expression of some of the relatively permanent characteristics of this activity.

The general world view which modern physics sketches for us is that of a reality comprised fundamentally of dynamically interacting events, as opposed to an essentially static Newtonian world of inert matter. As Whitehead rightly maintains, the more one takes science seriously the closer one comes to a process view of the world. But, on this view, the very meaning of 'order' becomes extremely problematic. There is no *a priori* ground to suppose that any single member or group of elements within the flux of events deserves the privileged status of absolute permanence. Hence there is no standard univocal meaning for 'pattern,' as a species of the genus 'order.' All instances of pattern that endure appear to do so under the threat of eventual annihilation. Not even the hallowed conservation laws of physics seem to be completely free from the possibility of change.

It thus requires an extraordinary leap of faith to hold that all aspects of order are reducible to abstract logico-mathematical pattern. It is highly unsatisfactory to appeal to mathematics itself, as the paradigm of rational system, to elucidate the nature of order. For mathematics is primarily a means to *express* order and pattern. It is therefore a question-begging approach, notwithstanding its popularity, to assume that abstract mathematical pattern and real pattern are identifiable. In fact, we glimpse here the fundamental complementarity of the rational and the empirical. On the one hand, the plausibility and adequacy of our efforts to account for the relatively permanent aspects of order and necessity have come more and more to rely upon mathematics for support. On the other hand, support is empty without empirical evidence, which frequently only comes to hand indirectly. In short, science provides strong grounds for supposing that mathematics is not merely a formal game, but none for supposing that the world is simply mathematical.

It is essential to be able to refer to different, distinguishable and recurrent aspects of order if one purports to say *anything* about what there is. Not only does the very notion of knowledge of things point to this fact, it is presupposed by the possibility of rational discourse. That possibility elicits the need for a rational account of order. The fact that mathematics works provides some evidence that, for all its air of theoretical ephemerality, pattern or structure may have as just a claim to be included in any account of the rational aspects of the world as any of its more substantial or accidental aspects, such as "other people, sticks, stones."[2] For if the existence of pattern is not to be ascribed to the internal workings of human minds, and to minds alone, the notion of order must be intimately bound up with the notion of an external reality. That is to say, the fact that there is external order follows from the assertion tht the world is no more the scene of total chaos than it is the fanciful product of free-floating mind or minds. Indeed, the attempt to conceive of a complete absence of order is like the attempt to conceive of a complete absence of mind. It is to render incoherent the very notion of conceiving. Thus the affirmation of external order is rational inasmuch as the notion of a world of pure chaos is perfectly unintelligible. And this last point is one of the most basic presuppositions of rational thought in any sphere of human cognitive activity.

While a process view of reality is, on the external side of things, a common sense realist view of the world, it is in no sense a naive realism. Indeed, it is highly doubtful if there could be a direct or uncluttered access to actual pattern.[3] This is partly because the world cannot be divided neatly into two compartments, with matter on one side, as the special concern of scientists and philosophers of science, and mind on the other side, as the special concern of psychologists and epistemologists. Under a process view, mind can only be adequately explained and described, if it can be explained at all, in terms of the events of process.[4] Mind is somehow derivative from the intrinsic order of events, an order which we deny on pain of renouncing the rationality of science. Moreover, a process view is naturally compatible with the evolutionary hypothesis that mind is not imposed upon or injected into certain types of events by some transcendental agent, but is rather an emergent characteristic of an evolutionary world.

In brief, mind is *in* and *of* the world. This point is in a certain sense obvious, at least to the post-Darwinian scientist. But it is worthy of constant reiteration in view of the ever-present temptation to speak of mind as if mindful events were somehow capable of viewing external reality from a privileged vantage point. This means that there is an important epistemological truth underlying the claim of idealism that *nothing* can be known which is not in some sense stamped with the workings of mind. The Kantian notion of perspective is implicated in all acts of viewing; indeed, the notion of perspective carries the connotation of intrinsically *limited* viewing. This is highly significant for the philosophy of mathematics, for there is no compelling reason to believe that there exists an utterly privileged perspective. The failure of Kant's own philosophy of mathematics indicates that it is unwise to pin one's hopes on such a perspective arising from mathematics.

The philosophical landscape, some of whose prominences I have just sketched in, indicates that the problem of the applicability of mathematics is unavoidably and profoundly complex. A thoroughgoing realist-process view of the world may be roughly characterized as evolutionary and monistic in its attitude towards matter. This view may be roughly described as monistic materialism but, on account of the unfortunate connotations of the last term, it is perhaps better designated by 'organic realism.'[5] Moreover, this sort of approach promises to be fruitless in the absence of ontological commitment, a point about which I shall say more later. But the epistemological and the ontological aspects of the problem of explaining the applicability of mathematics are not really completely separable. This fact is only partly explained by the insight that all knowledge is knowledge from a standpoint. An important further consideration turns on what is meant by the notion of explanation itself.

One immediate consequence of the organic realist point of view is that the traditional belief that mathematics somehow guarantees the objectivity of scientific explanation and knowledge is misleading, if not simply mistaken. This observation is more than a denial that mathematical statements bear some direct relation to objective reality. The fond hope that there can be completely objective knowledge of reality, or even of our cognitive capacities, seems doomed to disappointment. All expression, including mathematical expression, is the product of mind. And mind, being *in* the world, is not able to stand back, as it were, to obtain a clear and unequivocal grasp of any aspect of process, its own workings included. Hence it is doubtful if anything like 'objectivity' could be clearly defined or unequivocally understood.

On the face of it, then, a philosophy of mathematics sensitive to current empirical science would be highly incompatible with standard approaches to this specialized domain of philosophy. Here a common assumption is that the story of the connection between mathematics and the world can begin with the study of mathematical structures and concepts, rather than with the world. This reflects the widespread belief that the abstract naturally predominates over the concrete in questions of philosophical interest. But this assumption is closely bound up with the belief that mathematics invariably and automatically confers the virtues of certainty, determinateness, and objectivity on our otherwise shaky accounts of reality. We seem to have here a self-justifying circle of mistaken beliefs.

To escape from this vicious circle it is first necessary to renounce the common assumption that one must take sides in the perennial debate between realism and idealism. In the philosophy of mathematics, this debate is often conceived as if it involved a choice between dichotomous alternatives of Platonism and some form of constructivism. The real difficulty, however, involves a 'how' of reconciliation, not the 'which' of a choice between contraries. The issue turns, in the end, on what theory of meaning is held to be most realistic and reasonable.

A process-oriented realist philosophy of mathematics naturally embraces a holistic theory of meaning. All mathematical statements are, *prima facie,* part of a body of statements no one of which has a truth content which is entirely independent of a whole complex and interrelated network of logical and metaphysical concepts. A contrary view would require a prior demonstration, of the sort which Kant called transcendental, to show that individual mathematical statements are fully determinate in respect to meaning. Intuitionism, the most philosophically sophisticated of philosophies of mathematics, is committed to a belief in the possibility of such a justification. Likewise Platonism, as it is commonly understood, puts great stress on the notions of determinateness, truth and falsity of mathematical sentences.

But traditional Platonism, which postulates an objective mathematical reality, holds far too narrow a conception of the deep metaphysical issues which are involved.

The over-riding aim to find secure foundations for mathematical knowledge underlies the unreconciled duality of realism-idealism which both intuitionism and traditional Platonism uphold. In fact, it would seem that, for intuitionism, winning the debate between realism and idealism (or anti-realism) is crucial to its very *raison d'etre*.[6] But it is by no means clear that this view of the situation is warranted, given the complexity of the whole problem of the nature of mathematics.

Part of the trouble with intuitionism is that it makes little concession to the fact that the time-honoured concept 'truth' is highly problematic, even when applied to mathematical statements. A more cautious, and more realistic, view is that truth or falsity are concepts which attach primarily to sentences, but sentences need not attach clearly and unequivocally to reality. A simple "mirroring" view is no more intelligible when applied to mathematical language than it is when applied to ordinary language. Straightforward univocal correspondences between expressions and referents is vitiated by "the inscrutability of reference," in Quine's apt phrase. Indeed, it is not easy to see how even to begin to make sense of the notion of *determinate* reference. For the world is all that there is in just the way it is–in short, the Truth. And if the world is at basis shot through with mutability, any conceptual scheme, with its own peculiar perspective of true and false (and undecidable) sentences, is essentially a theory about Truth, and only more or less adequate to the expression of it. Reference, in short, is not only contextual, it would seem to be doomed to be forever approximate.

Similar considerations extend to the notion of proof. In fact, the thoroughgoing holist holds that there are no entirely unproblematical true sentences, at least none which do not, sooner or later, entail the assertion: "this is the way things *really* are in the world." But such claims can never be viewed in complete isolation from other truth claims. This means that the notion of proof cannot be completely separated from debatable metaphysical assumptions, and these include ontological propositions. But intuitionism, at least according to Dummett's account of it, is decidedly ambivalent about the proper nature of these kinds of statements.[7] The intuitionist can therefore never stray very far from the extreme idealist presupposition that mental constructions provide some sort of transcendental justification for meaning claims. But justification is not, and cannot be, forthcoming by virtue of the idealist's own insight that all knowledge, even knowledge of the transcendental (supposing this to exist) is contaminated by perspective.

Intuitionism, by emphasizing some important general philosophical problems connected with understanding, properly raises the discussion in the philosophy of mathematics above the level of discourse about logic and its special problems. In its laudable insistence upon the need for a theory of meaning it does show some awareness of how deep and complex the whole issue really is.[8] It raises into prominence the issue of the meaning of 'meaning,' and whether a theory of meaning should have priority over a theory of reality, or *vice versa*.

On this point intuitionism reveals a close kinship with positivism. Under both approaches the meaning of 'meaning' is closely linked to verificationism; explanation thereby becomes one-sidedly anthropocentric. The order of the external world is simply taken for granted. Both types of approach are thus unable to treat seriously the fact that mathematics works only in a *piecemeal* manner. For the evidence shows that mathematics merely *helps* to render partially transparent a world that is largely opaque to human understanding. Behind the question of why mathematics works is the prior metaphysical question of whether (and if not, why not) *everything* can be explained mathematically. The positivistic move tends to prejudge this question by assuming that the world is in principle entirely transparent to the mathematical methods of science. This move, in effect, simply glosses over the gap between the rational and the empirical; that is, between order as it finds expression in language and mathematical system, and order as it becomes manifest in the concrete world.

On the question of the applicability of mathematics to reality, the positivist in fact denies that there is anything here to be explained. Mathematics, on this view, is a deductive tool for winkling the consequences out of empirical hypotheses, and nothing else. The possibility that mathematics may somehow be expressive of the order prevalent in the world is simply dismissed. Yet to comment upon the applicability of mathematics, in whatever manner and however negatively or obliquely, is to make a metaphysical comment upon the notion of order. And it is just because this metaphysically loaded concept refuses, like the tormented ghost of Hamlet's father, to depart from center stage that the question of the applicability of mathematics requires a far more subtle answer than it normally receives.

2. Ontological Commitment

There is no such thing as a truth which is not evocative of the real. This indicates that reconciliation of the realist and idealist components of mathematical knowing requires reconciliation of the coherence and the correspondence views of truth. And this, in turn, requires a

recognition that there is a fundamental reciprocity between epistemology and ontology. Our discussion shows, however, that this reciprocity
is not generally recognized. Yet for this very reason it seems highly
unlikely that much progress can be expected if the discussion is confined
to the level of the philosophy of language. And this is where the
intuitionist's approach finally comes to rest. Hence on the applicability
question, the intuitionist must take away with one hand what he gives
with the other.[9]

By not taking the ontological side of the problem of order very
seriously, the intuitionist side-steps the crucial question of how to bridge
the gap between the rational and the empirical. This is due in part to a
misconceived sympathy for the dictum, commonly associated with
positivism, that it is only legitimate to talk about talk. Yet talk is
ultimately empty if it is never about things beyond itself. Quine's
position is particularly pertinent here, for while Quine is an eloquent
spokesman for the positivistic point of view, he is also outspoken on the
need for "ontological commitment." Moreover, he might, at first glance,
be mistaken for a realist.

Quine resolves the problem of the application of mathematics by,
in effect, dissolving the distinction between so-called pure and applied
mathematics: an artifical distinction, on his view, which leads to the
"disinterpretation" of mathematics–to the view that mathematics is
primarily formal and abstract, comprised of uninterpreted logically
connected sentences, and axiom schemata.[10] It is pointless, he says, to
look for an answer to the question of how the exact concepts of
mathematics mirror the inexact concepts of the physical world. For the
precision of mathematical concepts is the end result of an internal
process of refinement of our ordinary language idioms.[11]

Quine's approach has the undoubted merit of undermining the
mistaken notion that some sort of mirroring relationship can explain
the notion of reference. But his own response to the problem of the
applicability of mathematics fails to go beyond the realm of the
philosophy of language. Again we come to a dead end in the search for a
way to treat the problem of order. And it becomes even clearer that this
problematic is unlikely to dissolve under a programme of linguistic
reform.

The main trouble is that Quine's view of ontological commitment
does not require a commitment to any ontology. On the ontological
issues elicited by the applicability problem, Quine has this to say:

> The expressions 'five,' 'twelve,' and 'five plus twelve' differ from
> 'apple' in not denoting bodies, but this is no cause for disinterpretation;
> the same can be said of such unmathematical terms as 'nation' or
> 'species.' Ordinary interpreted scientific discourse is irredeemably
> committed to abstract objects–to nations, species, numbers, functions,

sets–as it is to apples and other bodies. All these things figure as values of the variables in our overall system of the world. The numbers and functions contribute just as genuinely to physical theory as do hypothetical particles.[12]

This is all very well, the holist might reply, for it is true that numbers, electrons, and apples must be accorded their due and rightful place in whatever system we use to describe and explain the world. Moreover, in attempts to come to terms with reality, some objects deserve to be accorded more substantiality than others. As Quine himself puts it, "there is nothing we can be more certain of than external things—some of them anyway—other people, sticks, stones."[13] Here we reach the nub of the realist-holist's difficulties: how should one bring these "things" together into some sort of coherent account without sacrificing "things," from chairs down to electrons, from cells up to minds, in whose existence we have good reason to be confident. It is not only an important but also a vital consideration for the realist that some ordinary empirical objects are much more ordinary than others, and that among these, as Quine suggests, there are some that deserve an award of maximum confidence. Furthermore, it does not seem possible to make much sense of the notion of confidence without eventually having to make a commitment to what one is confident about.

The situation would seem to call for a theory of matter. But, for Quine, it is only theory that matters: what we think about matter and not what matter is *per se*. Matter dissolves into structure; "structure is what matters to a theory, and not the choice of its objects."[14] And since all objects are theoretical, they can only be thought of as "values of variables." A scientific theory thus carries its own ontology with it, like a suit of clothes. Yet the clothes are those of the proverbial emperor: it is a mistake to take them seriously. It makes sense only to accept what there is according to one theory provided it can be linked to what there is according to another theory with translations which preserve structure. And structure itself is, in the end, nothing but a conceptual bridge linking sensory stimulation to sensory stimulation. Hence all Quinean "ontologies" are free-floating, and it makes no sense to ask what truth they contain. In sum,

> it is a confusion to suppose that we can stand aloof and recognize all the alternative ontologies as true in their several ways, all the envisaged worlds as real. It is a confusion of truth with evidential support. Truth is immanent, and there is no higher. We must speak from within a theory, albeit any of various.[15]

But for all its partial truth, such a view of truth, taken at face value, can lead nowhere but to a sterile formalism. Truth is a vacuous concept unless it is allowed that truth is not only immanent but is also transcendent. Some ontologies deserve to float less freely than others, even if they can never be firmly tied down to reality. Otherwise, it is hard to see why one should take scientific knowledge seriously enough to call it rational knowledge, with the attendant implication of getting something more or less right. In a word, we cannot get around the problem of accounting for the correctness or rightness of our sentences.[16]

Quine is fond of Neurath's analogy, whereby the progress both of science and of philosophy (which, in Quine's view, are continuous) is likened to the rebuilding of a ship at sea. The Quinean approach is mistaken inasmuch as it overlooks the fact that the analogy has two equally important facets, the vehicle and the medium. One cannot merely dismiss as irrelevant the sea on which the ship floats. A move to repair or extend existing structure presupposes that certain kinds and shapes of plank, fashioned so as to be able to perform particular functions, will serve better than others. A ship is not merely a structure; it has shape, gear and tackle of a kind governed by the type of seas in which it is meant to sail. We are not, and, if we are really serious about wanting *explanations,* cannot be entirely neutral in respect to our beliefs about what the sea is really like. To try to understand the world in terms of free-floating ontologies is no more satisfactory than to try to conceive of a ship while denying the possibility of having a conception of water.

Thus Quine's views on the applicability of mathematics are more akin to those of anti-realistic intuitionism than to realism, despite his confidence in "other people, sticks, stones." The differences, which appear at first glance to be large, are, at least where the philosophy of mathematics is concerned, not great. While the intuitionist properly insists on the need for a theory of meaning, an insistence which Quine generally regards as a complete mistake, both approaches ultimately ground their "ontologies" in sentences.[17] That is to say, both approaches simply leave the crucial question of concrete order dangling.

But if 'explanation' is to retain any of its ordinary meaning, other than being reduced to 'inter-theoretical translation,' the problem of order cannot be dodged forever. There is no half-way house in the matter of ontological commitment, not even in the philosophy of mathematics.

3. On Platonism

Quine's quasi-ontologies hover about, without ever settling, on what might, it they were allowed to roost, be a distinctly logical (i.e., predicate and class) version of Platonism. This raises the question whether the decision to take science seriously necessarily and naturally points us toward a logico-mathematical type of Platonism. Whitehead is rare among modern philosophers in taking this metaphysical bull directly by the horns. In fact he presents his readers with a stark and, for many with the tendency to mathematicize the world, unwelcome choice between two alternatives: either prepare to do metaphysics in the broadest and most general sense of the word, or give up all hope of making any sense out of mathematics.

As I noted in the second chapter, Whitehead holds that it is its connection with process that prevents mathematics from collapsing into mere tautology. This point is worth returning to briefly, for this view is intimately related to Whitehead's belief that some version of Platonism is necessary if our conception of the world itself is not to collapse into something analogous to tautology.

To reject the notion of process, as a general characterization of the way things really are, is, Whitehead might say, not only to fly in the face of current science, it is to assert that nothing really happens in the world. In other words, one would thereby be saying that the appearance of novelty is a mere illusion. From beginning to end the world's multifarious events are nothing but a rearrangement of parts. One might as well say that the world is given once and for all. For the world, on this view, is analogous to a tautological deduction, from which nothing emerges which was not already somehow present in the initial creation. But this is akin to a conception of the world as meaningless chaos: whatever happens is essentially devoid of reason. At the very least, it is a world for which the concept 'explanation' is vacuous. What is, just *is,* and it would be pointless to try to explain relationships which are merely contingent and accidental. They can only be described.

But all our actual modes of thought and practice belie the claim that this is really the way things are. And if empirical evidence is to count for anything at all, the truly rational move is to take reality, order and novelty seriously. Yet this is to invoke inevitably notions such as 'forms of order.' Hence we continually return to the ancient problem of how we should refer to, describe, and explain the variety of their manifestations. The question which Whitehead places squarely before the philosopher of mathematics is unavoidably and deeply metaphysical: is it possible to give an adequate account of order *without* having in the end to resort to an "eternal object" kind of explanatory device? While it is commonly held that such hypothetical entities have no place in a modern theory of reality, there are simply no grounds to support this view.

I have argued that the postulation of metaphysically ultimate objects is not in principle different from the postulation of scientific ultimate entities: both types of entities arise out of rational-empirical theory construction, whose method is that of retroductive conjecture. The question of their plausibility and usefulness turns in the end on the meaning of, in Quine's useful phrase, "evidential support." But what evidence deserves our greatest confidence is one of the perennial concerns of philosophy at large. And it is a major short-coming of the positivist approach that it prejudges, in a thoroughly unjustified way, what is to be admitted as evidence, as well as what should constitute a satisfactory and adequate explanation. On this ground alone Whitehead's approach is distinctly superior. With him we at least obtain a glimpse of the immense complexity of the difficulties that have to be faced if we hope to attain anything like adequacy in an explanation of the nature of mathematics.

4. *Whitehead on the Nature and Scope of Mathematics*

It is more than compatible with a thoroughgoing holistic (e.g., Whiteheadian) view that the rules and concepts of mathematics are the product of what might be called "mathematical intuition;" but an intuition of a kind more profound than that envisaged by intuitionism. Indeed, the evidence indicates that mental activity extends far beyond anything which could be encompassed by the notion of "mental constructions." In fact, it is more plausible to say that mind is capable, in certain of its manifestations, of responding more or less sensitively to actually existing patterns of regularity. After all, why should that which is in some sense an exemplar of the world's capacity for order not itself be in tune, to some extent, with actual patterns of order? Such an hypothesis suggests itself when science is taken seriously enough to locate mind *in* the world.

For the mind of an organism, human or otherwise, is closely bound up with the experiences of that organism. But experience of the world does not involve only the organism's ability to respond with enough acumen and alacrity to survive. At least in the case of the human organism, it involves the ability to extend its own scope into regions remote from ordinary sensory experience. While language, and mathematical language in particular, is instrumental in the discovery and the description of these remote aspects of reality, it is a highly eccentric assumption, which the "lingualistic" approach appears to advocate, that these aspects are somehow made out of the whole cloth of language. By contrast, it seems much more likely that the mind's rationality encompasses an intrinsic ability to respond to pattern, transcendent as well as immanent.[18]

One of the obstacles in the way of an adequate behaviouristic theory of meaning, of the sort to which intuitionism aspires, is its inability to account for unusual mental powers. Yet we constantly pay respect to the possibility that new expressions of pattern are capable of putting us into better touch with reality whenever we apply the word 'genius' to some particularly insightful individual. Traditional Platonism takes this consideration into account. And the traditional Platonist may not be altogether wrong–only too ready to find in mathematical *expressions* representatives of actual patterns. But expression of pattern is subject to human whim or error as well as to human genius, and dependent, as well, upon historical and cultural factors. Hence creative extensions and developments of mathematical pattern need not necessarily themselves be expressive of real pattern.

The Whiteheadian approach is arguably much more realistic in this respect. It can accommodate the proposition that a mathematical theory can express something of the character of the order which permeates process without being obliged to defend the untenable hypothesis that the theory is a complete or exhaustive expression of that order. Mathematical theories, and these include theories of logic, are as inherently limited as are all other theories. But this is a view which goes against the grain of the whole tradition of the philosophy of mathematics, so I will say more about it later.

In any case, this conclusion follows naturally from Whitehead's analysis of the meaning of order. In the first place, since mathematics expresses the systematic connectedness of the realm of eternal objects, it is knowledge of pure abstraction. That is, it is knowledge of the relations of necessity in the realm of possiblity. In the second place, it is knowledge of the necessary aspects of the contingent world in so far as it reveals aspects of ordered relatedness within events.

While mathematicians are free to make elaborate logical constructions independently of any consideration of actual physical events, mathematics is constantly shown to have connection to physical process. This is evident in the power of mathematics to provide connecting links between phenomena which have no 'immediately apparent relationship.[19] But mathematics pays a price for this power, and this distinguishes it from other forms of knowledge: it is at the furthest remove from the actual events of the world. In this sense mathematics and aesthetics are at opposite ends of a spectrum of abstractness, for the expressions of aesthetics remain comparatively close to the structure of actual events. These two branches of knowledge thus illustrate a distinct contrast. As Whitehead puts it,

> The distinctiion between logic and aesthetics consists in the degree of abstraction involved. Logic concentrates attention upon high abstraction, and aesthetics keeps as close to the concrete as the necessities of finite understanding permit.[20]

Under Whitehead's view, then, it is possible to compare various modes of knowing with one another and with mathematics in terms of their respective degree of abstraction. This means that the notion of their respective degree of abstraction. This means that the notion of abstraction must be linked to a general conception of truth. The Mathematics consists of what might be called static and timeless truths in the sense that it expresses something of the structure of the realm of eternal objects. But its high degree of abstractness limits its capacity to express truths about the real world. Modes of knowledge which are not so abstract as mathematics (that is, which deal with concepts which are closer to the actual events of the world), express truths of a higher order in the sense that they are of a lower degree of abstraction. However, such truths are contingent upon the present state of the world; they refer to the way things are "here-and-now." In other words, they are deficient in generality.

Whatever the loss in terms of immediacy in our knowledge of the events of the concrete world, Whitehead holds that its high degree of abstractness is the most impressive feature of mathematics. For the power of mathematics is undeniable: "The paradox is now fully established that the utmost abstractions are the true weapons with which to control our thought of concrete fact."[21] However, it must be stressed that a key word here is 'control.' Mathematics is indispensible in the endeavour to control physical events because it enables the physicist, for instance, to concentrate only upon those characteristics of events which transcend particular occasions.[22] In contrast, other forms of knowledge which differ from mathematics according to their respective emphasis upon particularity, approach the understanding of events with varying degrees of abstraction. So when Whitehead suggests that all science as it grows toward perfection becomes mathematical in its ideas, the notion of perfection must be read with a qualification. It should be understood that the term 'perfection' means 'complete abstraction." If the highest degree of abstractness is in fact what is desired, then the remark can be taken quite literally. Otherwise, the underlying intention of the system of knowledge must be taken into account. This will affect the meaning of the term 'perfection.' In aesthetics, for example, 'perfect knowledge' is not synonomous with 'mathematical' knowledge.[23] But even in its 'perfection' as complete abstraction, it is a mistake to dwell upon this aspect of mathematics in the absence of considerations that bear upon the notion of perspective. But before taking up this topic, is may be well to explore a little further the idea that mathematics is the purest form of abstract knowledge.

One immediate difficulty is to determine the extent to which mathematics, as it now stands, actually represents the abstract character of the realm of eternal objects. Here we meet what is actually a pseudo-problem: how to distinguish between examples of simple and of complex eternal objects in mathematical theories. For the difficulty extends far beyond that of mere identification.

In the first place, it must be kept continually in mind that eternal objects are significantly different from Platonic forms conceived as the sole repositories of intelligibility. For Whitehead, eternal objects are not *in themselves* intelligible, but rather *give* to the world its intelligibility. In other words, the complementary duality of eternal objects and actual events, which is central to Whitehead's metaphysical position, renders impossible a complete elucidation of the nature of eternal objects in terms of pure abstractions.[24] In this sense, the study of pure abstrctions, which is the study of pure mathematics, is a mere game. The question of the meaning of the abstract symbols and concepts is irrelevant, for there is no way of knowing with certainty whether or not a given mathematical pattern is expressive of a type of pattern which has achieved or could achieve realization in the current cosmic epoch. The most one can say is that the efficacy of mathematical systems testifies to the fact that the realm of possibility exemplifies patterned connectedness of only more or less clearly defined types of order.

While there are intuitively convincing aspects to Whitehead's examples of eternal objects, it is not surprising that obscurities arise in every attempt to discuss them. Whitehead offers a number of examples of eternal objects, some mathematical and some which refer to sense perception. He considers, for instance, a "definite shade of green," which, as a member of the lowest category of eternal objects (i.e., 'sensa')[25] ought to be comparatively unproblematical. But the simplicity of a particular shade of green changes into complexity when it is considered from the standpoint of its relations to other shades of green. These relationships involve not only quantitative difference but also qualitative differences. A particular shade of green, in terms of the hierarchy of organisms, is associated with electromagnetic radiation of a certain wavelength. Hence, it is reasonable to conjecture that it is connected to the activity of a particular species of primitive organism. But this organism will not likely be simple in the sense that it cannot be analyzed into more basic components. That is to say, the particular quality of the shade would seem more accurately to be described as the effect of the coordinated activities of a variety of primitive organisms, rather than as the effect of an organism of a single species. Moreover, if each primitive organism is ultimately analyzable as a contrast of eternal objects, it is difficult to see how it is possible to designate any of the effects, such as that exemplified by greenness, as simple.[26]

There are a number of problems of a more general nature which arise from this outline of a Whiteheadian philosophy of the mathematical sciences. One such problem, which has important epistemological implications, stems from Whitehead's fundamental commitment to the uniformity underlying the order of the world. When considered in terms of the realm of eternal objects, should one conclude that the term 'uniform' implies that there is just one true logic which expresses the "systematic completeness" of the realm of eternal objects? One notes that the scheme of systematic relationships includes many alternative routes linking the relational essences of the entire scheme. This feature of the realm of eternal objects accounts for the existence of formal structures which, although apparently distinct, nevertheless turn out to be logically equivalent. On the other hand, there are mathematical structures which are radically different. They contain incompatible features which cannot be reconciled because they represent distinct patterns of eternal objets. In other words, the definite status of each eternal object in the whole scheme, which includes alternatives, implies that the notion of perspective is indispensable to an adequate account.

For the present, it suffices to note that it is highly unlikely that any one humanly constructed system of logic would possess enough generality to encompass the entire relatedness of the realm of eternal objects. Hence, there are possibly many fundamentally different types of logical structure underlying mathematics, although these are not likely to be as numerous as the multitude of different mathematical structures themselves. Therefore, in view of the arbitrariness of human interests and of the finiteness of human thought processes, it is hardly surprising that both formal logic and mathematics should contain fundamentally different theories in a state of competition for pre-eminence.

5. The Formal Limitations of Mathematics

Despite their extreme formality, recent developments in the foundations of mathematics and logic seem to have some epistemological significance. While there is still no common agreement on an interpretation of the so-called limitative theorems of Goedel, Loewenheim, Skolem, Tarski, Church, and others, they have at least brought into question certain long-cherished beliefs about the nature of mathematics. It is no longer possible to assert with the confidence of past thinkers that the royal road to security in systems of knowledge lies in the development of rigorous mathematical structures. Moreover, the independence results of Goedel and Cohen, with respect to the continuum hypothesis, have undermined the belief that all well-formed mathematical problems must have, at least in principle, a unique solution. Nor is it the case that in any one branch of mathematics there is a unique representative theory. This doctrine of the uniqueness of mathematical truth,[27] extends to the belief that any representative theory unerringly reflects one true reality.

The ground began to slip from under the belief that mathematics is a unified subject with the discovery of non-Euclidean geometries. The existence of mathematically respectable competitors for the erstwhile unique and universally accepted Euclidean geometry did not merely affect the question of the place of geometry in mathematics. For the historially esteemed Euclidean system was thought to express important truths about the nature of the physical world. Not only was the uniqueness of mathematical truth put into question; the very notion of mathematical truth began to seem problematical. Since then, many other devleopments have rendered the doctrine of the uniqueness of mathematical truth even more doubtful. For example, a concentrated effort in the field of set theory has resulted in the creation of a number of feasible alternatives, and not just one optimal representative of set theory, in terms of which a unified mathematics could be expressed. Contrary to traditional expectations, there has grown up a plurality of mutually incompatible set theories which do not seem to have much in common except a restricted core.[28] The fact that set theory is at the base of the language of working mathematicians makes it impossible to maintain, without elaborate qualifications, that any given mathematical structure, however successful it may be in its applications, is the reflection of reality in any complete sense of the world. The connection between formal structures and their empirical counterparts is unlikely ever to turn out to be anything like an exhaustive and unambiguous matching of respective elements. Certain formal results of the limitative kind lend support to this conclusion.

The Loewenheim-Skolem theorem, for instance, states that any axiomatic theory which is embedded in elementary classical logic has a finite or countable model if it has any model at all. But the real number continuum, for instance, can be expressed in such a formal theory and one of its models is, as Cantor showed, a complex structure containing uncountable elements. The existence of a countable model of the real number system thus provides grounds for doubting that there is any one-to-one correspondence between the real continuum and physical reality. The situation is reminiscent of the existence of competitors for the true geometrical description of physical space. None of the competing geometries has claim to preeminence over the others, and all are linked in such a way that they stand or fall together. That is, the different geometries have been shown to be relatively consistent with respect to the real continuum. But none has been shown to be absolutely consistent. Which geometry is best suited to describe the actual geometrical relations of space-time is ultimately an empirical question. A similar conclusion applies to the possible models of the real number system.

Goedel's theorems also raise doubts about the exhaustiveness of any particular theory as a reflection of reality. One of his theorems states that no formal axiomatizable theory (satisfying certain minimal conditions such as set theory or number theory) admits of a formulation which is both consistent and complete. For if the system is consistent, there can always be found a formula which is known to be true (for extra-theoretical reasons) but which is not provable within the formal system. However, if an axiomatic theory were capable of exhaustively reflecting some aspect of reality, it should be possible to derive every true statement of the theory from the premises of the theory. But Goedel's theorem denies that every true statement within a formal theory can either be proved or disproved.

The significance of incompleteness in certain formal theories is still a controversial matter and the limitative theorems are capable of many interpretations.[29] But a general conclusion seems to follow: it is not safe to say that if a mathematical theory has anything to say about reality at all then all its parts must equally apply to reality.[30] In short, the limitative theorems of the foundations of mathematics and logic are consistent with, if they do not actually entail, the conclusion that mathematics consists of a plurality of co-existing but independent and competitive theories which share common elements but which are different in fundamental respects.[31]

Whitehead's views on the nature of mathematics and logic are wholly compatible with the above observations. While regarding systematic thought as necessary, indeed indispensable, for understanding, Whitehead points out that it is always marred by "a tingle of pedantry." In other words, systematic thought has built-in limitations. There are no exceptions to this rule: not even logic can be exempted. For systematic thought relies in the end upon finite deductive systems which, however formalized, cannot escape the constraints of perspective. This, then, appears to be the general significance of the limitative theorems. As Whitehead remarks,

> Today, even Logic itself is struggling with the discovery embodied in a
> formal proof, that every finite set of premises must indicate notions
> which are excluded from its direct purview.[32]

The significance is not so much philosophical as it is methodological. It points to the inappropriateness of the type of philosophical enquiry which has, in the second chapter, been described as Euclidean.

But this observation does not deny the value of the Euclidean enterprise *tout court*. The contribution of axiomatized deductive systems to the advancement of knowledge is undeniable. It is to say rather than there is a radical non-Euclidean element to knowledge acquisition which ineluctably emerges when Euclidean systems are interpreted. The non-Euclidean factor can be subsumed under the notion of perspective. The situation is characterized by what seems, at first glance, to be a paradox: systematic formalization both contributes to the advance of knowledge and at the same time constricts and hinders its growth. The reason is that the inadequacies of a particular perspective eventually predominate and overbalance its advantages. The paradox is only the result of "the finite intellect [dealing] with the myth of finite facts." Hence Whitehead's succinct summary of the scope and power of scientific knowledge deserves continual reiteration, especially in the light of current hubristic attitudes towards science:

> Science is always wrong, so far as it neglects this limitation. The conjunction of premises, from which logic proceeds, presupposes that no difficulty will arise from the conjunction of the various unexpressed presuppositions involved in these premises. Both in science and in logic you have only to develop your argument sufficiently, and sooner or later you are bound to arrive at a contradiction, either internally within the argument, or externally in its reference to fact.[33]

The Whiteheadian approach may thus be generally characterized in its epistemological aspect as placing primary emphasis upon the notion of perspective. He is suggesting, in fact, that this concept is our chief means to prevent the much-lauded rationality of science from dissolving into the irrationality of myth. It thus seems appropriate to conclude my study with a brief glance at some of the implications for the philosophy of mathematics of a Whiteheadian conception of perspective.

6. Perspective and the Philosophy of Mathematics

In this book I have concentrated mainly upon the ontological aspects of issues most of which invoke in one way or another a general principle that is at the heart of Whitehead's theory of organism: the principle of relativity. This philosophical principle, which asserts the complex interconnectedness of the events of nature, is not only in accord with the theoretico-empirical results of modern physics,[34] it is closely bound up with the epistemological notion of perspective.

Ordinary experience and common sense indicate that any given field of knowledge presupposes a restricted field of applicability with respect to its particular collections of key concepts. These would seem to be only more or less clearly grounded in a finite group of primitive presuppositions. In the absence of some *a priori* reason to the contrary, there are no grounds to preclude the possibility that should two modes of knowing employ only slightly different variants of a single concept, profound and significant differences may result. It seems more likely that cognitive systems are inherently incommensurable, rather than otherwise. It is possible that a slight alteration in a primitive concept, either in its meaning or in its relation to other primitives, may effect far-reaching changes in the entire structure. One might even go so far as to say the very notion of abstract knowledge is synonymous with non-interchangeability of different modes of knowing.

Primitive concepts embody what Collingwood speaks of as "absolute presuppositions;" that is, what he aptly calls "the mental furniture of a certain age."[35] In his view, these basic assumptions "are not 'derived from experience,' but are catalytic agents which the mind must bring out of its own resources to the manipulation of what is called 'experience' and the conversion of it into science and civilization."[36] The question of the source of the resources of mind is, however, not so easily dismissed in terms of "ready-made," or even inherited, furniture. As I have suggested earlier, it is a natural hypothesis, under a thoroughly holistic view of the world, that the mind may not create catalytic agents out of its own resources so much as itself be a catalytic agent, bringing into being the expression of and the means to develop pattern. Be this as it may, the *prima facie* evidence is that our grasp of the world is uncertain and limited: absolute presuppositions are neither easy to identify nor easy to articulate. This obstinate fact always stands between our attempt to explain the relation between some particular mode of thought and the world.

Hence adequacy in explanation presupposes adequacy of perspective. It is one of the strengths of Whitehead's approach, then, that he explicitly employs the term 'perspective' in his interpretation of the metaphysical meaning of 'experience':

> Each entity, of whatever type, essentially involves its own connection with the universe of other things. This connection can be viewed as being what the universe is for that entity either in the way of accomplishment or in the way of potentiality. It can be termed the perspective of the universe for that entity.[37]

He believes, with good reason, that there is a strong tendency in human thought to ignore this important factor:

> Our danger is to take notions which are valid for one perspective of the universe involved in one group of events and to apply them uncritically to other events involving some discrepancy of perspective.[38]

One good reason to grant primacy to the notion of perspective, therefore, is that it provides a necessary prophylactic for the prevention of the Fallacy of Misplaced Concreteness.

Whitehead's conception of perception conforms to the general tenet of holism that final truth is not attainable, at least not if the act of cognition is conceived as primarily embedded in the world as a dynamic entity. In the actual world, everything is just what it is, and the relations between things are just what they are, but not everything can be understood all at once.[39] This fact may be expressed in terms of an epistemological complementary duality: this duality is in fact implicit in Whitehead's conception of the general principle of relativity. Analogous to the complementary dualities previously discussed, there is a complementary duality of knower and known. The knower cannot be completely separated from the things known, nor can the thing known be completely expressed in terms which exclude reference to the knower.[40]

This means that any particular attempt to systematize knowledge delineates a foreground and a background: to know that which is in the foreground depends upon the knower making a finite selection from among a multitude of alternative concepts. The background is neglected, but this does not entail its permanent irrelevance. Moreover, under the Whiteheadian view, the analysis of what is known ultimately involves reference to necessity, that is, to abstract relations whose ground is the realm of eternal objects. But reference to this realm can bring into play factors of necessity which may have no direct bearing upon actual events. Whatever the merits of this type of answer, Whitehead here unequivocally responds to the perennially vexed question why it never seems possible to fit any field of knowledge with a clear-cut and immutable boundary which distinctly separates its foreground from its background. Boundaries of conceptiual systems seem always subject to displacement either by the incorporation of new concepts either as a result of logical inference or creative imagination, or by the alteration of the relative emphasis or meaning of the entities in the foreground.[41]

A simple illustration from mathematics can be found in the changing fortunes of the concept of number. Shifts in perspective are evident in the various terminologies employed at different stages in the growth of the concept. For example, the term 'irrational' as applied to number is now understood to mean 'non-rational,' where 'rational' has a purely technical connotation. There was a time, however, when the term signified that such numbers lay beyond the scope of the proper meaning of number.[42] Similarly, the notion of complex number, now regarded as the logical generalization of the concept of real number, carried with it, for a time, the stigma of 'imaginary.' Every branch of mathematics or science bears witness to significant alterations in meaning of fundamental concepts resulting from shifts in perspective. Perhaps it was partly due to the insecurity created by inevitable shifting perspectives that the desire for purely formal foundations came to be seen to be urgent. But whatever the reason, the ideal of mathematical expression has become essentially formalistic: rigorous logico-deductive, pruely abstract structures with uninterpreted symbolisms are believed by many to be the final bastions against the intrusions of unexpected and embarassing anomalies. Nevertheless, inasmuch as mathematical structures actually express truths about reality, the notion of perspective remains critically relevant. In brief, to take a purely formal approach to the meaning of 'meaning' is to evade the key issue altogether.

This applies as well to the fundamental concepts which underlie all rational discourse. Logic, in whatever form it is conceived, is an expression of connectedness. Formal logic is the codification of the rules by which concepts can be shown to have 'reasonable togetherness'; that is, stand in logical relationship. Here Whitehead draws our attention to the putatively simple and basic connective 'and.' As a word expressive of togetherness, it refers to a relationship from the standpoint of a particular perspective. But there is always room for ambiguity to enter in the repeated use of conjunctions. As Whitehead observes,

> In logical reasoning, which proceeds by the use of the variable, there are always two tacit presuppositions–one is that the definite symbols of composition can retain the same meaning as the reasoning elaborates novel compositions. The other presupposition is that this self-identity of each variable can be preserved when the variable is replaced by some definite instance.[43]

In short, the repetition of a conjunction in a logical argument presupposes that the initial perspective retains its relevance throughout all stages of the argument.

In the purely formal context of abstract systems the term 'consistency' simply means non-contradiction. But in the fullest sense of the word, which applies once the system is applied to the world, maximum consistency resides in the necessary connections which are exemplified between and within entities actually present in the process of the world. Hence any departure from the description of the world as it actually *is* opens the door to inconsistency. And if Whitehead is essentially correct in his metaphysical analysis of necessity, a systematic description of actual processes, as in an attempt to apply a theory of mathematics, very likely elicits factors of necessity which are impossible to distinguish completely and clearly from factors which may have no bearing upon actuality. Under this view, then, it would seem that an element of inconsistency is present from the outset in every mode of abstraction.

Again, there are possible ambiguities present in the simplest expression of non-conjunction. In this context, the inconsistency of a pair of propositions, which refer in some manner to actuality, may be localized inconsistency. As Whitehead puts it, such an inconsistency

> is the fact that the two states of things which constitute the respective meanings of a pair of propositions cannot exist together. It denies a possible conjuction between these meanings.[44]

But inconsistency in this sense may possibly be the result of limitations inherent in the narrowness of the chosen pespective, and may not be present in a broader perspective.

There are good reasons, therefore, for Whitehead to regard words expressive of conjunction as "the death-traps for accuracy of reasoning."[45] There is no resolving difficulties connected with the use of ambiguous words of conjunction, and with problems of consistency in general, without, in the final analysis, embarking upon a critical examination of perspectives. We are constantly led back to large and complex metaphysical problems, even in the most rigorously formal of contexts.

Indeed, the more rigidly rigorous the pursuit of logical consistency, the more obscure becomes its relevance to actuality. For a high degree of consistency is obtainable only in those areas of knowledge which, like mathematics, approach a high degree of abstraction. But here pure logical consistency is what Whitehead calls "an easy intellectual consistency,"[46] i.e., questions about its relevance to actuality, which is where the real difficulties lie, are simply ignored.

The full implication of the term 'perspective' enters when questions about the consistency of the specialized sciences are raised. Here, "inconsistency is relative to the abstraction involved."[47] The more specialized the science, the narrower is its perspective of the world and the more likely it is to suffer from inconsistency as it attempts to go beyond the boundaries implicit in its presuppositions.[48] Under the Whiteheadian view, then, it is reasonable to expect to find a kind of inverse relationship between consistency and scope in any system of natural knowledge. In other words, the more we demand of the former the less we are likely to attain in the latter. This point, in fact, provides a concise summary of what, under a Whiteheadian view, we may expect to attain in the way of exact knowledge from the natural sciences.

7. Conclusion

In this essay I have tried to delineate a skeleton of a philosophy of mathematics and the natural sciences which might serve as an adequate framework upon which to build a more solid and detailed anatomy. My study does not, therefore, lead to a single conclusion so much as it indicates a plurality of beginnings. For inasmuch as Whitehead's approach is on the right track, he shows clearly how complex and wide-ranging the problem of the applicability of mathematics really is. In my final remarks I will try to sketch in some of the more salient philosophical difficulties that lie ahead. These indicate once again that the crux of the problem of the applicability of mathematics centers more upon notions associated with perspective than upon those associated with logical structure.

I have argued that it is unlikely that an adequate and satisfactory philosophy of mathematics and the natural sciences will ever arise from the barren metaphysics of the purely formalistic point of view. In particular, the view that logic ultimately guarantees the security of our most trusted systems of knowlege becomes, under the Whiteheadian view, more than merely doubtful. For even in the purely abstract domain of formal systems it does not seem reasonable to hope to attain anything like secure foundations. This is because the construction and application of logical system inevitably elicits limited perspectives. Moreover, belief in the soundness of any system presupposes belief in the adequacy of the primitive concepts in its foundations. And even if it could, *per impossible,* be shown that these were fully adequate for the given purpose, we can never be certain that the deductive procedures may not lead us to inappropriate or even misleading conclusions. The point is aptly summarized by Whitehead thus:

> There can be no logical test for the possibility that deductive procedure, leading to the elaboration of compositions, may introduce into relevance considerations from which the primitive notions of the topic have been abstracted. The mutual conformity of the various perspectives can never be adequately determined.[49]

History on the whole vindicates Whitehead's concern with the notion of perspective. In fact, the discovery, early in this century, that logical paradoxes infect the very basis of modern mathematical discourse (i.e., the language of sets) implies more than that the Euclidean quest for absolutely secure foundations of logic and mathematics is a quixotic one. It illustrates well the dangers and perplexities that result when the importance of perspective is not taken into account. First Russell showed that ordinary logic, in conjuncition with the naive concept of class, gave rise to deep perplexities.[50] It gradually became evident that mere logical precision was no guarantee against the appearance of paradoxes. As Whitehead describes the response to Russell's discovery, it was found necessary to introduce the theory of types "to correct the omissions of the original premises."[51] The concept of class, which to the naive mind appears to be intuitively self-evident, cannot be trusted when viewed under certain perspectives. Or perhaps it is better to say: when viewed in such a way as to neglect the importance of perspective. For the theory of types, in so far as it is metaphysical in nature,[52] may perhaps be regarded as a formal means to treat the notion of relevant perspective. In any case, it seems that we cannot with complete confidence ever assure ourselves that we are safe from unpleasant surprises of the sort Russell happened upon, even with strict regulation of the premises of whatever set theory we happen to be considering. That this point is generally acknowledged perhaps implies a tacit awareness that choice of perspective may make all the difference.

But such speculations indicte only a small part of what lies ahead as ground in need of further exploration. For it would seem that there are few standard concepts currently employed in the philosophy of mathematics which deserve immunity from critical reassessment.

One of the most notable casualties in the ranks of notions which have traditionally occupied the forefront of the quest for certain and secure knowledge is that of proof. Its importance cannot now be taken for granted. Indeed, Whitehead suggests that the human demand for proof merely illustates how uncertain and tentative is human apprehension of the patterns of order within the world. This is because an act of understanding is the attempt to apprehend and coordinate a "succession of details of self-evidence."[53] Understanding is, for Whitehead, synonymous with the experience of self-evidence because for him the ground of order lies in the realm of eternal objects and this in all its connectedness is simply what it is; the grasp of any one of its patterns can only be the grasp of the self-evident. Thus proof is not essentially a procedure by which truth is established and understanding thereby guaranteed. Rather, it is a process whereby the self-evident is disclosed to finite minds. It is thus a "feeble second-rate procedure" which renders itself unnecessary inasmuch as it reveals self-evidence.[54]

This observation leads us into an area of enquiry which is just as pertinent to the philosophy of mathematics as it is to more humanistic disciplines. I mean the investigation of understanding itself. For the primary goal of any human cognitive enterprise, as Whitehead points out, is the penetration of the understanding into the multifarious connectedness of the world. We have seen that mathematics is but one, albeit an invaluable, aid to this penetration. Even here success is only fitful, and requires considerable effort. While the pervasive demand for proof is scarcely surprising, given the limited powers of the human mind, it is nonetheless only one stage of the route toward the unattainable ideal of complete understanding.

Much misunderstanding seems to be traceable to the common notion that proof is firmly tied to a bivalent theory of truth. But considerations of perspective indicate that the notions of truth and falsehood, despite their technical importance, are secondary when it comes to the investigation of understanding. For these notions in fact take their meaning in the end from considerations which inevitably elicit factors belonging to both the realms of necessity and of contingency. From a purely abstract point of view, the truth of a logico-mathematical proposition or theory depends upon the extent to which the proposition or theory actually expresses the patterned connectedness of the realm of pure potentialities. In other words, a proposition in pure mathematics may be true if it expresses some facet of the systematic internal relatedness within the realm of eternal objects. But this interpretation of mathematical truth, if rigidly applied, would result in a purely formal and so essentially meaningless notion of truth. This is because pure potentialities are totally devoid of definite and determinate character. Or, as Whitehead puts it, they are eternal objects in a state of disconnectedness.[55]

A propostion, then, in the profound Whiteheadian sense, is a complex entity that only partially reflects the necessity of the realm of eternal objects. On this view, its relations to other propositions cannot be analyzed completely in a purely logical manner. On the other hand, should it be the case that a proposition refers to actuality, it is still wrong, says Whitehead, to insist that it be regarded unequivocally as either true or false. This dichotomy overlooks the fact that a judgement may often need to be suspended. For every proposition implicitly evokes a particular perspective; however, such a thing, as we have seen, cannot be precisely determined. In general,

> every proposition refers to a universe exhibiting some general systematic metaphysical character. . . . A proposition can embody partial truth because it only demands a certain type of systematic environment, which is presupposed in its meaning. It does not refer to the universe in all its detail.[56]

Thus a proposition, as an incomplete abstraction from actual events, is a hybrid, a kind of bridge between the necessary and the contingent. It therefore must be regarded as more in the nature of a theory than as a factual statement capable of being classified as either true or false.[57] Whitehead's views are thus fully in accord with one of the central tenets of a thoroughgoing holism: propositions are essentially theories about reality. The lesson is as replete with interest as it is disturbing for the orthodox view. For if that most common and ubiquitous of philosophical conceptual tools, the proposition, is so fraught with profound difficulties, then it seems highly likely that most of the notions which we now take so much for granted are in need of a radical conceptual overhaul.

At any rate, there are good reasons to suppose that the field of enquiry in the philosophy of mathematics and the natural sciences is very broad indeed. This discipline has traditionally held itself aloof from controversial topics of the sort mentioned above. But now that the basis of the special status of mathematics among cognitive systems has dissolved, the philosophy of mathematics can no longer afford to look the other way. For like all other philosophies, it is ultimately concerned with the attempt to utter sentences that contain a modicum of truth. But if sentences, mathematical or otherwise, are to be meaningful, in any ordinary sense of the word, they must sooner or later appeal to notions that provide the term 'truth' itself with meaning.

The general conclusion is that such notions owe their intelligibility primarily to the ontological commitments that they represent. In this essay I have attempted to argue that the time is once again ripe for the making of such commitments. Whitehead's metaphysics may or may not be the most plausible answer to the vexed question of what sort of commitment is actually best suited to our current state of knowledge of the world, especially of our scientific knowledge. He would be the first to acknowledge the likelihood of its eventual replacement by a better theory. But come what may, Whitehead's work will stand as an extremely rare, profound, and valuable lesson in how to take the world and science seriously enough to be able to do justice to much-neglected and pressing problems not only in the philosophy of mathematics and the natural sciences but in other areas as well. The Whiteheadian approach also brings out clearly the fact that the philosophy of mathematics stands on just as firm, or infirm, a ground as does any other specialized philosophy. Hence the most general conclusion to which this whole discussion points is that to the extent that the last point is overlooked, to that extent the philosophy of mathematics is in danger of fading into complete irrelevance.

NOTES

Chapter One. Introduction

1. Eugene P. Wigner, "The Unreasonable Effectiveness of Mathematics in the Natural Sciences," *Communications on Pure and Applied Mathematics,* Vol. XIII, 1960, pp. 1-14.

2. Burtt's remarks in this context are as pertinent as ever. He observes that the early philosophers of science initiated a "metaphysical barbarism of a few centuries," wherein the practical successes of modern science were believed to justify the neglect of metaphysics. "Metaphysics they tended more and more to avoid, so far as they could avoid it; so far as not it became an instrument for their further mathematical conquest of the world." See E. A. Burtt, *The Metaphysical Foundations of Modern Physical Science* (New York: Anchor Books, 1954), pp. 305-6.

3. An outstanding exception to the tendency to adopt one or the other of these two exteme positions is Hermann Weyl. In his classic works, especially in the book *The Philosophy of Mathematics and the Natural Sciences* (Princeton: Princeton University Press, 1949), Weyl discusses a wide range of difficulties connected with our large question. He draws upon a deep familiarity with the technical aspects of recent scientific advances and illustrates their problematic nature with copious references to the metaphysical reflections of great thinkers of the past. His own reflections point him towards the philosophical stance of "epistemological idealism," whose fundamental tenet is that it is unintelligible to hold that "quality disjoint from consciousness can be attributed as a property as such to a thing as such." (P. 111) However, this view does not lead inexorably to the truth of intuitionism. See Section 3, note 12.

4. W. B. Yeats, *Collected Poems,* "Blood and the Moon."

5. I shall expand a little further on this designation in Section 1 of Chapter 4.

6. L. Susan Stebbing, *Philosophy and the Physicists* (London: Methuen, 1937), p. ix.

7. *Op. cit.,* pp. 229-30. Burtt describes Newton as exemplifying all three main types of metaphysical notions actually held by those thinkers who decry metaphysics: 1) He uncritically takes over many of the ideas of his age on ultimate questions, 2) he tends to make a metaphysics out of his method, and 3) he cannot help playing carelessly and unsystematically with metaphysical notions insofar as these are thrust upon him by his positivistic investigations.

8. ESP, p. 95.

9. This assumes that science is being taken seriously enough to give the concepts of matter and of evolution their proper due. I will discuss this point further in Chapter 4.

10. For an excellent discussion of the historical background of the concepts of matter and the physical see Ivor Leclerc, *The Nature of Physical Existence* (London: George Allen and Unwin, 1972).

11. It is worth noting that Kant does not completely downgrade the importance of the notion of matter: for him it figures among the necessary

conditions of experience. Indeed, he sides with Leibniz against Descartes in maintaining a "dynamic" view of matter. See John E. Smith, "Kant's Doctrine of Matter," in Ernan McMullin, *The Concept of Matter in Modern Philosophy* (Notre Dame: University of Notre Dame Press, 1978), pp. 141–152. The trouble is, as Smith observes, "there is a something-less-than-perfect integration" in Kant's epistemological and cosmological views on matter; the "long arm of epistemology" ultimately prevails. His pre-critical thinking, in fact, is much more relevant to a Whiteheadian dynamic view of matter. For Kant insists upon a reciprocity between activity and passivity. Under the view taken in this essay, these concepts are prime examples of what I shall call (in the next section) complementary concepts. For a description of Kant's views on this particular reciprocity, see Leclerc, *op. cit.,* Chapter 22.

12. When viewed in this light, the putative clarity and claim to priority of one of Kants's basic "forms of intuition," the pure intuition of time, fades into obscurity. Hence one of the fundamental planks in the programme of intuitionism, which rests upon the premise of the intuitive clarity of the concept of time, has a much more slippery character than Brouwer, for example, is prepared to admit. It requires that many pertinent questions be entirely ignored and so can never provide a sturdy enough platform upon which to try to lay the foundations for the whole of mathematical knowledge.

13. On the other hand, it would be a complete mistake to hold that the generic notion of experience can be explained in terms completely free from reference to human experience. For if it is allowed that analogy plays a central role in understanding, an attempt to reach a "purified" conception of experience of this sort would issue in no conception at all. The centrality of analogy in metaphysical thinking is a topic which I explore in Chapter 4.

14. For an attempt to show how certain Whiteheadian conceptions of experience and value accord well with aspects of purely physical causal relationships in the context of modern physics, see J. M. Burgers, *Experience and Conceptual Activity* (Cambridge, Mass.: M.I.T. Press, 1965).

15. For this reason, it seems worthwhile to hold on to the timeworn term 'matter' despite its deeply ingrained connotation of valueless inert 'stuff.' In any case, the term is sufficiently vague and general to be able to accommodate the necessary (if Whitehead is essentially correct) radical conceptual turn-around.

16. PR, p. 4.

17. The phrase 'trancendental deduction' may be generally applied to any attempt to establish foundations for objectively valid knowledge by showing that not only do our metaphysical categories describe the world as it seems to us but also that they described the world in the only way it could possibly be for us. The search for such an argument is central to Kant's thought. R. Scruton correctly remarks that, "if valid, the transcendhead is saying, in effect, that Kant's failure is inevitable since this notion is akin to the notion of an absolute proof, which is an impossible ideal.

18. For instance, Whitehead refers to the "unbridled" rationalism of the middle ages which, he says, seeks to establish truth by predominantly metaphysical analysis. On the other hand, he decries the "unimaginative" empiricism of Aristotle, who seeks, for example, for an explanation of motion in what sustains motion. See SMW, p. 47. The closest modern equivalent of the rationalism of the middle ages is perhaps the "mathematical materialism" of the post-Galilean tradition. I shall say more about this in Chapter 4.

19. For a detailed critique of the notion that the ideal form of knowledge, and particularly of scientific knowledge, is the deductive system, see Rom Harre, "The Mythology of Deductivism," in *The Principles of Scientific Thinking* (Chicago: University of Chicago Press, 1970).

20. In a word, Hume's famous apophthegm still rules: Philosophical writing that does not contain "any abstract reasoning concerning quantity or number," or "experimental reasoning concerning matter of fact and existence," should, he notoriously says, be committed to the flames, "for it can contain nothing but sophistry and confusion."

21. Quoted by W. E. Hocking, "Whitehead On Mind and Nature," in P. A. Schilpp, *The Philosophy of Alfred North Whitehead* (New York: Tudor, 1951), p. 391.

22. It is on just this vital point that Kant is open to severely damaging criticism. He cannot explain his utter confidence in the synthetic apriority of the truths of Euclidean geometry. Cf. Jonathan Bennett, *Kant's Analytic* (Cambridge: University Press, 1966). As Bennett rightly observes, even if the world must obey a geometry, there are no grounds for insisting that it do so exactly and always (p. 29).

23. *Op. cit.,* p. 25.

24. That this is the primary source of Kant's failure to reconcile the rational and the empirical is perhaps evident in Kant's own account. For, as Scruton notes, "This synthesis is somewhat confusingly described by Kant: sometimes it seems to be a 'process' whereby experience is generated, at other times a kind of 'structure' which experience contains." *Ibid.*

25. For a good short account of Whitehead's Leibnizian rationalism see Charles Hartshorne, "Whitehead and Contemporary Philosophy," in Ivor Leclerc, *The Relevance of Whitehead* (London: Geo. Allen and Unwin, 1961), pp. 21–43.

26. Ian Hacking, *Why Does Language Matter to Philosophy?* (Cambridge: Cambridge University Press, 1975), p. 33.

27. Quoted by W. E. Hocking, *op. cit.,* p. 385. For a short and valuable account of Whitehead's theory of perception, see Hartshorne, *op. cit.*

28. PNK, p. 15.

29. While not being describable as a naive realist, Whitehead has sympathy for the motivating idea of naive realism. In referring to what he calls the indefensible half-way house of Russell's more sophisticated realism, he

observes approvingly that "The naive realist conceives mentality as adventuring amid realities, not amid dreams." (Quoted by Hocking, *ibid.*)

Chapter Two. Whitehead on Mathematics and Philosophy

1. SMW, p. 19.

2. IM, p. 2. This work, intended as an exposition for the student and layman of some fundamental mathematical concepts, contains many valuabale philosophical insights. It was first published in 1911, at the time of the completion of the writing of *Principia Mathematica*. Thus the term 'mathematics' should be understood to include logic as well. I shall discuss Whitehead's position on logicism in the next section.

3. See Imre Lakatos, "Infinite Regress and Foundations of Mathematics," *The Aristotelian Society,* Supplementary vol. no. 36 (1962), pp. 155–184. Lakatos defines the attempt to establish foundations for mathematics as the attempt to obtain for mathematics a secure place in knowledge despite the strictures of skepticism.

4. Such premises, says Lakatos, are to be established in the Euclidean programme by the "natural light of Reason, specifically by arithmetical, geometrical, moral, etc. intuition." *Ibid.,* p. 159.

5. *Ibid.* In Lakatos' usage, the term 'empiricist' is meant to cover a broad range of entities and propositions which, provided only that they occupy the bottom level of the deductive system, can be drawn from factual, arithmetical or metaphysical contexts. Lakatos, in fact, follows Popper in the version of empiricism which holds that there are no perfectly well-known empirical terms at the primitive level; all terms are theoretical and an empiricist theory is thus entirely conjectural.

6. *Ibid.,* p. 158.

7. PR, p. 8.

8. As for Russell, according to Lakatos he was forced to retreat from his early Euclideanism into Inductivism, thereby choosing "confusion rather than facing and accepting that what was interesting in mathematics is conjectural." See *ibid.,* pp. 167–179.

9. See L. E. J. Brouwer, "Intuitionism and Formalism," in Paul Benacerraf and Hilary Putnam, *Philosophy of Mathematics* (New Jersey: Prentice Hall, 1964), p. 67.

10. For a purely constructivist view of this problem, see Errett Bishop, "The Crisis in Contemporary Mathematics," *Historia Mathematica,* vol. 2, 1975, p. 514. He remarks that "the only reason mathematics is applicable is because of its inherent constructive content." The explanation of the empirical significance of mathematics derives, under this view, from the assumption that statements about mathematical constructions are empirical statements involving the least possible risk of error. Hence the practical efficacy, as well as the security, of formal systems rests ultimately upon the dubious self-evidence of basal

intuitions and the debatable propriety of constructive methods. What has been completely overlooked is the imaginative aspect of mathematical thinking: it as if this were an epiphenomenon, not to say a kind of aberration. I will return to this aspect of the problem a little later.

11. N. R. Hanson, *Patterns of Discovery* (Cambridge: Cambridge University Press, 1965). Hanson cites Kepler's work on the orbit of the planet Mars as a prime example of the retroductive method. He also cites the work of Galileo, Newton, Einstein and Planck in this context.

12. As Hanson puts it, "the physicist often seeks not a general description of what he observes, but a general pattern of phenomena within which what he observes will appear intelligible." *Ibid.,* p. 109.

13. Hanson observes that research in modern theoretical physics "might be described as observation statements in search of a premise." *Op. cit.,* p. 108.

14. Cf. Sir Karl Popper, who succinctly remarks that scientific explanation "is the reduction of the known to the unknown." See *Conjectures and Refutations* (New York: Basic Books, 1963), p. 63.

15. The unignorable factor of human ingenuity in mathematical creation should give us notice that the term 'interesting' is not a gratuitous addition to Whitehead's description: indeed, it is a major, but somewhat hidden, factor behind the application of the retroductive method in any of its instances.

16. M, p. 881.

17. PM, p. v.

18. MT, p. 105.

19. PM, p. v.

20. PM, p. vi.

21. M, p. 880.

22. See Bertrand Russell, *The Principles of Mathematics* (London: Allen and Unwin, 1907), pp. 3–4, in which the explicit aim is "to arrive at certainty in regard to. . . the questions [of] the nature of number, of infinity, of space, time and motion, and of mathematical inference itself."

23. *Ibid.*

24. A vivid illustration of their fundamentally different outlooks is given by Russell in *Portraits from Memory* (London: Allen and Unwin, 1956), p. 41. Russell reports Whitehead as saying to him: "You think the world is what it looks like in fine weather at noonday; I think it is what it seems like in the early morning when one wakes from a deep sleep."

25. M, p. 881.

26. Hence Whitehead makes a purely logical attempt to overcome the shortcomings of *Principia Mathematica* (that is, to solve the logicist's problem of basing arithmetic on logical constructions "abstracted from the metaphysical notion of types, and from the particularities of history"): see Alfred North Whitehead, "Indication, Classes, Numbers, Validation," in ESP, pp. 313–331. Here he puts forward the notion of 'validation-value' as more important than the traditional notion of 'truth-value,' in keeping with his overall conviction

that the structural aspects of logic (and mathematics) are more fundamental than the truth-transmission aspects.

27. Whitehead's answer to the dilemma is his entire theory of organism wherein the world (as "one") is conceived as a self-differentiating entity; it gives rise to a plurality of distinct but interrelated actual entities (the "many"). See Chapter 3, section 7 for a short description of Whitehead's theory of becoming.

28. M, p. 882.

29. UA, p. vi.

30. UA, p. vii (my emphases).

31. Conventionalism has recently been much talked about in the philosophy of mathematics. This seems to reflect the influence of analytic philosophy. Indeed, as Benacerraf and Putnam observe, "so much of the literature of analytic philosophy has been devoted to discussions *pro* and *con* conventionalism that very little would be left of any important bearing on the philosophy of mathematics if it should turn out that conventionalism is fundamentally and completely wrong." Paul Benacerraf and Hilary Putnam (eds.), *Philosophy of Mathematics* (New Jersey: Prentice-Hall, 1964), p. 19. Yet it seems very likely that there is a large measure of truth in the assertion that statements of pure mathematics are "true by convention" or "true by the rules of the language." And it is also highly probable that there is a strong element of conventionalism in what physics or philosophy decides is worthy of attention. The latter may mean nothing more than that, in Whitehead's words, "Nature is patient of interpretation in terms of Laws which happen to interest us." AI, p. 136. As for the role played by convention in the making of mathematics, he might add that what captures our interest never comes in flashes of absolutely clear insight, uncluttered by extraneous or arbitrary factors.

32. In claiming that mathematics is a collection of tautologies, which may serve to guide us in our empirical search for knowledge, A. J. Ayer describes the implications of this view as follows: "A being whose intellect was infinitely powerful would take no interest in logic and mathematics. For he would be able to see at a glance everything that his definitions implied, and, accordingly, could never learn anything from logical inference which he was not fully conscious of already." See the article "The A Priori," in Benacerraf and Putnam, *op. cit.,* p. 300. (This article is reprinted from *Language, Truth and Logic.*) But this omniscient being has presumably learned that it is possible to describe the world in terms of its mathematical and logical characteristics, and it would be question begging of a high order to say that he would need to use *only* mathematical terms to do this. So the question of the relation between the mathematical and the nonmathematical remains unresolved.

33. UA, pp. vi-vii. See MT, *passim,* for a general exploration of some of the epistemological implications of this notion.

34. M, p. 881.

35. *Ibid.*

36. IM, p. 39.

37. IM, p. 22.

38. Noting that it was once a widespread belief that the manipulation of symbols could lead, in some mysterious way, to valid proofs of propositions, Whitehead remarks, "Nothing can be more mistaken. A symbol which has not been properly defined is not a symbol at all. It is merely a blot of ink on paper which has an easily recognized shape. Nothing can be proved by a succession of blots, except the existence of a bad pen and a careless writer." IM, p. 64.

39. IM, p. 40.

40. ESP, p. 107. Algebra, he adds, evolved as "the study of patterns involved in the various ways of assembling numbers." ESP, p. 108.

41. UA, p. v. For a good survey of this early work, see Victor Lowe, *Understanding Whitehead* (Baltimore: Johns Hopkins Press, 1962 and 1966), chapters 6 and 7. The algebras which Whitehead has in mind are Hamilton's quarternions, Grassmann's calculus of extension, and Boole's symbolic logic.

42. *Ibid.*

43. Cf. C. S. Pierce, who usefully distinguishes between mathematics and philosophy by observing that in the former the reasoning is "frightfully intricate," but based upon self-evident premises; while in the latter the reasoning is simple, but based upon abstruse conceptions. In other words, the types of reasoning involved seem to be of quite different kinds. The explanation of mathematical reasoning must, says Pierce, take account not only of the logical aspects but all those other aspects that involve "the construction of a diagram, the mental experimentation, and the surprising novelty of many deductive discoveries." See "The Nature of Mathematics," in Justus Buchler (ed.), *Philosophical Writings of Peirce* (New York: Dover Pub. Inc., 1955).

44. IM, p. 6.

45. IM, p. 4. Mathematics, says Whitehead, expresses not only "what is general in what is particular" but also "what is permanent in what is transitory." See also SMW, p. 34: "mathematics is the science of the most complete abstractions to which the human mind can attain."

46. Observing that the addition of vectors in the plane is analogous to the formal definition of addition of complex numbers, Whitehead says: "We have been guided merely by the most abstract of pure mathematical considerations; and yet at the end of them we have been led back to the most fundamental of all the laws of nature, laws which have to be in the mind of every engineer as he designs an engine and of every naval architect as he calculates the stability of a ship. It is no paradox to say that in our most theoretical moods we may be nearest to our most practical applications.' IM, p. 71.

47. PR, p. 5.

48. PR, p. 10.

49. PR, p. 8.

50. PR, p. 42.

51. Whitehead misleads his readers somewhat in this respect, for he speaks rather confidently at times of certain colours and geometrical relationships as examples of eternal objects. See, for example, SMW, p. 166.

52. See, for example, MT, p. 92: "This discussion is a belated reminder to Plato that his eternal mathematical forms are essentially referent to process."

53. As an example of a proposition generally, but mistakenly, regarded as a tautology, Whitehead cites the phrase 'twice-three is six.' Rather than being a tautology, the phrase refers to "a process and its issue," i.e., to a form of process in which two triplets combine in a way which conforms to the (usually only tacitly acknowledged) "principle of sustenance of character." Furthermore, the issue of the process is a group with the arithmetical character of 'six' only if the above-mentioned principle (that there is no loss of individuation) does not fail (MT, pp. 88–95). This principle applies even to statements like 'six equals six,' for "the very notion of number refers to the process from the individual units to the compound group." MT, p. 93. Nevertheless, this principle is not, for Whitehead, a necessary characteristic of process. Such characteristics of process which can be regarded as absolutely necessary are those which constitute the ultimate metaphysical categories. As my earlier discussion indicates, there is no good reason to think that mathematical abstractions belong to these categories. See also Robert Palter, "The Place of Mathematics in Whitehead's Philosophy," *Journal of Philosophy*, vol. 58, 1961, pp. 565–76, for another discussion of this point.

54. For a discussion of Platonism and intuitionism in which the deter- minateness of the truth or falsity of individual statements is held to be central to the whole question of the meaning of mathematical propositions, see Michael Dummett, *Elements of Intuitionism* (Oxford: Clarendon Press, 1977).

55. Dummett, for instance, refers to the Platonist's "realistic view of mathematical reality," as opposed to the intuitionist's view in which "mathematical reality is . . . not something existing independently of ourselves [but instead is] simply the product of our own thought." See *ibid.*, pp. 381–2.

56. Cf. Robert Palter, "The Place of Mathematics in Whitehead's Philoso- phy." Palter identifies three senses of 'mathematics' in Whitehead's philosophy: 1) mathematics as 'logic,' concerned with the truths of pure abstraction; 2) mathematics as 'natural knowledge,' concerned with the application of mathematics to natural processes; and 3) mathematics as 'cosmology,' concerned with the metaphysical truth of propositions. An arithmetical proposition is true in the latter sense only if it expresses truths about the relations of ultimate metaphysical entities.

Chapter Three. Zeno's Paradoxes: Mathematical and Metaphysical Responses

1. *IS, p. 215.*
2. See "The Problem of Infinity Considered Historically," in Wesley C. Salmon, ed., *Zeno's Paradoxes* (Indianapolis and New York: Bobbs-Merrill Co., 1970), pp. 45-58.
3. The notion that Zeno was intent upon discrediting the particular doctrine of Pythagoreanism is due to Paul Tannery. I shall instead adopt the view that Zeno was a faithful disciple of Parmenides and that Zeno's arguments were directed against *all* competing philosophies.
4. Cf. G. E. L. Owen, "Zeno and the Mathematicians," in Salmon, *op. cit.*, pp. 139-163, who stresses the Eleatic essence of Zeno's arguments: "Zeno's major question . . . is: if you say there are many things in existence how do you distinguish your individuals?" (p. 141).
5. See, for example, Carl Boyer, *The History of the Calculus and its Conceptual Development* (New York: Dover, 1959), pp. 24-25. He states that "the four [Zenonian] paradoxes are, of course, easily answered in terms of the concepts of the differential calculus." Since the latter is based upon the logically valid theory of infinite classes, the paradoxes present no logical difficulty but rather "the difficulties . . . are those of conceiving intuitively the nature of the continuum and of infinite aggregates."
6. The paradox of the Arrow introduces a further complication in that it depends for its intelligibility upon an understanding of material substance and its properties, and, in particular, upon its relation to space and time. Thus a major source of dissatisfaction with standard formulations of this paradox lies in the questionable assumption that the fundamental relation between material body and space-time is analogous to that between object and container.
7. See Owen, *op. cit.*, who suggests that the concept of a line segment as a locus of points was Newton's response to the problematic conception of a line segment as an aggregate of parts rather than a direct response to Zeno's arguments, as some writers have suggested. Hence it is ultimately a reaction to the Greek discovery of incommensurables, where most of our present-day troubles with numbers begin.
8. See the article "Logical Paradoxes" in *Essays in the Philosophy of Mathematics* (Leicester: Leicester University Press, 1965), pp. 12-22.
9. It is interesting, and somewhat ironical, that the achievement of respectability, which the concept of the actual infinite owes to Cantor, had for him much more than formal significance in that it contributed to the successful "arithmetization" of analysis. He regarded his work on the consistent formulation of hierarchies of transfinite cardinal and ordinal numbers as a contribution to metaphysics, and as an important step toward understanding God and the world. See Herbert Meschkowski, *Probleme des Unendlichen,*

Werk und Leben Georg Cantors (Braunschweig: Friedr. Vieweg Sohn, 1967). In fact, among the modern supporters of the exact-correspondence hypothesis, the metaphysical aspects have merely been ignored.

10. The system of real numbers includes not only the rational numbers (i. e., fractions, whose infinite multiplicity is accessible to the intuition as the ideal limits of endless repetitions of sub-divisions of a finite line segment), but even greater multiplicities of numbers which, as the Pythagoreans first discovered, cannot be represented as ratios of integers. Among these are the transcendental numbers which are more numerous, according to Cantor's theory, than the denumerable, but actually infinite, rational numbers. To the modern mind, their existence, not to mention their uncountable multiplicity, should perhaps be as astonishing and upsetting as the discovery of incommensurables was to the Pythagoreans.

11. For an interesting exploration of this aspect of Zenonian paradoxes, see Jose A. Benardete, *Infinity; An Essay in Metaphysics* (Oxford: Clarendon Press, 1964). He appositely observes that "the beauty of the 'bisection' paradox [is that] it points up in a peculiarly trenchant form the conceptual gap between mathematics and reality." P. 26.

12. Salmon, p. 32.

13. Adolf Gruenbaum, *Modern Science and Zeno's Paradoxes* (Middletown, Conn.: Wesleyan University Press, 1967), p. 119. See also Adolf Gruenbaum, "The Resolution of Zeno's Metrical Paradox of Extension for the Mathematical Continua of Space and Time," Chapter 6 of *Philosophical Problems of Space and Time,* Boston Studies in the Philosophy of Science, vol. 12, 2nd edn. (Dordrecht-Holland: D. Reidel, 1973). A verson of this article appears as "Zeno's Metrical Paradox of Extension," in Salmon, pp. 176–99 (reprinted from *Modern Science and Zeno's Paradoxes,* chapter 3).

14. *Modern Science and Zeno's Paradoxes,* p. 116.

15. *Ibid.,* p. 117.

16. *Ibid.,* p. 133.

17. *Ibid.*

18. *Ibid.,* pp. 130–31.

19. In fact, Gruenbaum's use of the adjective 'customary' is essential to his point. Without it, one would require a further assumption to the effect that the standard Cantorian formulation of measure theory is the only feasible basis upon which to model a rival denumerable measure theory. The question of whether or not it is appropriate to turn to an alternative conception involving a countable structure to space-time will be taken up later.

20. *Ibid.,* p. 135.

21. Adolf Gruenbaum, "Modern Science and Refutation of the Paradoxes of Zeno," *The Scientific Monthly,* November, 1955, pp. 234–9. See p. 238.

22. See also *Modern Science and Zeno's Paradoxes,* pp. 109–111.

23. In this context, it should be borne in mind that the mathematical theory of the calculus, which is intimately connected in its development with the

theory of real numbers, and which has been so useful in physics, can be described as a device for treating average approximations efficiently and economically by means of the notion of ideal limits of approximations.

24. Gruenbaum acknowledges this circularity only in the case of Zeno's problem of motion (e.g., the Dichotomy and the Achilles) where he sees the force of Zeno's arguments as directed not against the consistency of the mathematical theory of motion but against the applicability of the mathematical theory of continuity to time. However, Gruenbaum's defence of the postulate of continuous (dense) time is based upon an assumption of the continuity of space: "In the context of the Dichotomy and the Achilles . . . the mathematical considerations applied to a finite *space* interval . . . can be *legitimately* carried over to a finite time interval. . . ." (*Ibid.,* p. 63) It would seem, then, that the circularity would carry over as well.

25. One may go so far as to say that the mathematical approach begins with a fallacy, which Whitehead has called the Fallacy of Misplaced Concreteness. This is the assumption that abstract entities, which are incorporated into a system under the guiding principle of internal consistency, have concrete existence.

26. "The Zenonians either explicitly or tacitly adduced Physical Grounds for *demanding* specified kinds of additivity for length (and duration) in stated types of physical manifolds of space and time." Adolf Gruenbaum, *Philosophical Problems of Space and Time,* p. 811. (emphasis in original)

27. The remark pertains to crystals, in which the duality is "the general contrast between fixed internal constitution and variable conditions." *Op. cit.,* p. 291.

28. *Op. cit.,* p. 43. The other two attempts to resolve the continuum problem center respectively upon the concept of the infinitesimal and upon the modern Cantorean set-theoretic concept of the actual infinite.

29. *Ibid.* Zeno's paradox of the stadium, if it is interpreted as being predicated upon the discreteness of space and time, is related to this objection.

30. *Ibid.,* p. 41.

31. *Ibid.* (The passage is from a letter to Remond, *Philosophische Schriften,* III, p. 622.)

32. Cf. Ivor Leclerc, "Kant's Second Antinomy, Leibniz, and Whitehead," *Review of Metaphysics, 20,* 1966, pp. 24–41, who claims that after Leibniz, and in the context of twentieth century advances in physical science, Whitehead has so far had "the most penetrating insight" into the fundamental problem of the discrete versus the continuous, and into other related dualities which emerge in the discussion of this problem.

33. Indeed, he sees the root of the contradictions in set theory in that feature of the mathematizing method which treats "a field of constructive possibilities as a closed aggregate of objects existing in themselves." *Op. cit.,* p. 50.

34. Weyl himself supports this view when he points out, with reference to mensuration, that complete accuracy is a limiting idea. He also makes the

insightful observation, which seems somewhat at odds with the programme of intuitionism, that "Even so one can understand the necessity and expediency of exact mathematics: the exact theory provides the framework for approximate verifications." *Ibid.,* p. 143.

35. *Modern Science and Zeno's Paradoxes,* p. 111.

36. For a discussion of this point see, for example, the article by C. W. Kilmister, "Beyond What?" in *Quantum Theory and Beyond,* pp. 117-27. He advocates a search for a combinatorial basis of quantum mechanics, and suggests that the hypnotic power of the real number system is a hindrance to progress in this area.

37. PR, p. 35.

38. *Ibid.*

39. PR, pp. 35-36.

40. PR, p. 68.

41. PR, p. 35.

42. PR, p. 68.

43. PR, p. 69.

44. Whitehead appears to have thrown many of his critics off the track of his own thought with his observation that an "inadequate mathematical knowledge" hinders William James' treatment of Zeno. (PR, p. 68) A correct description of Whitehead's approach to Zeno's problems is not that of Gruenbaum: he criticizes Whitehead according to the interpretation that Whitehead's interest, together with James,' is to deny "the appropriateness of the formal mathematics of linear continuity to time." (*Op. cit.,* p. 45) While it may be a consequence of Whitehead's views that it is inappropriate to carry over to the physical world all the characteristics of the formal system, this is in fact not his main intention. Whitehead's response to Zeno is essentially at the philosophical level: the mathematical argument seems more of a (misleading) afterthought.

45. PR, p. 73. Here we have the means to come to terms with Aristotle's observation, which Weyl and the intuitionists endorse, "That which moves does not move by counting." (Weyl, *op. cit.,* p. 54)

46. PR, p. 68.

47. PR, p. 69.

48. *Ibid.*

49. For a discussion of the difficult problem of the relation between form and actuality, see Ivor Leclerc, "Form and Actuality," in Ivor Leclerc (ed.), *The Relevance of Whitehead,* pp. 169-189.

50. Thus Whitehead observes, "So long as the atomic character of actual entities is unrecognized, the application of Zeno's method of argument makes it difficult to understand the notion of continuous transmission which reigns in physical science." PR, p. 307.

51. Cf. V. C. Chappell, "Whitehead's Theory of Becoming," in George L. Kline, ed., *Alfred North Whitehead, Essays On His Phisosophy* (Englewood

Cliffs, N.J.: Prentice-Hall, Inc., 1963). After criticizing Whitehead's use of an argument of Zeno, Chappell points out, correctly I think, that such arguments have only a minor role to play in his thought.

52. See note 42.

53. Whitehead misleads us somewhat with his reference to James' remark that experience is atomistic. He quotes James as saying that our "acquaintance with reality grows literally by buds or drops of perception" which "come totally or not at all." (PR, p. 68) Be this as it may, psychological considerations centered upon the characteristics of human perception are of little help in clarifying Zeno's problems. The difficulty lies in the inadequacy or the incoherence or the obscurity of the conceptual apparatus which we emply to describe and explain the apparently undeniable fact that the world is the scene of events which display the characteristics of both atomicity and continuity.

54. PR, p. 284.

55. PR, p. 285. In the mental pole, there is, says Whitehead, "always a contingency left open for immediate decision." PR, p. 284. This "conceptual aim" cannot be divided. We thus find here the justification for calling an actual entity a "quantum in solido." See p. 283.

56. As Whitehead puts it, "The actual entity is the product of the interplay of physical pole with mental pole. In this way potentiality passes into actuality, and extensive relations mould qualitative content and objectifications of other particulars into a coherent finite experience." PR, p. 308.

57. See PR, p. 284. "The divisions of the [extensive] region [of the actual entity] are not divisions which are; they are divisions which might be."

58. PR, p. 284.

59. PR, p. 285.

60. A certain character of 'openness' can be ascribed to the lower end of the hierarchy of organisms. This character is in accord with current research in elementary particle physics where the more fundamental the particle is the harder it is to detect, i.e. the more elusive it is in terms of its distinguishing characteristics.

Chapter Four. On Philosophizing Adequately about Science, Mathematics, and Reality

1. In "Saggiatore" (Opere, p. 232). Quoted by H. Weyl, op. cit., p. 112.

2. See "The Scope and Language of Science," in The Ways of Paradox, (Cambridge, Mass.: Harvard University Press, 1979 revised edn.), p. 232.

3. Ibid., p. 237.

4. "There is nothing," says Quine, "we can be more confident of than external things–some of them anyway–other people, sticks, stones." Theories and Things (Cambrdige, Mass.: Harvard University Press, 1981), p. 2.

5. SMW, p. 73.

6. I hesitate to call Quine himself a materialist, for despite his profession of

belief in "other people, sticks, stones," his ontological commitment to matter itself is highly equivocal. On the other hand, Quine calls himself a "robust realist," a description which, given his predilection for a logical point of view, is highly debatable.

7. As reported by W. E. Hocking, "Whitehead as I Knew Him," in Kline, pp. 7–17.

8. Thus R. Harre justly observes that "nowhere is the scholasticism of the deductivist approach to] the philosophy of science more clearly evident than in the treatment of theoretical terms." With reference to the 'famous' problem (as expressed by C. G. Hempel): "The use of theoretical terms in science gives rise to a perplexing problem: why should science resort to the assumption of hypothetical entities when it is interested in establishing predictive and explanatory correlations among observables," Harre rightly responds that "science is certainly not interested in establishing *only* predictive and explanatory correlations among observables." See *The Principles of Scientific Thinking*, p. 21. In fact, in reporting these correlations, scientists cannot avoid making tacit estimations of their meaningfulness, by appealing to implicit metaphysical presuppositions. These inevitably creep in, if only through assertions that some correlations are more right than others, and that getting it right is what makes the doing of science more significant than the playing of a mere game.

9. The case of Hobbes is interesting in this respect. As Anthony Quinton points out, it is not for his attempts to embed his entire thought in a consistent mechanical materialism that Hobbes is remembered. Rather his social and political theories are usually studied in isolation from his metaphysics, despite the fact that Hobbes insisted that the latter were integral to his materialistic monism. See Anthony Quinton, "Hobbes," in *Thoughts and Thinkers* (London: Duckworth, 1982).

10. For a discussion of this point with reference to the mind-body problem, see Marx W. Wartofsky, "Toward a Critical Materialism," in *Models* (Dordrecht: D. Reidel Pub. Co., 1979).

11. That science is a refinement of common sense is a view which is central to W. V. Quine's position. See, for instance, *Ways of Paradox*, pp. 233 ff.

12. As A. Quinton points out, "The critics of idealism . . . have remained, from Hume to Russell and beyond, unshakeably loyal to fundamental idealists presuppositions, in particular to the principle that all we directly and certainly know is the contents of our own minds." *Op. cit.,* p. 135.

13. In addition to Stebbing's work, which I have already cited, an important general critique of the idealist attempt to interpret scientific thought is given by Dorothy Emmet, in *The Nature of Metaphysical Thinking* (New York: St. Martin's Press, 1966). The failure of the strict idealist approach is closely bound up with an uncritical predilection for a strict deductivist methodology. This ideal cannot be consistently realized, for, as Emmet observes, even McTaggart, "the most rigorous of the English idealists in following a strictly deductive

method . . . had to introduce one empirical premise at the outset (that 'something exists')." P. 84.

14. Richard M. Rorty, *Philosophy and the Mirror of Nature* (Princeton: Princeton University Press, 1979), p. 336.

15. *Ibid.*, pp. 376–77.

16. *Op. cit.*, p. 371.

17. *Ibid.*, p. 372.

18. *Op. cit.*, Chapter VIII

19. Aside from the obvious merit of supplying a warrant for Occam's razor in the perennial mind-body debate, this world picture has the additional advantage of encouraging an appropriate attitude of humility and wonder, a state of mind which seems only to afford embarassment to the "systematic" philosopher.

20. Hilary Putnam, *Reason, Truth and History* (Cambridge: Cambridge University Press, 1981), p. 55.

21. *Ibid.*, p. 50.

22. See W. E. Hocking, "Whitehead on Mind and Nature," in P. A. Schilpp, *The Philosophy of Alfred North Whitehead* (New York: Tudor, 1951), pp. 400–401.

23. *Ibid.*, p. 400.

24. That this can result in some very odd notions of explanation is evidenced by Quine, who is reported by P. F. Strawson as confidently saying (in conversation) that he had reduced "everything down to number." While this may be something of an exaggeration, it seems to express a widely held (albeit usually in a more covert manner) ideal.

25. *Ibid.*

26. *Ibid.*

27. Thus many scientists claim that modern physics does not offer us a 'picture' of the physical world in any ordinary sense of this word. See, for example, the remarks of P. A. M. Dirac on quantum theory in *The Principles of Quantum Mechanics*, 4th edition (Oxford: Clarendon Press, 1958). He notes that the trend in physics is to "extend the meaning of the word 'picture' to include any *way of looking at the fundamental laws which makes their self-consistency obvious.*" (p. 10, emphasis in original) In a word, the aim towards comprehensive system has supplanted more ordinary demands for comprehensibility. See also Chapter Two, Section 2.

28. See, for instance, W. V. Quine, *Theories and Things*, who defines naturalism as the view that "it is within science itself, and not in some prior philosophy, that reality is to be identified and described." (P. 21)

29. For example, the complex system of a molecule displays emergent properties in the sense that the properties of the system as a whole are not deducible from or fully explicable in terms of the properties of the component systems of nucleons and electrons.

30. The qualification "more or less" is very likely indispensable because so-called complex entities, such as biological organisms, generally exhibit many types of organization exemplifying quite distinct types of order which range from purely random conjunctions through physico-chemical processes to purposive behaviour.

31. See Harre, *op. cit.*, pp. 285 ff., for a detailed discussion of Boscovitch's arguments.

32. This is not to suggest that the course of science ought to have taken a different path, or that many philosophic programmes which appeal in some overt or covert way to the incoherent metaphysics of scientific materialism, are wholly mistaken. Progress in science, or in philosophy for that matter, does not proceed in a straight line: rather it follows paths of a kind which make the title of A. Koestler's study of the Copernican revolution in astronomy, *The Sleepwalkers,* so particularly apt. Many important discoveries seem to be the result of researches whose fundamental goal turns out, in the end, to have been illusory.

33. Ernan McMullin, *The Concept of Matter in Modern Philosophy* (Notre Dame: University of Notre Dame Press, 1978), p. 49. See also Hanson, *op. cit.,* pp. 99 ff, who lists a number of distinct uses and interpretations of Newton's second law of motion.

34. McMullin observes that "There seems to be good reason to suppose . . . that the notion of mass itself (i.e., an intrinsic measure of response or resistance to motion) is a 'classical' one, useful in the Newtonian approximation, but no longer even definable in a full relativity theory." *Ibid.,* p. 292.

35. See D. Emmet, *op. cit.,* for a good discussion, from an epistemological point of view, of the importance of analogy for metaphysical thinking. She claims, rightly I think, that metaphysical thinking is primarily analogical thinking. The analogical relation, she says, is "some correlation of elements within experience, considered (analogically) as throwing light on a mode of interconnection in events and processes beyond our experience. The ground for drawing the analogy is the recognition that our experience itself arises within a situation of interrelated processes. Hence we seek to give an indirect indication of their possible character in analogical terms, and we must understand the 'realist' element in scientific concepts in this sense." (P. 92.)

36. It is by no means clear, however, that a description of the role of models in scientific Homeotypal explanation can be reduced to purely heuristic terms. For a discussion of this topic, see Marx Wartofsky, "Metaphysics as a Heuristic for Science." He argues for the indispensability of metaphysical notions in scientific thought and notes that "the heuristic force of metaphysics lies in its closeness to our primary modes of understanding and explaining: by means of the *story,* the re-enactment of nature in dramatic form." *Op. cit.,* p. 40. One might add that there are stories within stories–some of these, I am suggesting, possess a significance which is not fully captured by the phrase "reenactments of nature." For a machine can be made to "reenact" the movements of a human

organism, without having any great significance for explanations of human behaviour.

37. See Emmet, *op. cit.,* who cites Meyerson as the origin of the suggestive term 'rapport.'

38. The terminology is Emmet's. As she notes, the prime example of an illustrative analogy is that of "mechanism." This came to be used in physics (e.g., in the early work on field theory of Kelvin and Maxwell) not as a metaphysical model of "how nature works" but rather as a "regulative principle," or guiding principle of method. See *ibid.,* pp. 88–9.

39. One finds it, for example, in accounts of modern biology where its metaphysical implications are covertly used to shore up rigidly neo-Darwinian accounts of the theory of evolution. Here one frequently meets with a wholly uncritical implicit endorsement of the muddled metaphysics of scientific materialism.

40. See Chapter 1, note 7.

41. Cf., for example, Hanson, *op. cit.,* p. 120, who, in an otherwise interesting and insightful discussion of explanation, too quickly glosses over the possibility that there are degrees of abstraction with the observation: "Explanations must not involve the explicans in the explicandum. Thus it is no explanation to say of a red thing that it is red because it is composed of red particles:–the totality of a class cannot be explained by any member of the class." The answer to this overly logical way of thinking is that the issue of the meaning of explanation must not be confused with problems of logical classification.

Chapter Five. The Model in Physical Science

1. The controversies surrounding the attempts at interpretation do not arise from the predilections of groups of scientists for preferred formalisms. Indeed, abstract formal systems often turn out to have the happy characteristic of interchangeability. Consider, for example, the compatibility of wave mechanics with matrix mechanics in formal quantum theory. That two apparently distinct formal systems, each developed from a different point of view, should converge in the sense of being formally transformable one into the other, is one of the more impressive features of formal quantum theory.

2. A. B. Pippard, "Particles and Waves," in *Quanta and Reality* (Cleveland: World Publishing Co., 1964), p. 28.

3. *Ibid.,* p. 27.

4. Instances of the suggestive powers of models abound in the history of science. For example, Einstein's use of a model portraying the properties of liquid solutions, in order to determine the size of molecules, led him to a new method for calculating Avogadro's number. See Banesh Hoffman and Helen Dukas, *Albert Einstein, Creator and Rebel* (New York: New American Library paperback, 1972), p. 56.

5. See M. Hesse, "Models and Matter," in *Quanta and Reality*, pp. 49–57. For Hesse the model is essential to scientific progress: "If we were forbidden to talk in terms of models at all, we should have no expectations at all, and we should then be imprisoned for ever inside the range of our existing experiments." Pp. 56–7. As Hesse points out, a glance at the language of physicists as it appears in technical journals indicates that the model is important for its intrinsic content.

6. Hesse describes the model as possessing both positive and negative analogies. The latter are aspects of the model which have no correlates in the formalism. These are usually tacitly ignored.

7. Indeed, as Hesse remarks, "What criteria for reality could we have in physics other than the satisfaction of our expectations for objects of a certain type?" *Ibid.*, p. 56.

8. It is important for the philosopher, however, to disclose as much of the tacit component as is possible. The analysis of basic language is metaphysical analysis. In Collingwood's description of metaphysics, it is analysis of absolute presuppositions. Indeed, as he points out, "all analysis is metaphysical analysis; and since analysis is what gives its scientific character to science, science and metaphysics are inextricably united, and stand or fall together." R. J. Collingwood, *An Essay on Metaphysics* (Chicago: Henry Regnery Co., Gateway edition, 1972), pp. 40–41.

9. For a brief description of the experiment conducted with an electron microscope see Pippard, *op. cit.*, pp. 26–27. He summarizes his position thus: "Between the moment when the electron leaves the filament and the moment when it arrives at the [target] screen we must deny ourselves the luxury of looking at it."

10. For a detailed study of the Copenhagen Interpretation, especially of Bohr's and Heisenberg's contributions, see Aage Petersen, *Quantum Physics and the Philosophical Tradition* (Cambridge, Mass.: M. I. T. Press paperback, 1968). Petersen finds Bohr's epistemological writings stylistically difficult and obscure with respect to terms like 'closed;' nevertheless, he believes that Bohr's and Heisenberg's views "contain the deepest insight into the quantum problem obtained thus far." P. 92.

11. See C. F. von Weizsaecker, "The Copenhagen Interpretation," in Ted Bastin, ed., *Quantum Theory and Beyond*, who interprets the Copenhagen Interpretation to mean that "quantum theory does not reject particular models but the very concept of 'models'." P. 27.

12. Neils Bohr, *Atomic Theory and the Description of Nature* (Cambridge: University Press, 1961), p. 18 (emphasis in original).

13. Cf. Peterson, *op. cit.*, p. 146, who describes this altered view of the interpretation problem as the "clarification of the conditions that the quantum formalism sets for unambiguous application of physical concepts."

14. Bohr, *ibid.*, p. 4.

15. *Ibid.*, p. 54.

16. See *ibid.*, p. 19. The term 'complementarity,' says Bohr, serves to remind

us that our difficulties in interpreting the quantum theory "arise from the fact that all our ordinary verbal expressions bear the stamp of our customary forms of perception, from the point of view of which the existence of the quantum of action is an irrationality."

17. Bohr, pp. 62–69.

18. This idea Bohr seems never to have explained fully. Cf. Petersen, p. 110, who remarks that the important terminology of 'possibilities of observation' and 'possibilities of definition,' are introduced by Bohr with "minimum preparation and explanation."

19. *Op. cit.*, p. 16 (emphasis in original).

20. *Op. cit.*, p. 26.

21. *Ibid.*, p. 27.

22. *Ibid.*, p. 27.

23. *Ibid.*, pp. 27–8.

24. *Ibid.*, p. 30.

25. *Ibid.* Von Weizsaecker does offer an hypothesis based on the notion of 'irreversability' as to why the mind is 'classical' or, in Bohr's terminology, why our space-time intuition is unalterable. See pp. 28–30.

26. See *Op. cit.*, p. 56: "The concepts of classical physics are just a refinement of the concepts of daily life and are an essential part of the language which forms the basis of all natural science."

27. Cf. Petersen, *Op. cit.*, p. 179: "It appears impossible to justify the assertion that the scope of unambiguous physical communication coincides with the limits of what can be stated in ordinary classical physical terms."

28. *Op. cit.*, p. 70. See also p. 18 where quantum theory is described as "a rigorous re-interpretation, based upon the idea of correspondence, of the classical theories."

29. Cf. Petersen, *Op. cit.*, who views the principle as being more suitable than the concept of complementarity for bringing "the meeting of quantum physics and traditional philosophy into sharper focus." P. 33.

30. Cf. Hanson, *Op. cit.*, who points out that the principle of correspondence requires "a spectrum of intelligible assertability through which a single formula S can range within a language. . . ." P. 152. The effort to conceive of classical physics as a limiting case of quantum physics ignores the fact that they use languages which spring from a different stock: "The punctiform mass, a primarily kinematical conception, is the starting point of classical particle theory. The wave pulse, a primarily dynamical conception, is the starting point of quantum theory." P. 154.

31. Cf. Petersen, *op. cit.*, who remarks that, while the Copenhagen Interpretation has been very successful in clarifying measurement problems requiring analysis of important physical concepts, "interestingly enough, it has not required an equally thorough analysis of a concept like physical reality." P. 28.

32. It is perhaps true to say that the situation in quantum physics has contributed to a large amount of philosophical confusion. As one commentator

aptly puts it, it is a situation "which must be unique in the history of science where the practitioners of a scientific theory which has reached the stage of being regarded as a finished product habitually work with a jumble of elements taken from a variety of different conceptual frameworks none of which, singly, is adequate to present the facts that are known, and each of which is partly or even largely incompatible with the rest." Ted Bastin, *Quantum Theory and Beyond*, p. 8.

33. SMW, p. 135.

34. The special theory asserts the invariance of the laws of physics under transformations between inertial coordinate systems.

35. Victor Guillemin, *The Story of Quantum Mechanics* (New York: Scribner's Sons, 1968), p. 170. Guillemin also remarks that the variety of particles seems to be endless, and all display "a volatility of the most extreme sort, a dance of creation and annihilation." Even the so-called stable particles, stable in the sense of being capable of existing forever if left alone, may, under the right circumstances, be prodded into "acts of annihilation."

36. Werner Heisenberg, *Physics and Philosophy* (New York: Harper, 1958), p. 160.

37. Heisenberg, as one of the founders of the Copenhagen Interpretation, restricts the term 'happens' to the act of obseration. He is not in sympathy with the proponents of hidden variable theory, such as David Bohm, who insist that the term 'happens' applies to the interior of a quantum phenomenon in some ordinary sense of the word. That is to say, the fact that we at present lack the ability to speak about such 'happenings' does not mean that there is no underlying process or event even taking place.

38. *Ibid.*, p. 160.

39. *Ibid.*, pp. 71–2.

40. See R. J. Collingwood, *The Idea of Nature* (Oxford: Clarendon Press, 1945), for a discussion of the irresolvable dilemma in which Ionian natural scientists found themselves in their search for a primary substance. The Ionic cosmology, in Collingwood's assessment, leads to a *reductio ad absurdum* since their conception of matter "cannot be distinguished from the conception of the void." P. 51.

41. The principle of relativity, for example, has remarkable consequences for the whole of future physics. See John Archibald Wheeler, "From Relativity to Mutability," in Jagdish Mehra, ed., *The Physicist's Conception of Nature* (Dordrecht-Holland: D. Reidel Pub. Co., 1973), pp. 202–47. In noting some of the negative consequences of relativity, such as the meaninglessness of the concept of 'total energy' or of 'total momentum' in a closed universe, or the transcendence of the laws of conservation of particle number in black hole physics, Wheeler summarizes his review by proposing a new law: " 'There is no law except the law that there is no law;' or more briefly, 'Ultimate *MUTABILITY* is the central feature of physics'. " P. 242.

42. *Op. cit.*, p. 160.

43. Referring to the fact that particle physics has revealed two new kinds of

forces, the strong and the weak, Guillemin notes that "the conception of force has been broadened to encompass the cause of various kinds of particle interactions other than attraction and repulsion, the strength of the force being guaged by the rapidity with which it can produce its effects." *Op. cit.,* p. 171.

44. The pre-eminence of 'particle' over 'field', or vice versa, is not a settled matter among physicists. In quantum field theory, for example, it is held that "fields alone are real, that *they* are the substance of the universe, and that particles are merely the momentary manifestations of interacting fields." On the other hand, "the activities of the fields seem particle-like because fields interact very abruptly and in very minute regions of space." *Ibid.,* pp. 175–76.

45. SMW, p. 102.

Chapter Six. The Model of Organism in Physical Science

1. AI, pp. 157–8. The doctrine of Simple Location asserts that a natural fact, such as a bit of matter, can be completely described in its spatio-temporal characteristics by specifying its location "in a definite finite region of space, and throughout a definite finite duration of time, apart from any essential references of the relations of that bit of matter to other regions of space and to other durations of time." SMW, P. 58. Whitehead maintains, contrary to this doctrine, a general principle of relativity in his theory of organism.

2. Cf. Heisenberg, *op. cit.,* who states, "In modern quantum theory there can be no doubt that the elementary particles will finally also be mathematical forms." Pp. 71–2. In direct contrast, Whitehead's whole approach stresses that "the fact is more than the formulae illustrated." AI, p. 158.

3. See note 2, chapter 5.

4. See, for example, R. Hagedorn, "What happened to our elementary particles? (Variations of a theme of Jauch)," in Charles P. Enz and Jagdish Mehra, eds., *Physical Reality and Mathematical Description* (Dordrecht-Holland: D. Reidel Pub. Co., 1974), pp. 100–10. Hagedorn suggests the following recursive definition of an elementary particle: "An elementary particle is a particle which cannot, in a unique and reproducible way, be decomposed into elementary particles" (pp. 105–6). Under this definition, most particles are "highly complicated dynamical composite systems," with the possible exception of electrons, neutrinos, and protons. However, even this small group of 'really' elementary particles does not have complete security. In the theory of quarks it is conjectured that the proton, for example, is a composite entity.

5. See Hesse, *op. cit.,* who notes that as well as the model having features which conform with observations (positive analogies) and features which do not (negative analogies), there are also features which can be called neutral analogies. The latter contain important implications for the physical theory, for they suggest expectations of future physical behaviour and may lead to the discovery of new phenomena. See also M. Hesse, "Models and Analogies in

Science," in Paul Edwards, ed., *The Encyclopedia of Philosophy*, vol. 5, (New York: Collier Macmillan, 1967), pp. 354–9. In this article, Hesse defines a 'theoretical model' as one whose 'surplus meaning' is exploited in prediction and explanation, where the 'surplus meaning' of a model is the set of familiar features which may or may not carry over to the formal theory (the explanandum). From this point of view the model of organism is full of surplus meaning, a measure of this surplus being the great complexity of the interwoven net of ideas which it invokes, as witnessed by Whitehead's theory of organism.

6. For a critique of the "Newtonian-Euclidean sub-conscious" which permeates all common-sense thinking, see Milic Capek, *The Philosophical Impact of Contemporary Physics* (Princeton, N. J.: D. Van Nostrand, 1961).

7. See Chapter 3, section 7.

8. Cf. A. O. Lovejoy, *The Revolt Against Dualism* (La Salle, Illinois: Open Court, 1955). He remarks that "the human animal . . . does not for the most part live where its body is–if an organism's life is made up of what it really experiences; it lives where the things are of which it is aware, upon which its attention and feeling are directed." P. 15.

9. Such an entity, as Whitehead puts it, is "secluded within a finite region of space, and changes in its circumstances [can] only arise from forces which [form] no essential part of its nature." AE, P. 149.

10. It is a continual challenge to the ingenuity of the experimental physicist to detect weakly interacting particles which are predicted by the formal theory. For example, the neutrino, whose existence was theoretically postulated by Dirac, has been detected, albeit indirectly, only comparatively recently.

11. See, for example, David B. Cline, Alfred K. Mann and Carlo Rubbia, "The Search for New Families of Elementary Particles," *Scientific American*, January, 1976, pp. 44–54. In describing sub-atomic behaviour, they write: "The neutrinos have no electric charge and therefore do not feel the electromagnetic force; as leptons they are also excluded from feeling the strong force. They can interact only by the weak force and as a result they scarcely interact with matter at all." P. 47.

12. A criterion for life, as Whitehead points out, is originality of response to external stimuli. See PR, p. 104: "An organism is 'alive' when in some measure its reactions are inexplicable by *any* tradition of pure physical inheritance."

13. Hence Whitehead's theory of organism contains a complicted theory of feeling, or 'prehension.' See the article "Time," in IS, pp. 240–7. In this article Whitehead states that "the category of Prehension expresses how the world is a system of organisms," where the term 'organism' for Whitehead means a temporal process of organization. P. 241. At the purely physical level, one is speaking of, "blind physical perceptivity" or, as he puts it elsewhere, "pure physical feeling" which accounts for "the transference of energy in the physical world." See PR, p. 246.

14. Thus Whitehead's theory of organism is both creative and evolutionary. As Whitehead puts it, matter in the materialistic theory merely changes its external relations; thus change is "purposeless and unprogressive." But nature exhibits the evolution of complex organisms from antecedent states of less complex organisms. Hence "the emergence of organisms depends on a selective activity which is akin to purpose." SMW, p. 107.

15. It is worth noting in passing that this line of thought is not entirely new. Whitehead observes that F. Bacon touched upon the notion that physical entities must be able to "feel" one another: "It is certain," says Bacon, "that all bodies whatsoever, though they have no sense, yet they have perception; for when one body is applied to another . . . Whether the body be alterant or altered, evermore a perception preceedeth operation; for else all bodies would be like to one another." Quoted in SMW, p. 41.

16. The doctrine of vitalism, according to Whitehead, combines a doctrine of mechanistic materialism (to which he is adamantly opposed) with some *ad hoc* component of vital control which is required to account for the actions of living bodies. See SMW, p. 102.

17. The concept of mental pole must be carefully distinguished from that of mental process. In fact, in Whitehead's philosophy of organism, mental processes presuppose physical processes and, in particular, physical feeling; consciousness is a relatively rare and rarefied form of feeling. See PR, book 3, chapter 5.

18. IS, p. 240 (emphasis in original). The reference is to Descartes' conception of substance.

19. *Ibid.,* p. 242.

20. See Chapter 1, section 3.

21. Whitehead puts great emphasis on periodicity as a fundamental concept in science. See, for example, IM, Chapter 5: "The whole life of Nature is dominated by the existence of periodic events, that is, by the existence of successive events so analogous to each other that, without any straining of language, they may be termed recurrences of the same event." (P. 123) Again, in a later work, Whitehead suggests that the discovery of the idea of periodicity was "a flash of divine genius, penetrating to the inmost nature of things." SMW, p. 37.

22. Cf. Leon Rosenfeld, "The Wave-Particle Dilemma," in Mehra, *op. cit.,* pp. 251–63: "The whole framework of quantum mechanics has its origin in the consideration of multiply periodic systems." (P. 255) That this should not be surprising would seem to follow from the theoretical conjunction of Planck's equation $E=hf$ with Einstein's equation $E=Mc^2$ whereby even the internal energy of mass acquires a vibratory character.

23. Cf. Wheeler, in Mehra, *op. cit.,* who goes so far as to say, "nature conserves nothing; there is no constant in physics that is not transcended; or, in one word, mutability is a law of nature." P. 202.

24. The common conception of the electron as a point charge of electricity is meaningless in the organic view. In formal calculations, concerning the interaction of an electron and an electromagnetic field, this assumption leads to infinite singularities which some physicists remove by 'working rules.' However, Dirac suggests that "the natural way to remove them is to say that the electron is not a point charge, but the charge is distributed over a certain region." P. A. M. Dirac, "Development of the Physicist's Conception of Nature," pp. 1–14, in Mehra, *op. cit.*, see p. 11. It is a short step from this view to the organic conception of electric charge as that characteristic of a physical organism which concerns the kind of interaction which will take place if it is subjected to a particular set of conditions.

25. Indeed, the detection of neutrinos is indirect and inferential; their presence becomes manifest through the presence of other particles in certain interactions. The apparently 'insubstantial' entities in electromagnetic wave phenomena have already received partial recognition of substantiality. This is evident in technical terminology such as 'radiation pressure,' or 'hard' and 'soft' radiation.

26. It is interesting that Whitehead in his early writings uses a terminology which emphasizes the cognizable aspect of the forms, calling them 'recognita.' See Chapter 7 for a more detailed discussion of the theory of eternal objects.

27. It is argued that Plato himself did not advocate a pure transcendence theory or a pure immanence theory but instead was the first philosopher to attempt to merge the dual aspects into one theory. See Collingwood, *The Idea of Nature,* pp. 55–72. Whitehead clearly is trying to do just this.

28. See PR, p. 327. The notion of "universal system" is one which is indispensable for the intellectual comprehension of the physical universe, and indeed is one which is presupposed in science. As Whitehead puts it: "Apart from these [mathematical] relations as *facts* in nature, such science is meaningless, a tale told by an idiot and credited by fools." *Ibid.* (emphasis added). I will return to this point in the next chapter.

29. For example, most formulations of the various problems of Zeno, contain, at least implicity, assumptions about the nature of the fundamental structure of physical reality. And, as I have argued, it is just these assumptions which create the major difficulties.

30. Cf. Collingwood, *The Idea of Nature* pp. 17–27. He proposes a principle of minimum space and time as follows: any natural process or function can exist only in an appropriate amount of space and time. The principle is, in fact, in accord with recent conjectures of some physicists who, granting that the velocity of light is the maximum possible in the physical world, designate the quantum of time as the chronon of the quantum of space as the hodon. See also Capek, *op. cit.,* pp. 232ff., who points out that these quanta should be incorporated in a quantum of space-time, which he calls a "pulsation of time-space," in order to counter the pre-relativistic assumption inherent in any reference to the concepts which treats them as independent.

31. It is interesting that Heisenberg, in his description of the genesis of the principle of uncertainty, uses phrases which contradict the notion of nature-at-an-instant, and which evoke the concept of the model of organism. He remarks that the principle of uncertainity grew out of the observation that the path of an electron in a cloud chamber "was not an infinitely thin line with well-defined positions and velocities . . . [but was actually] a sequence of points which were not too well-defined by the water droplets, and the velocities were not too well defined either." He notes further that "the wave packet representing the electron is changed at every point of observation, that is, at every water droplet in the cloud chamber," a situation which is exactly what one would expect with the model of organism. see W. Heisenberg, "Development of Concepts in the History of Quantum Theory," in Mehra, *op. cit.,* pp. 264–75 (especially pp. 269–70).

32. Lowe lists "five or six" important influences from physics, and four from mathematics, as contributing stimuli to Whitehead's metaphysical speculations. The "weightiest" influence from physics, he says, was the development of vector methods. *Op. cit.,* p. 166. Whitehead seems to be referring to pre-quantum physics when he maintains that he arrived at his conception of the world by reason of his studies in mathematics and mathematical physics. See SMW, p. 152.

33. Cf. Palter, *Whitehead's Philosophy of Science,* who notes a puzzling lack of reference in Whitehead's published work to post–1924 developments in quantum theory.

34. For a critique of this aspect of Whitehead's theory of primates see Abner Shimony, "Quantum Physics and the Philosophy of Whitehead," *Boston Studies in the Philosophy of Science,* vol. 2, Robert S. Cohen and Marx W. Wartofsky, eds, (New York: Humanities Press, 1965), pp. 307–330. See also J. M. Burgers, "Reply to Shimony," *ibid.,* pp. 331–342, who rightly suggests that Shimony misses the point that what is at stake is not whether or not Whitehead's metaphysics accords with existing quantum mechanics but whether or not his metaphysics is adequate for the interpretation of what at present lacks a coherent interpretation. In other words, Shimony approaches the problem from the wrong direction in that he leans too heavily on an inadequate classical language.

35. The major part of the discussion which follows is based upon Chapters 7 and 8 of SMW. The theory of primates, in Whitehead's words, is tentatively offered "as an example of the sort of possibilities which the organic theory leaves open for physical science." SMW, p. 135.

36. SMW, p. 132.

37. SMW, p. 25.

38. According to Whitehead, spatio-temporal relations are only very special examples of relations of extension. That they should be selected by thought as the "permanent ground for objectival distinction" in the apprehension of sense-objects as thought objects, is perhaps the result of their comparative

simplicity. See AE, p. 134. The connection between order and extensionality is discussed in more detail in section 5.

39. See, for example, "Space, Time, and Relativity," in IS, pp. 90–107. The act of experience, Whitehead says, is a perception of "a whole formed of related differentiated parts. The relations between these parts possess certain characteristics, and time and space are the expressions of some of the characteristics of these relations." P. 100.

40. SMW, p. 133.

41. SMW, p. 131.

42. SMW, p. 134. Both sets of conditions are, of course, consistent with the "accepted electromagnetic laws," which are supposed to hold throughout all space, "including the interior of a proton."

43. SMW, pp. 133–4.

44. Palter, *loc. cit.,* believes this conjecture to be unwarranted.

45. The latter are described as those which force upon a primate changes in its proper space-time system. SMW, pp. 132–3. As an example, Whitehead cites the neutral atom, regarded as composed of an association of differently charged species of primate, but whose overall neutrality shields it from the production of a change in its space-time system which would be caused by an electric field.

46. In the terminology of the philosophy of organism, this means that a physical organism is properly called a 'society.' Society is an important secondary concept in Whitehead's metaphysical system and refers to a complex interwoven pattern or nexus of actual entities. It exists as a unit by reason of a common element of form, which Whitehead calls its "defining characteristic." The latter is a complex eternal object. Since actual entities and eternal objects constiitute the two fundamental metaphysical catagories, this means that even a very primitive physical organism is a complicated rather than an essentially simple entity.

47. SMW, p. 110.

48. SMW, p. 153.

49. *Ibid.*

50. SMW, p. 154.

51. The individuality of elementary particles is represented also by the so-called quantum numbers, of which electric charge is one instance. See, for example, Cline, Mann and Rubbia, *op. cit.:* "Quantum numbers describe the properties of a particle in the same way that a list of facial features might describe a person. The complete list of quantum numbers defines the particle uniquely; together with the mass, such a list represents all one can possibly know about the particle." P. 45.

52. SMW, p. 154.

53. Cf. SMW, p. 102: "Energy is merely the name for the quantitative aspect of a structure of happenings; in short, it depends on the notion of the functioning of an organism."

54. SMW, p. 154.

55. *Ibid.*

56. See SMW, p. 103: It is "very unlikely that there should be an infinite regress in nature."

57. PR, p. 91.

58. For example, quantum field theory postulates the existence of four fundamental types of particle which account for the interactions of matter. These are called mesons, photons, W-particles and gravitons, the exchange of which is said to account for the strong force, the electromagnetic force, the weak force and the gravitational force respectively. The latter two types of particle are still undetected.

59. Indeed, Whitehead remarks that "a field can be viewed as a possibility of action, but as a possibility which represents an actuality." AE, p. 150.

60. In Whitehead's view, "The low-grade organism is merely the summation of the forms of energy which flow in upon it in all their multiplicity of detail. It receives, and it transmits; but it fails to simplify into intelligible system." PR, p. 254.

61. PR, pp. 177.

62. "No intelligible definition of rest and motion is possible for historic routes including them, because they correspond to no inherent spatialization of the actual world." *Ibid.*

63. See note 35.

64. This important point will be explored further in Chapter 7. This must not be understood as an assertion that non-quantitative forms of mathematics are excluded from physical science. As his earliest work indicates, Whitehead is very much aware of the power of abstract mathematical theories, quantitative and non-quantitative, to organize our knowledge of nature. Indeed, Whitehead views the spatio-temporal continuum as "the general system of relatedness of all possibilities, in so far as that system is limited by its relevance to the general fact of actuality." SMW, p. 162.

65. In Whitehead's theory of primates, the primate moves in a manner analogous to that of a wave-packet; that is, by the continual dissolution and reformulation of a certain pattern. Thus he postulates two different types of vibration: the previously mentioned 'vibratory organic deformation,' and 'vibratory locomotion.' The two notions, when used together to describe the coming into being and the relative motions of primates, imply that the life-histories of primates must be displayed diagrammatically as sequences of detached dots. See SMW, p. 136.

66. In Whitehead's view, according to his theory of multiple space-time systems, "if two primates do not continue either mutually at rest, or mutually in uniform relative motion, at least one of them is changing its intrinsic space-time system. The laws of motion express the conditions under which these changes of space-time systems are effected. The conditions for vibratory *locomotion* are founded upon these general laws of motion." SMW, p. 132.

67. As Whitehead puts it: "The modern thought-object of science . . . has the complexity of the whole material universe. In physics, as elsewhere, the hopeless endeavour to derive complexity from simplicity has been tacitly abandoned. What is aimed at is not simplicity, but persistence and regularity. In a sense regularity is a sort of simplicity. But it is the simplicity of stable mutual relations, and not the simplicity of absence of types of internal structure or of type of relation." AE, p. 149.

68. As Whitehead describes the situation, "The science of physics conceives a natural occasion as a locus of energy. Whatever else that occasion may be, it is an individual fact harboring that energy. The words electron, proton, photon, wave-motion, velocity, hard and soft radiation, chemical elements, matter, empty space, temperature, degradation of energy, all point to the fact that physical science recognizes qualitative differences between occasions in respect to the way in which each occasion entertains its energy. These differences are entirely constituted by the flux of energy, that is to say, by the way in which the occasions in question have inherited their energy from the past of nature, and in which they are about to transmit their energy to the future." AI, p. 185.

69. SMW, p. 126. Kant's observation (from the section 'Of the Axioms of Intuition' in the *Critique of Pure Reason)* is interesting because it adumbrates Whitehead's method of extensive abstraction, whereby he constructs points and moments as ideal limits of objects given in sense perception. See Palter, *Whitehead's Philosophy of Science,* for an exposition of this method. It is worth noting that the method of extensive abstraction was not designed by Whitehead with the intention of literally deducing all aspects of continuity, especially those concerned with a non-denumerable infinite class of entities, from sense-data. Palter suggests that when Whitehead assumes Cantor-Dedekind (i. e., non-denumerable) continuity for the moments of a given time-system, he is thinking of a definition of continuity in terms of "subsets of, or 'cuts' in, that denumerably infinite class of moments which is, in principle at least, available to sense-perception." *Loc. cit.,* p. 61.

70. PR, p. 288. "For our epoch, extensive connection with its various characteristics is the fundamental organic relationship whereby the physical world is properly described as a community. There are no important relationships outside the extensive scheme."

71. PR, p. 66.

72. The concept of measurability, along with those of shape, dimension, and the concepts of metrical geometry, are "additional determinations of real potentiality arising from our cosmic epoch." PR, p. 66.

73. Thus Whitehead observes: "So far as mere extensiveness is concerned, space might as well have three hundred and thirty-three dimensions, instead of the modest three dimensions of our present epoch. . . . Indeed the sheer dimensionality of space, apart from the precise number of dimensions, is such an additional fact, not involved in the mere notion of extension." PR, p. 289.

74. PR, p. 286.

75. PR, p. 288.

76. PR, p. 284.

77. "A member of this species can only function relationally: by a necessity of its nature it is introducing one actual entity, or nexus, into the real internal constitution of another actual entity. Its sole avocation is to be an agent in objectification." (PR, p. 291) Whitehead suggests, speaking of physical energy, that an eternal object of the objective species is involved in the particular *form* of the flux of energy while an eternal object of the subjective species is involved in the *intensity* of the energy. See PR, p. 292.

78. PR, p. 292.

79. "All scientific measurements merely concern the systematic real potentiality out of which [the contemporary actualities of the world] arise. This is the meaning of the doctrine that physical science is solely concerned with the mathematical relations of the world." PR, p. 326.

80. PR, pp. 91.

81. "The metaphysical characteristics of an actual entity–in the proper general sense of 'metaphysics'–should be those which apply to all actual entities. It may be doubted whether such metaphysical concepts have ever been formulated in their strict purity–even taking into account the most general principles of logic and mathematics." PR, p. 90.

82. This is what Whitehead means when he states: "Continuity concerns what is potential; whereas actuality is incurably atomic." PR, p. 61.

83. M, p. 881.

84. This is the position of A. Gruenbaum: see Chapter 3.

85. The term mass-effect is used here in order to distinguish the organic concept, which refers to a mode of interaction, from the Newtonian (materialistic) concept of mass. In the materialistic theory, the concepts of mass and force exhibit a certain circularity. Mass in conceived as an intrinsic property of matter and force as an external agency acting upon passive matter. Newton's second law of motion, however, defines force as the product of mass and acceleration. This leads, as Whitehead observes, to a confused notion of both concepts: "The familiar equation of elementary dynamics, namely, mf=P, now becomes mf=mf. It is not easy to understand how an important science can issue from such premisses." See PNK, pp. 16–19.

86. To the extent that the organic pattern of a society becomes less pronounced, the society may be treated as "a mere aggregation of effects. . . . Accordingly, the characteristic laws of inorganic matter are mainly the statistical averages resulting from confused aggregates." SMW, p. 110.

87. *Ibid.*

88. One might conjecture that the difference between classical and quantum physics disappears in the realm of large quantum numbers because the quantum society behaves in a manner similar to an aggregate of organisms in a material society. In other words, the correspondence principle of quantum mechanics perhaps merely reflects the blurring of distinctions which occur at

the imprecise boundaries between different levels of the hierarchy of organisms.

89. This is the case also in biology where the life-histories of individual organisms can be followed; nevertheless, the principal aim is to find general laws which transcend individual cases.

90. PR, pp. 205–6.

91. See PR, Chapter 3, Part II, where Whitehead emphasizes that " 'order' is a mere generic term: there can only be some definite specific 'order,' not merely 'order' in the vague."

92. In Whitehead's terminology, this is the doctrine of law as Immanent; he contrasts this doctrine with the doctrines of law as Imposed, of law as Description, and of law as Conventional Interpretation. See AI, pp. 111 ff.

93. PR, p. 90.

94. PR, p. 92.

95. PR, p. 90.

96. For this reason, "The phrase 'cosmic epoch' is used to mean that widest society of actual entitites whose immediate relevance to ourselves is traceable." PR, p. 91.

97. Whitehead conceives of the nature of this epoch as one dominated by electromagnetic occasions. "The electromagnetic society exhibits the physical electromagnetic field which is the topic of physical science." It is pervaded by even more special societies, such as the "regular trains of waves, individual electrons, protons, individual molecules, societies of molecules, such as inorganic bodies, living cells, and societies of cells such as vegetable and animal bodies." PR, p. 98.

98. PR pp. 90–1.

99. "The term 'disorder' refers to a society only partially influential in impressing its characteristics in the form of prevalent laws. This doctrine, that order is a social product, appears in modern science as the statistical theory of the laws of nature, and in the emphasis on genetic relation." PR, p. 92.

100. "In so far as this dominance approaches completeness, the systematic law which physics seeks is absolutely dominant. In so far as the dominance is incomplete, the obedience is a statistical fact with its corresponding lapses." PR, p. 98.

Chapter Seven. Mathematics and Necessity

1. One of Whitehead's more concise expressions of the principle is as follows: "Our experience requires and exhibits a basis of uniformity, and . . . in the case of nature this basis exhibits itself as the uniformity of spatio-temporal relations." P Rel, p. v.

2. PR, pp. 3–4 [emphases added].

3. The test of idealism for Whitehead is "the refusal to conceive reality apart from explicit references to some or all of the characteristic processes of

mentality." See "Philosophical Aspects of the Principle of Relativity," in IS, p. 136.

4. *Ibid.,* p. 137.

5. For a concise summary of Whitehead's philosophy of natural science see A. H. Johnson's introduction to IS, pp. xi-xli.

6. On the general character of the latter discipline he says that "What we ask from the philosophy of science is some account of the coherence of things perceptively known." CN, p. 29.

7. See Palter, *Whitehead's Philosophy of Science,* for a thorough discussion of Whitehead's theory of relativity. Palter sums up the difference between Whitehead's and Einstein's approaches to the theory of relativity thus: "One might say Einstein supposes that matter (or the gravitational field) is ontologically prior to space-time while events are simply intersections of world-lines of particles; and Whitehead supposes that events are ontologically prior to space-time, while matter is simply a contingent characteristic of certain events." P. 213.

8. Whitehead describes this two-termed relationship as leading to the concept of a divided or bifurcated nature, one nature being that which is apprehended in awareness and the other being that which causes the awareness, the two natures meeting only in the mind. (See CN, pp. 26–48) Hence nature is conceived as "two systems of reality, which, in so far as they are real, are real in different senses. One reality would be the entities such as electrons which are the study of speculative physics. This would be the reality which is there for knowledge; although on this theory it is never known. For what is known is the other sort of reality, which is the byplay of the mind. Thus there would be two natures, one is the conjecture and the other is the dream." (CN, p. 30)

9. See "Uniformity and Contingency," in IS, p. 114.

10. *Ibid.*

11. P Rel, p. 26.

12. *Ibid.*

13. As Whitehead puts it: "There is essentially a beyond to whatever is observed. I mean by this that the event is known as being related to other events which it does not include." CN, p. 186.

14. CN, p. 187.

15. IS, p. 140. "We ask whether this interior is occupied with condensed matter or is empty, and whether this matter be hot or cold, solid or gaseous, because we know that the uniform systematic spatio-temporal relations must supply entities which have the status of forming the interior of the earth."

16. See SMW, pp. 120ff. Each of these must be uniform and, it would seem to follow, each should exhibit some more general uniform relatedness which connects them all. But Lowe, for instance, believes that it is not possible to reconcile the early theory of the uniformity of spatio-temporal relatedness with the later notion that spatio-temporal relatedness is the outcome of the nature

of occurrences which are peculiar to a given epoch. See *Understanding Whitehead,* p. 237.

17. CN, p. 28.

18. See Chapter 2, section 5.

19. IS, p. 142.

20. V. Lowe, for instance, interprets Whitehead as asserting that a rational description of actual things would be impossible without forms of definiteness, but notes that this does not prove that the forms must be eternal. The assertion amounts to saying, says Lowe, that if the forms of definiteness are not eternal, "we must either write metaphysics as if they were or not write metaphysics." *Op. cit.,* pp. 318–19.

21. See CN, p. 189: "Recognition and abstraction essentially involve each other. . . . We cannot abstract without recognition and we cannot recognize without abstraction. Perception involves apprehension of the event and recognition of the factors of its character."

22. IS, p. 63.

23. IS, pp. 62–3 (emphasis added).

24. See, for example, IS, p. 63: "Objects and events [are] fundamentally different sorts of entities disclosed in nature with certain determinate relations to each other."

25. PR, p. 48.

26. *Ibid.*

27. As Whitehead himself puts the point, "throughout the universe there reigns the union of opposites which is the ground of dualism." AI, p. 190. Cf. Dorothy Emmet, *Whitehead's Philosophy of Organism,* 2nd. ed. (London: Macmillan, 1966), who notes that Whitehead's entire work, and especially his major work, illustrates the absence of any dualism of the 'vicious' kind: "'Process' and 'Reality' imply and demand one another. . . . There is thus no dualism between the Realms of Being and Becoming." pp. 134–5.

28. Chapter 6, section 2.

29. PR, p. 22.

30. See "Of What Use Are Whitehead's Eternal Objects," in George L. Kline, ed., *Alfred North Whitehead: Essays on his Philosophy* (Englewood Cliffs, N. J.: Prentice-Hall, Inc., 1963), pp. 102–16.

31. SMW, p. 107.

32. Thus value, too, is a generic concept. At the ground of physical order, value must be analyzed, according to Whitehead, in terms of the becoming of actual entities in respect of the selection of certain characteristics from among many possibilities. Hence, "the organism is a unit of emergent value, a real fusion of the characters of eternal objects, emerging for its own sake." SMW p. 107; see also pp. 103–4.

33. With characteristic sensitivity for the vivid in expression, Whitehead finds just the right phrase in Tennyson's interpretation of the mechanistic conception of the world: " 'The stars,' she whispers, 'blindly run.' " See SMW, pp. 77–8.

34. The differences in physical entities are, moreover, only explicable in terms of value, for if eternal objects are graded as to their relevance for a particular actual occasion, "these grades can be expressed only as relevance of value." SMW, p. 162.

35. SMW, p. 178. In Whitehead's metaphysics, the concept of God is sometimes expressed as the ultimate Principle of Limitation or Determination. This closely resembles the concept which, in Aristotle's metaphysics, is expressed as the Prime Mover.

36. "The only alternative to this admission," says Whitehead, "is to deny the reality of actual occasions." *Ibid.*

37. Cf. SMW, p. 158: "It is the foundation of the metaphysical position which I am maintaining that the understanding of actuality requires a reference to ideality." There are, of course, other approaches to the construction of a metaphysical theory whose structure includes a realm of potentiality. V. Lowe discusses some alternatives; see *op. cit.,* pp. 320–1. However, he notes that a theory of pseudo-eternal potentials would be "no more than half Whiteheadian."

38. See SMW, p. 163: "The *analytical character* of the realm of eternal objects is the primary metaphysical truth concerning it. By this character it is meant that the status of any eternal object A in this realm is capable of analysis into an indefinite number of subordinate relationships of limited scope."

39. SMW, p. 161.

40. SMW, p. 158. The significance of the phrase "untrue propositions" is that the degree of achieved value in an actualization is a function of what is definitely excluded or rejected, not merely omitted, in terms of possibilities.

41. SMW, p. 159.

42. For example, the events which make up the world are internally related in the sense that any one event is "found only where it is and how it is." SMW, p. 160.

43. SMW, p. 162 (emphasis in original).

44. SMW, p. 159. Whitehead also describes the aspect of disconnectedness in terms of isolation. Eternal objects in the realm of possibility are "devoid of real togetherness: they remain within their "their relationships as possibilities are expressible without reference to their respective individual essences." SMW, p. 165. This means that the concept of abstraction, which I shall examine in the next section, must be analyzed in such a manner as to take into account the determinateness and the indeterminateness of eternal objects.

45. "The individual essence is merely the essence considered in respect to [the eternal object's] uniqueness." SMW, p. 159.

46. The relational essence of an eternal object is "the perfectly definite status of that object as a relatum in the general scheme of relationship." SMW, p. 164.

47. "There can be no occasion which includes [an eternal object] in all its determinate relationships; for some of these relationships are contraries." SMW, p. 163.

48. Indeed, the topic of the finiteness of knowledge is treated in this way in Whitehead's philosophy of science. See, for example, P Rel, pp. 22 ff.

49. "The difficulty which arises in respect to internal relations is to explain how any particular truth is possible. In so far as there are internal relations, everything must depend upon everything else. Apparently, therefore we are under the necessity of saying everything at once." SMW, p. 163.

50. SMW, p. 165.

51. SMW, p. 164.

52. SMW, p. 164.

53. ESP, p. 138.

54. This property would also account for the arresting fact that distinct formal systems of mathematics or logic, while possessing apparently quite different starting points and subject-matter, often turn out to be essentially the same system. They exemplify, in effect, the same relational essence, or patterns of relational essences. This conjecture is in accord with Whitehead's declaration that "the mere relational essence of each eternal object determines the complete uniform scheme of relational essences, since each object stands internally in all of its possible relationships." SMW, p. 164.

55. SMW, p. 165.

56. See SMW, p. 158: The justification is to be sought "(i) in our direct knowledge of the actual occasions which comprise our immediate experience, and (ii) in their success as forming a basis for harmonising our systematised accounts of various types of experience, and (iii) in their success as providing the concepts in terms of which an epistemology can be framed."

57. As Whitehead unequivocally states, "mathematics is the science of the most complete abstractions to which the human mind can attain." SMW, p. 34.

58. SMW, p. 25.

59. SMW, pp. 25–6.

60. SMW, p. 26.

61. SMW, p. 166.

62. SMW, p. 167.

63. SMW, p. 167.

64. SMW, p. 170.

65. This is consistent with the notion of the constructed hierarchy because if an abstractive hierarchy is finite it has only one member in its maximum grade. This property follows from a formal condition of the hierarchy which Whitehead calls its 'connexity.'

66. "There is a connected hierarchy of concepts applicable to the occasion, including concepts of all degrees of complexity." Hence, "it is impossible to complete the description of an actual occasion by means of concepts." SMW, pp. 169–70.

67. This point will be discussed more fully in the last chapter.

68. Thus there are, in much of standard applied mathematics, many instances of pure mathematical concepts which appear to have no physical

significance. One example is the use of complex numbers in electrical circuit theory.

69. This is the kernel of truth in the positivistic claim that mathematics is nothing but, in Carl Hempel's words, a "theoretical juice extractor," an analytical tool for extracting the implications from empirical assumptions. See "On the Nature of Mathematical Truth," in Benacerraf and Putnam, pp. 366–81.

70. SMW, p. 22.

Chapter Eight: Aspects of a Whiteheadian Philosophy of Mathematics

1. Victor Lowe, *Understanding Whitehead*, p. 84.

2. The reference is to W. V. Quine. I shall comment further on this point in Section 2.

3. Hence the position taken here is antithetical to what H. Putnam calls "metaphysical realism:" the view that there is somewhere one true theory, and a true and complete correspondence between that theory and "external" things. See "Why There Isn't a Ready-Made World," in *Synthese 51* (1982), pp. 141–167. On the other hand, the position which Putman calls "internal realism" (see Chapter 4) is also unsatisfactory–it is in fact akin to the Quinean view of realism, about which I shall say more later.

4. Such "events" are of course not Humean events, whose character is such that mind is always set over against them, puzzled by its inability to perceive any co-ordinating factors in apparently causally related sequences of independent and atomistic occurrences.

5. This is, in fact, one of the phrases Whitehead uses to describe his theory. See, for instance, PR, p. 309.

6. In Michael Dummett's view," intuitionism represents the only sustained attempt by the opponents of a realist view to work out a coherent embodiment of their philosophical beliefs." Moreover, he goes so far as to say that intuitionistic mathematics is "pointless without the philosophical motivation underlying it." Hence, if intuitionism loses the philosophical battle, "the practice of intuitionistic mathematics itself and the metamathematical study of intuitionistic systems will alike become a waste of time." See *Elements of Intuitionism*, pp. viii-ix.

7. In Dummett's view, "the intuitionistic ontology would be a *consequence* of the intuitionistic theory of meaning, not a premiss for it." *Ibid.,* p. 382.

8. But by this very token there is, *pace* Dummett (see note 6), no "philosophical battle" over realism and idealism (or anti-realism) whose outcome can greatly affect the practice of intuitionistic mathematics. Apart from describing another legitimate way to do mathematics, intuitionism has perhaps no deeper significance for the philosophy of mathematics than has logicism. Just as the latter helps us to become clearer about the difference between mathematics and pure logic, intuitionism points up some differences

in the subject-matter which result from distinguishing between ways of doing mathematics.

9. Thus at one point Dummett says, "In making mathematical statements, we are not purporting to describe an external reality." (*Ibid.*, p. 383) Nevertheless, it is still open to the intuitionist, he adds, to affirm non-mathematical or material-object statements which *do* refer to an external reality.

10. See W. V. Quine, *Theories and Things*, pp. 149–50.

11. Quine does not say that *all* mathematical language derives from ordinary language vocabulary through the "sharpening and regimenting" of appropriate idioms. In mathematical creation, the basic vocabulary is extended by means of analogy and reinterpretation. These analogical reinterpretations "have fostered the unfortunate conception of mathematics as basically uninterpreted." *Ibid.*, p. 150.

12. *Ibid.*, pp. 149–50.

13. *Ibid.*, p. 2.

14. *Ibid.*, p. 20.

15. *Ibid.*, pp. 20–1.

16. Thus Hilary Putnam rightly observes that if we abandon the notions of "justification, rational acceptability, warranted assertability, right assertability, and the like, completely, then 'true' goes as well, except as a mere device for 'semantic ascent,' that is a mere mechanism for switching from one level of language to another." See "Why Reason Can't be Naturalized," *Synthese 52* (1982), p. 20.

17. Both philosophies are thus representatives of what Ian Hacking has aptly called "linguistic idealism" or "lingua-lism:" indeed, they seem to lean towards the extreme version of this world-view in which "to be is to be spoken of," that is, "something is real only insofar as it enters into communication." See *Why Does Language Matter to Philosophy?* p. 182. Quine rightly insists that philosophers need an explicit standard of "what constitutes assumption of objects," but his well-known formula ("to be is to be the value of a variable") leads to a realism founded upon high abstractions. As he describes himself, he is a "Predicate and Class Realist . . . a deep-dyed realist of abstract universals." (*Op. cit.*, p. 184)

18. While such speculations are not at present popular, this appears to be as much the result of contingent factors in the development of Western philosophy as it is the product of decisions about what it might be reasonable to think. According to Ian Hacking, there has been, since the seventeenth century, a radical transformation in our modes of understanding. In the current philosophical climate, the proper objects of philosophizing are nothing like the abstract objective entities, called ideas, which once providing the link between the rationalist Cartesian *ego* and the world external to it. We live now in a "heyday of sentences," wherein "the sentence is the simple object taken as fundamental in the explanation of truth, meaning, experiment, and reality."

(*Op. cit.*, p. 159) I am suggesting that a middle ground needs to be found, somewhere between the lingualistic empiricism of the present day and the rationalistic idealism of the past.

19. Indeed, this characteristic is just what distinguishes mathematics from games such as chess. As Whitehead observes, "In mathematical science connections between things are exhibited which, apart from the agency of human reason, are extremely unobvious." SMW, p. 19.

20. MT, pp. 60–1.

21. SMW, p. 32.

22. Thus the price of the generality sought for in science, as Whitehead vividly expresses it, is that "science, in its perfection, relapses into the study of differential equations. The concrete world has slipped through the meshes of the scientific net." MT, p. 18.

23. For Whitehead's views on the connection between mathematics and aesthetics see his lecture entitled "Mathematics and the Good," reprinted in IS, pp. 187–221. Here he describes mathematics as "the intellectual analysis of types of pattern." Aesthetics also involves the analysis of pattern, as in the analysis of a picture in terms of geometrical and color patterns. But he insists that "pattern is only one factor in our realization of experience:" the relationship between individual characteristics is of vital importance in aesthetics. On the other hand, Whitehead believes that the mathematical analysis of pattern is in its infancy, and "in the next two thousand years the overwhelming novelty in human thought will be the dominance of mathematical understanding." See pp. 199–200. This should not be interpreted as saying that mathematical understanding is the most complete form of understanding. On the contrary, "by reason of the greater concreteness of the aesthetic experience, it is a wider topic than that of the logical experience. Indeed, when the topic of aesthetics has been sufficiently explored, it is doubtful whether there will be anything left over for discussion." MT, p. 62.

24. Thus Whitehead observes that "the endeavour to understand eternal objects in complete abstraction from the actual world results in reducing them to mere undifferentiated nonentities." PR, p. 257.

25. This category consists of simple eternal objects which "do not express a manner of relatedness between other eternal objects. They are not contrasts, or patterns." PR, p. 114.

26. Whitehead is, of course, aware of the complexity of his own theory of eternal objects and the sort of difficulty mentioned here. He observes, with reference to the question of the simplicity and the complexity of eternal objects, that "we may doubt whether 'simplicity' is ever more than a relative term, having regard to some definite procedure of analysis." PR, p. 133.

27. Cf. Stephen Koerner, "On the Relevance of Post-Goedelian Mathematics to Philosophy," in Lakatos, *Problems in the Philosophy of Mathematics,* pp. 118–132. Koerner describes the doctrine as "not admitting, or at least not considering, the possibility that conflicting mathematical theories can with

equal correctness be abstracted from experience." P. 120. He also notes that "all major philosophers from Plato to Kant and most later ones regard the postulates and theorems of mathematical theories as true in the actual world, however much they differ in their conception of it." P. 119.

28. See Andrzej Mostowski, "Recent Results in Set Theory," in Lakatos, *op. cit.*, pp. 82–96. Mostowski notes that among the multitude of competing set theories there is none which can claim a central place in mathematics. Indeed, "only their common part could claim such a position; but it is debatable whether this common part will contain all the axioms needed for a reduction of mathematics to set theory." Pp. 94–5.

29. See, for example, Stephen F. Barker, "Realism as a Philosophy of Mathematics," in Bulloff Jack J.; Holoyke, Thomas C.; Hahn, S. W.; eds., *The Foundations of Mathematics* (New York: Springer-Verlag, 1969). Barker offers an interesting epistemological interpretation of Goedel's theorem (as an alternative to the interpretation which views the result as putting into question the reality of mathematical objects): the theorem indicates "an essential limitation in the expressive power of symbolism; the limitation being that no symbolism can fully succeed in characterizing a system of objects as rich as the natural numbers." P. 4.

30. Koerner's interpretation also supports this conclusion: "An incomplete system of interpreted axioms cannot describe the actual or possible world completely." *Op. cit.*, p. 129.

31. For a discussion of the view that Goedel's second theorem has no philosophical significance whatever, see John Tucker, "Goedel and Epimenides," *Proceedings of the Aristotelian Society*, LIX, 1958–59, pp. 25–48. Tucker is mainly concerned to show that the theorem has no bearing on the Epimenidean puzzles of self-reference, since it merely guarantees the existence of a certain case of self-description. In the absence of interpretation Goedel's results "are concerned only with numbers and the relations between them." (p. 35) Tucker's point, that difficulties only arise as a consequence of the interpretation given to the formal result, is an important one: it reminds us once again that there are no philosophical problems within formal mathematics itself. Problems arise only when certain interpretations of formal mathematics conflicts with prior philosophical assumptions: indeed, paradoxes, as we have seen, seem to be useful mainly for drawing attention to the shortcomings of these preconceptions.

32. MT, p. 2.

33. MT, p. 10.

34. Indeed, Whitehead points out that "the general principles of physics are exactly what we should expect as a specific exemplification of the metaphysics required by the philosophy of organism." PR, p. 116.

35. R. J. Collingwood, *Essay on Metaphysics*, p. 265.

36. *Ibid.*, p. 197.

37. MT, p. 66.

38. MT, p. 67.

39. As Whitehead observes, a complete understanding is "a perfect grasp of the universe in its totality." MT, p. 42. A complete understanding, therefore, would encompass the act of understanding itself. But this engenders an infinite regress which is scarcely within the compass of a finite intellect.

40. The contrary view seems hopelessly entangled in a Cartesian conception of a free-floating ego. But, as Whitehead emphatically and succinctly puts the point, "the notion of intelligence in pure abstraction from things understood is a myth." *Ibid.*

41. The view that there are potentially far-reaching effects inherent in even slight modifications of conceptual systems receives support from studies of conceptual change in the history of science. Conceptual "leaps," seem to have, in I. Bernard Cohen's words, a "fine structure." Cohen argues that our understanding of the "logic" of scientific creation/discovery will best progress if we emphasize "difference between successive generations of concepts," rather than "their apparent and undifferentiated similarities." He cites Galileo's creative work as exemplifying "transformations" of existing conceptual structures, as opposed to the introduction of "revolutionary" new concepts. See "History and the Philosopher of Science," in Frederick Suppe (ed.), *The Structure of Scientific Theories* (Urbana: The University of Illinois Press, second edition, 1977), pp. 308–49.

42. This is evident in the terminology of the medieval period, when such numbers were referred to as *numeri surdi* and *numeri ficti.*

43. MT, p. 107.

44. MT, p. 53. Whitehead goes on to point out that there are profound difficulties involved in the concept, for there is yet another form of 'togetherness' invoked by the very judgement of inconsistency: "This is the sort of perplexity that Plato alluded to, when he makes one of his characters say, 'Not-being is a sort of being.' "

45. *Ibid.* He suggests that "the contradictions, famous in ancient and modern logic, arise from such ambiguities. Many words which are not formally conjunctions, are expressive of a conjunctive meaning. For example, the word *class* has all the manifold ambiguity of the word *and.*" MT, p. 54.

46. MT, p. 55.

47. *Ibid.*

48. Whitehead sums up this point as follows: "The expansion of any special topic changes its whole meaning from top to bottom. As the subject matter of a science expands, its relevance to the universe contracts. For it presupposes a more strictly defined environment." *Ibid.*

49. MT, p. 106. The conclusion, applicable to all estimations of the comprehensiveness of formal logical methods, is, as Whitehead concisely puts it, that deductive logic "has not the coercive supremacy which is conventionally conceded to it." *Ibid.*

50. It is worth noting that for Cantor, the originator of set theory, the

concept of class held profound implications of a metaphysical nature. In contrast to Dedekind's more naive description of a set as "a sack," Cantor poignantly and prophetically speaks of a set as "an abyss." See Herbert Meschkowski, *Probleme des Unendlichen* (Braunschweig: Friedr. Vieweg und Sohn, 1967), p. 89.

51. MT, p. 106.

52. See Chapter 2, note 26.

53. MT, p. 47.

54. MT, p. 48. "Unless proof has produced self-evidence and thereby rendered itself unnecessary, it has issued in a second-rate state of mind, producing action devoid of understanding."

55. It is worth noting that Whitehead's approach here is in agreement with the shift in emphasis in current foundational investigations, which stresses the notion of provability as opposed to the "truth" of formal systems. For Whitehead, the question of truth or falsehood is wholly inappropriate at purely formal levels of discourse. This view is reflected in his basic ontological principles. For instance, he holds that "truth or falsehood are always grounded upon a reason" and, according to the ontological principle, "a reason is always a reference to determinate actual entities." It follows that "there can be no reason upon which to found the truth or falsehood of an eternal object." PR, pp. 256–7.

56. PR, p. 11.

57. Granted that a theory affords ground for action as well as a vehicle for understanding, a promising course to follow in trying to explain the function of propositions is indicated in Whitehead's observation that what we should look for in propositions are those that are *interesting* rather than true. He adds that a proposition is likely to be true if it is interesting, for action in accordance with a true proposition is more apt to be successful. AI, p. 244.

BIBLIOGRAPHY

This short bibliography lists works that either have been cited in the text or have been influential in my choice of topics and approach.

Ayer, A. J. "The A Priori," in Benacerraf and Putnam, pp. 289–301. (Excerpted and reprinted from *Language, Truth and Logic.*)

Barker, Stephen F. "Realism as a Philosophy of Mathematics," in Bulloff, Jack J.; Holyoke, Thomas C.; Hahn, S. W.; editors. *The Foundations of Mathematics.* New York: Springer-Verlag, 1969.

Bastin, Ted; editor. *Quantum Theory and Beyond.* Cambridge: University Press, 1971.

Benacerraf, Paul and Hilary Putnam, editors. *Philosophy of Mathematics.* New Jersey: Prentice-Hall, 1964.

Benardete, Jose A. *Infinity; An Essay in Metaphysics.* Oxford: Clarendon Press, 1964.

Bennett, Jonathan. *Kant's Analytic.* Cambridge: University Press, 1964.

Bishop, Errett. "The Crisis in Contemporary Mathematics," *Historia Mathematica, 2,* 1975, pp. 507–17.

Bochner, Salmon. *The Role of Mathematics in the Rise of Science.* Princeton, N.J.: Princeton University Press, 1981.

Bohr, Niels. *Atomic Theory and the Description of Nature.* Cambridge: University Press, 1961.

Boyer, Carl. *The History of the Calculus and its Conceptual Development.* New York: Dover, 1959.

Brouwer, L. E. J. "Intuitionism and Formalism," in Benacerraf and Putnam, pp. 66–77.

Buchler, Justus; editor. *Philosophical Writings of Peirce.* New York: Dover, 1955.

Burgers, Johannes. *Experience and Conceptual Activity.* Cambridge, Mass.: M. I. T. Press, 1965.

———. "Reply to Shimony," in *Boston Studies in the Philosophy of Science, 1,* Robert Cohen and Marx Wartofsky; editors. New York: Humanities Press, 1965, pp. 331–342.

Burtt, E. A. *The Metaphysical Foundations of Modern Science.* Garden City, N. Y.: Doubleday and Co. Ltd, Anchor Books edition, 1954.

Capek, Milic. *The Philosophical Impact of Contemporary Physics.* Princeton, N. J.: D. Van Nostrand, 1961.

Chappell, V. C. "Whitehead's Theory of Becoming," in Kline, pp. 70–80.

Cline, David B., Alfred K. Mann, and Carlo Rubbia. "The Search for New

Families of Elementary Particles," *Scientific American*, January, 1966, pp. 44–54.

Cohen, I. Bernard. "History and the Philosophers of Science," in Suppe, pp. 308–49.

Collingwood, R. J. *An Essay on Metaphysics*. Chicago: Henry Regnery, Gateway edition, 1972.

———. *The Idea of Nature*. Oxford: Clarendon Press, 1945.

Dirac, P. A. M. "Development of the Physicist's Conception of Nature," in Mehra, *The Physicist's Conception of Nature*, pp. 1–14.

———. *The Principles of Quantum Mechanics*, 4th edition. Oxford: Clarendon Press, 1958.

Dummet, Michael. *Elements of Intuitionism*. Oxford: Clarendon Press, 1977.

Eddington, Sir Arthur. *The Philosophy of Physical Science*. University of Michigan Press, 1958.

Emmet, Dorothy. *The Nature of Metaphysical Thinking*. New York: St. Martin's Press, 1966.

———. *Whitehead's Philosophy of Organism*, 2nd edition. London: MacMillan, 1966.

Enz, Charles P. and Jagdish Mehra, editors. *Physical Reality and Mathematical Description*. Dordrecht-Holland: D. Reidel, 1974.

Goodstein, R. L. *Essays in the Philosophy of Mathematics*. Leicester: Leicester University Press, 1965.

Gruenbaum, Adolf. "Modern Science and Refutation of the Paradoxes of Zeno," *The Scientific Monthly*, November, 1955, pp. 234–9.

———. *Modern Science and Zeno's Paradoxes*. Middletown, Conn.: Wesleyan University Press, 1967.

———. "The Resolution of Zeno's Metrical Paradox of Extension for the Mathematical Continua of Space and Time," Chapter 6 of *Philosophical Problems of Space and Time, Boston Studies in the Philosophy of Science*, vol. 12, 2nd edition. Dordrecht-Holland: D. Reidel, 1973.

Guillemin, Victor. *The Story of Quantum Mechanics*. New York: Scribner's Sons, 1968.

Hacking, Ian. *Why Does Language Matter to Philosophy?* Cambridge: University Press, 1975.

Hagedorn, R. "What happened to our elementary particles? (Variations on a theme of Jauch)," in Enz and Mehra, *Physical Reality and Mathematical Description*, pp. 100–110.

Hall, Everett. "Of What Use Are Whitehead's Eternal Objects?" in Kline, pp. 102–16.

Hanson, Norwood Russell. *Patterns of Discovery*. Cambridge: University Press, 1961.

Harré, Romano. *The Principles of Scientific Thinking*. Chicago: University of Chicago Press, 1970.

Harré, R. and E. H. Madden. *Causal Powers*. Oxford: B. Blackwell, 1975.

Harris, Errol E. *The Foundations of Metaphysics in Science.* London: Geo. Allen and Unwin, 1965.

Hartshorne, Charles. "Whitehead and Contemporary Philosophy," in Leclerc, *The Relevance of Whitehead,* pp. 21–43.

Heisenberg, Werner. "Development of Concepts in the History of Quantum Theory," in Mehra, *The Physicist's Conception of Nature,* pp. 264–75.

———. *Physics and Philosophy.* New York: Harper, 1958.

Hempel, Carl G. "On the Nature of Mathematical Truth," in Benacerraf and Putnam, pp. 366–381. (Reprinted from *The American Mathematical Monthly,* vol. 52, 1945, pp. 543–56).

Hesse, Mary B., "Action at a Distance," in McMullin, pp. 119–37.

———. "Models and Analogies in Science," in Paul Edwards, ed., *The Encyclopedia of Philosophy,* vol. 5, pp. 354–359. New York: Collier Macmillan, 1967.

———. "Models and Matter," in *Quanta and Reality,* Cleveland: World Publishing Co., 1964, pp. 49–57.

Hocking, William E. "Whitehead as I Knew Him," in Kline, pp. 7–17.

———. "Whitehead on Mind and Nature," in Schilpp, pp. 383–404.

Hoffman, Banesh and Helen Dukas. *Albert Einstein, Creator and Rebel.* New York: New American Library paperback, 1972.

Kalmar, Laszlo. "Foundations of Mathematics–Whither Now?" in Lakatos, *Problems in the Philosophy of Mathematics,* pp. 187–94.

Kilmister, C. W. "Beyond What?" in Bastin, *Quantum Theory and Beyond,* pp. 117–27.

Kline, George L.; editor. *Alfred North Whitehead: Essays On His Philosophy.* Englewood Cliffs, N. J.: Prentice-Hall, Inc., 1963.

Koerner, Stephen. *Kant.* Harmondsworth, Mddx.: Penguin Books, 1960.

———. "On the Revelance of Post-Goedelian Mathematics to Philosophy," in Lakatos, *Problems in the Philosophy of Mathematics,* pp. 118–132.

———. *The Philosophy of Mathematics.* London: Hutchinson University Library, 1960.

Lakatos, Imre. "Infinite Regress and Foundations of Mathematics," *The Aristotelian Society,* Supplementary vol. 36, 1962, pp. 155–84. Reprinted in *Mathematics, Science and Epistemology,* vol. 2, edited by J. Worrall and G. Currier. Cambridge: University Press, 1978.

———, editor. *Problems in the Philosophy of Mathematics.* Proceedings of the International Colloquium in the Philosophy of Science. London, 1965, vol. 1. Amsterdam: North-Holland Pub. Co., 1967.

Leclerc, Ivor. "Kant's Second Antinomy, Leibniz, and Whitehead," *Review of Metaphysics,* 20, 1966, pp. 24–41.

———. *The Nature of Physical Existence.* London: Geo. Allen and Unwin, 1972.

———, editor. *The Relevance of Whitehead.* London: Geo. Allen and Unwin, 1961.

————. *Whitehead's Metaphysics*. London: Geo. Allen and Unwin, 1958.

Lovejoy, A. O. *The Revolt Against Dualism*. La Salle, Illinois: Open Court, 1955.

Lowe, Victor. *Understanding Whitehead*. Baltimore: Johns Hopkins Press, paperback edition, 1966.

Margenau, Henry. *The Nature of Physical Reality*. New York: McGraw Hill, 1950.

McMullin, Ernan; editor. *The Concept of Matter in Modern Philosophy*. Notre Dame: University of Notre Dame Press, revised edition, 1978.

Mehra, Jagdish; editor. *The Physicist's Conception of Nature*. Dordrecht-Holland: D. Reidel, 1973.

Meschkowski, Herbert. *Probleme des Unendlichen*. Braunschweig: Friedr. Vieweg und Sohn, 1967.

Mostowski, Andrzej. "Recent Results in Set Theory," in Lakatos, *Problems in the Philosophy of Mathematics*, pp. 82–95.

Owen, G. E. L. "Zeno and the Mathematicians," in Salmon, pp. 139–163.

Palter, Robert. "The Place of Mathematics in Whitehead's Philosophy," *Journal of Philosophy,* vol. 58, 1961, pp. 565–776.

————. *Whitehead's Philosophy of Science*. Chicago: University of Chicago Press, 1960.

Petersen, Aage. *Quantum Physics and the Philosophical Tradition*. Cambridge, Mass.: M. I. T. Press paperback, 1968.

Pippard, A. B. "Particles and Waves," in *Quanta and Reality*. Cleveland: World Publishing Co., 1964, pp. 25–33.

Popper, Sir Karl. *Conjectures and Refutations*. New York: Basic Books, 1963.

————. *Objective Knowledge*. Oxford: Clarendon Press, 1973.

Putnam, Hilary. *Reason, Truth and History*. Cambridge: University Press.

————. "Why There Isn't a Ready-Made World," *Synthese, 51,* (1982), pp. 141–67.

————. "Why Reason Can't Be Naturalized," *Synthese, 52,* (1982), pp. 3–23.

Quine, W. V. *Ontological Relativity*. New York: Columbia University Press, 1969.

————. *The Ways of Paradox*. Cambridge, Mass.: Harvard University Press, revised and enlarged edition, 1976.

————. *Theories and Things*. Cambridge, Mass.: Harvard University Press, 1981.

Quinton, Anthony. *Thoughts and Thinkers*. London: Duckworth, 1982.

Rorty, Richard M. *Philosophy and the Mirror of Nature*. Princeton: Princeton University Press, 1979.

Rosenfeld, Leon. "The Wave-Particle Dilemma," in Mehra, *The Physicist's Conception of Nature,* pp. 251–63.

Russell, Bertrand. *Portraits from Memory*. London: Geo. Allen & Unwin, 1956.

————. *The Principles of Mathematics*. London: Geo. Allen and Unwin, 1907.

Salmon, Wesley C.; editor. *Zeno's Paradoxes*. Indianapolis and New York: Bobbs-Merrill Co., 1970.

Schilpp, P. A.; editor. *The Philosophy of Alfred North Whitehead.* New York: Tudor, second edition, 1951.

Scruton, Roger. *Kant.* Oxford: Oxford University Press, 1982.

Shimony, Abner. "Quantum Physics and the Philosophy of Whitehead," *Boston Studies in the Philosophy of Science, 2,* Robert S. Cohen and Marx W. Wartofsky, editors. New York: Humanities Press, 1965, pp. 307–330.

Smith, John E. "Kant's Doctrine of Matter," in McMullin, pp. 119–37.

Stebbing, L. Susan. *Philosophy and the Physicists.* New York: Dover, 1958.

Suppe, Frederick; editor. *The Structure of Scientific Theories.* Urbana, Ill.: The Univeristy of Illinois Press, second edition, 1977.

Tucker, John. "Goedel and Epimenides," *Proceedings of the Aristotelian Society, 59,* 1958–59, pp. 25–48.

Von Weizsaecker, C. F. "The Copenhagen Interpretation," in Bastin, *Quantum Theory and Beyond,* pp. 25–31.

Wartofsky, Marx. "Metaphysics as Heuristic for Science," in *Boston Studies in the Philosophy of Science, 3,* Robert Cohen and Marx Wartofsky, editors. Dordrecht: D. Reidel, 1968, pp. 123–72.

———. *Models.* Dordrecht: D. Reidel, 1979.

Weyl, Hermann. *Philosophy of Mathematics and Natural Science.* Princeton: Princeton University Press, 1949 (revised and augmented English edition, based on a transaltion by Olaf Helmer).

Wheeler, John Archibald. "From Relativity to Mutability," in Mehra, *The Physicist's Conception of Nature,* pp. 202–47.

Wigner, Eugene P. "The Unreasonable Effectiveness of Mathematics in the Natural Sciences," *Communications on Pure and Applied Mathematics,* 13, (1960), pp. 1–14.

Whitehead, Alfred North. *Adventures of Ideas.* New York: Macmillan Free Press Paperback, 1967.

———. *The Aims of Education and Other Essays.* New York: Macmillan Free Press Paperback, 1967.

———. *The Concept of Nature.* Cambridge: University Press, 1964.

———. *An Enquiry Concerning the Principles of Natural Knowledge.* Cambridge: University Press, 1955.

———. *Essays in Science and Philosophy.* London: Rider, 1948.

———. *The Function of Reason.* Boston: Beacon Press paperback edn., 1958.

———. "Indication, Classes, Numbers, Validation," in *Essays in Science and Philosophy, pp. 227–240.*

———. *The Interpretation of Science,* Selected Essays. A. H. Johnson, editor. Indianapolis: Bobbs-Merrill, paperback edition, 1961.

———. *An Introduction to Mathematics.* Oxford: University Press Paperback, 1958.

———. "Mathematics," *Encyclopaedia Britannica,* 11th edition, pp. 878–83.

———. *Modes of Thought.* New York: Macmillan, Free Press Paperback, 1968.

———. "On Mathematical Concepts of the Material World," *Philosophical*

Transactions, Royal Society of London, Ser. A, CCV (1906), pp. 465–525.

————. "The Organisation of Thought," first published in 1917, reprinted in AE and IS.

————. *The Principle of Relativity.* Cambridge: University Press, 1922.

————, and Russell, Bertrand. *Principia Mathematica,* vol. 1, 2nd edition. Cambridge: University Press, 1963.

————. *Process and Reality.* New York: Macmillan; The Free Press, Corrected edition, edited by D. R. Griffin and D. W. Sherburne, 1978.

————. *Science and the Modern World.* New York: Macmillan; Free Press Paperback, 1967.

————. *A Treatise on Universal Algebra, with Applications,* vol. 1. Cambridge: University Press, 1898.

INDEX

254